P9-ECN-173

INHUMAN

INHUMAN VOL. 2: AXIS. Contains material originally published in magazine form as INHUMAN #7-11. First printing 2015. ISBN# 978-0-7851-8780-6. Published by MARVEL WORLDWIDE, INC., a subsidiary of MARVEL ENTERTAINMENT, LLC. OFFICE OF PUBLICATION: 135 West 50th Street, New York, NY 10020. Copyright © 2014 and 2015 Marvel Characters, Inc. All rights reserved. All characters featured in this issue and the distinctive names and likenesses thereof, and all related indicia are trademarks of Marvel Characters, Inc. No similarity between any of the names, characters, persons, and/or institutions in this magazine with those of any living or dead person or institution is intended, and any such similarity which may exist is purely coincidental. **Printed in Canada.** ALAN FINE, EVP - Office of the President, Marvel Worldwide, Inc. and EVP & CMO Marvel Characters B.V.; DAN BUCKLEY, Publisher & President – Print, Animation & Digital Divisions; JOE QUESADA, Chief Creative Officer; TOM BREVOORT, SVP of Publishing; DAVID BOGART, SVP of Operations & Procurement, Publishing; C.B. CEBULSKI, SVP of Creator & Content Development; DAVID GABRIEL, SVP Print, Sales & Marketing; JIM O'KEEFE, VP of Operations & Logistics; DAN CARR, Executive Director of Publishing Technology; SUSAN CRESPI, Editorial Operations Manager; ALEX MORALES, Publishing Operations Manager; STAN LEE, Chairman Emeritus. For information regarding advertising in Marvel Comics or on Marvel.com, please contact Niza Disla, Director of Marvel Partnerships, at ndisla@marvel.com. For Marvel subscription

WRITER
CHARLES SOULE

ARTISTS
PEPE LARRAZ (#7-8) &
RYAN STEGMAN (#9-11)

COLORIST
RICHARD ISANOVE

LETTERER
VC'S CLAYTON COWLES WITH JOE SABINO (#9)

COVER ART
RYAN STEGMAN

ASSISTANT EDITORS
DEVIN LEWIS & CHARLES BEACHAM

EDITOR
NICK LOWE

INHUMANS CREATED BY STAN LEE & JACK KIRBY

COLLECTION EDITOR:
SARAH BRUNSTAD
ASSOCIATE MANAGING EDITOR:
ALEX STARBUCK
EDITORS, SPECIAL PROJECTS:
JENNIFER GRÜNWALD & MARK D. BEAZLEY
SENIOR EDITOR, SPECIAL PROJECTS:
JEFF YOUNGQUIST
BOOK DESIGNER:
NELSON RIBEIRO

SVP PRINT, SALES & MARKETING:
DAVID GABRIEL
EDITOR IN CHIEF:
AXEL ALONSO
CHIEF CREATIVE OFFICER:
JOE QUESADA
PUBLISHER:
DAN BUCKLEY
EXECUTIVE PRODUCER:
ALAN FINE

MILLIONS OF YEARS AGO, WHEN HUMANKIND WAS IN ITS INFANCY, AN ALIEN CIVILIZATION CALLED THE KREE EXPERIMENTED ON ANCIENT HOMO SAPIENS. THE EXPERIMENTS CREATED A NEW RACE WHO CALLED THEMSELVES INHUMANS, AN EVOLUTIONARY LEAP OVER THEIR CAVE-DWELLING BRETHREN.

TO PROTECT THE EARTH FROM AN ATTACK LED BY THANOS, BLACK BOLT, KING OF THE INHUMANS, ENLISTED THE HELP OF HIS BROTHER MAXIMUS THE MAD TO DETONATE A MASSIVE BOMB IN THE FLOATING INHUMAN CITY ATTILAN. THOUGH THE PLAN HELPED TO HOLD OFF THE MAD TITAN, THE EXPLOSION SENT THE CITY CRASHING INTO THE HUDSON RIVER AND RELEASED A CLOUD OF TERRIGEN MIST ACROSS THE GLOBE, AWAKENING SUPERHUMAN ABILITIES IN ANYONE WITH TRACES OF INHUMAN DNA. THOSE WHO SURVIVED EXPOSURE ARE NO LONGER MERELY HUMAN. THEY ARE...

INHUMAN

WITHDRAWN

NEITHER BLACK BOLT NOR MAXIMUS HAVE BEEN HEARD FROM SINCE ENACTING THEIR PLAN, LEAVING MEDUSA, THE INHUMANS' QUEEN, TO PICK UP THE PIECES OF THEIR ONCE GREAT SOCIETY—AND PICK UP THE PIECES SHE HAS. FROM THE RUBBLE OF THE FALLEN CITY, THE QUEEN AND HER SURVIVING SUBJECTS HAVE BUILT NEW ATTILAN, AN ISLAND REFUGE FOR INHUMANS OLD AND NEW. WITH MEDUSA LEADING THE CHARGE, INHUMANS HAVE TAKEN THEIR NUHUMAN RELATIVES UNDER WING AND ARE WORKING TOGETHER TO FIND THEIR FOOTING IN THE AFTERMATH OF DISASTER.

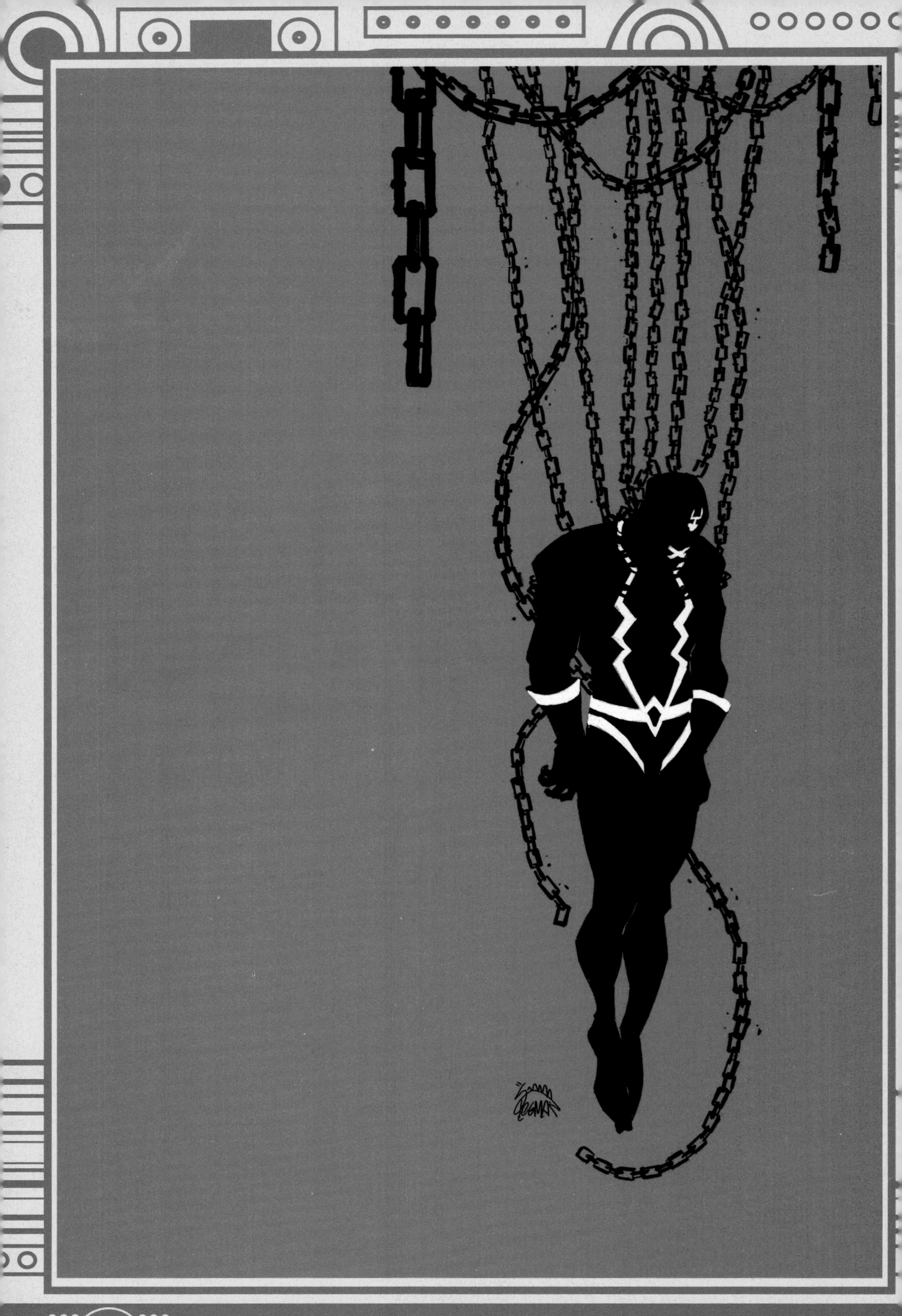

7 PART SEVEN: OUT OF THE DARKNESS

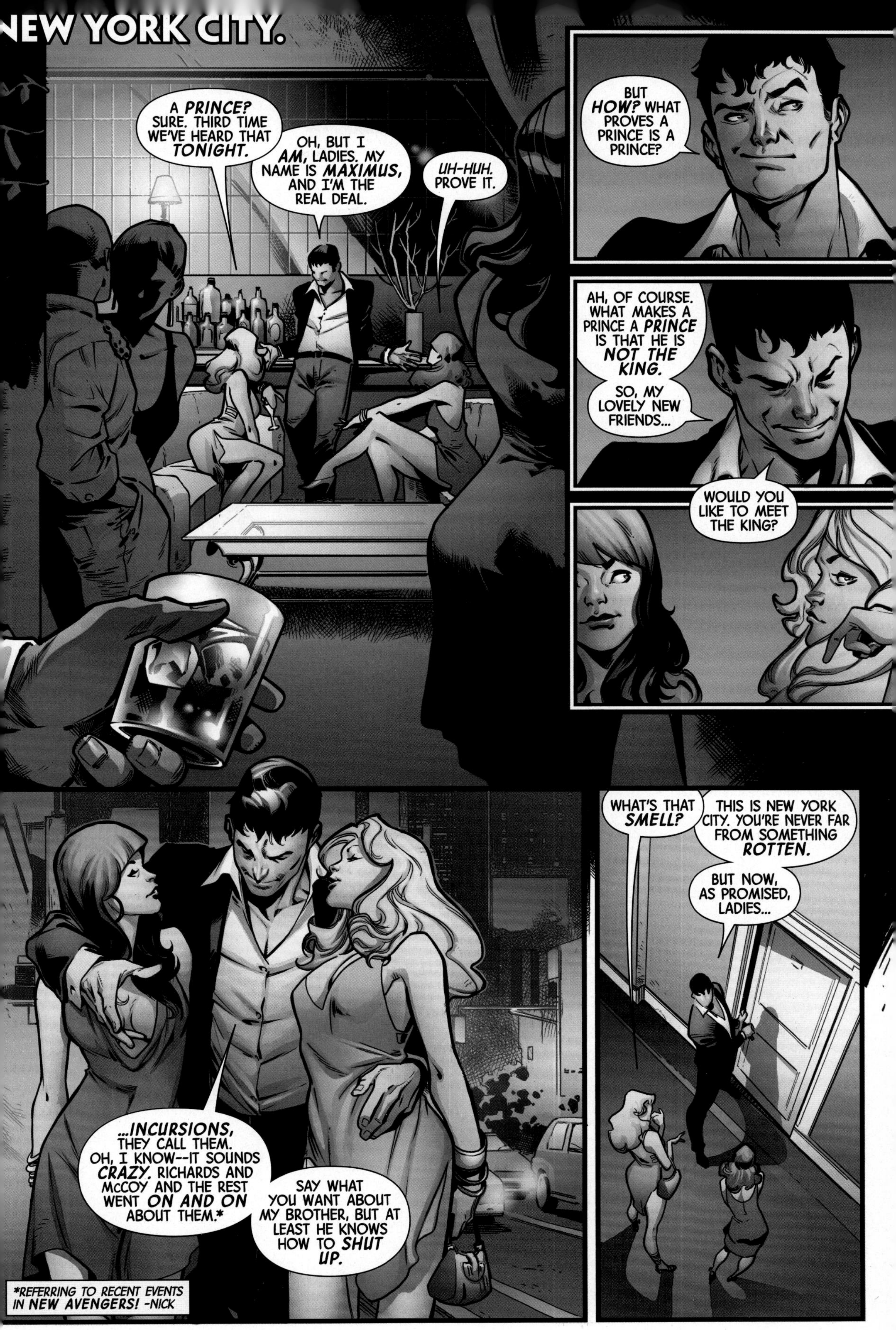
NEW YORK CITY.
A PRINCE? SURE. THIRD TIME WE'VE HEARD THAT TONIGHT.
OH, BUT I AM, LADIES. MY NAME IS MAXIMUS, AND I'M THE REAL DEAL.
UH-HUH. PROVE IT.
BUT HOW? WHAT PROVES A PRINCE IS A PRINCE?
AH, OF COURSE. WHAT MAKES A PRINCE A PRINCE IS THAT HE IS NOT THE KING.
SO, MY LOVELY NEW FRIENDS...
WOULD YOU LIKE TO MEET THE KING?
...INCURSIONS, THEY CALL THEM. OH, I KNOW--IT SOUNDS CRAZY. RICHARDS AND McCOY AND THE REST WENT ON AND ON ABOUT THEM.*
SAY WHAT YOU WANT ABOUT MY BROTHER, BUT AT LEAST HE KNOWS HOW TO SHUT UP.
*REFERRING TO RECENT EVENTS IN NEW AVENGERS! -NICK
WHAT'S THAT SMELL?
THIS IS NEW YORK CITY. YOU'RE NEVER FAR FROM SOMETHING ROTTEN.
BUT NOW, AS PROMISED, LADIES...

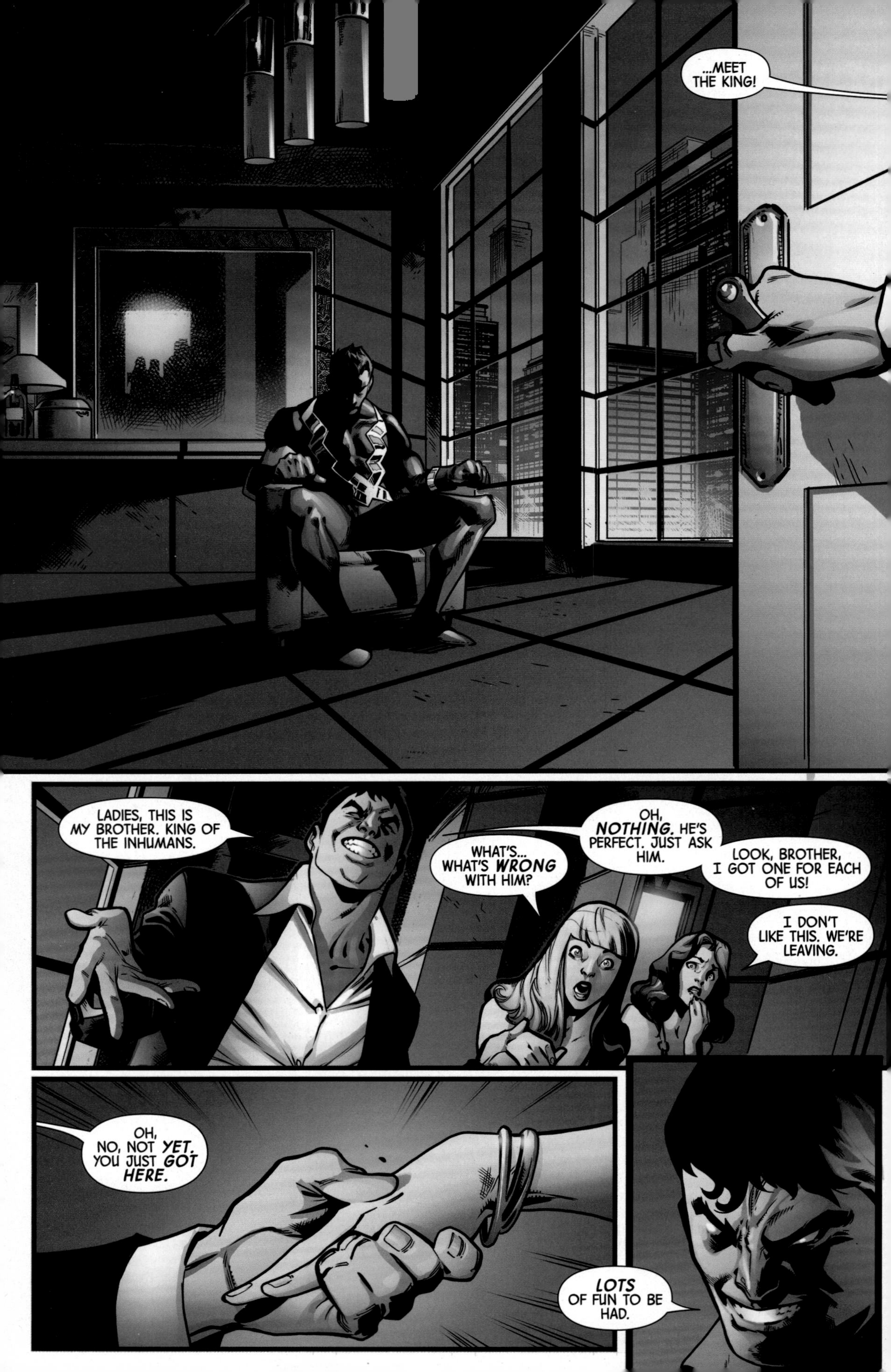
...MEET THE KING!
LADIES, THIS IS MY BROTHER. KING OF THE INHUMANS.
WHAT'S... WHAT'S WRONG WITH HIM?
OH, NOTHING. HE'S PERFECT. JUST ASK HIM.
LOOK, BROTHER, I GOT ONE FOR EACH OF US!
I DON'T LIKE THIS. WE'RE LEAVING.
OH, NO, NOT YET. YOU JUST GOT HERE.
LOTS OF FUN TO BE HAD.

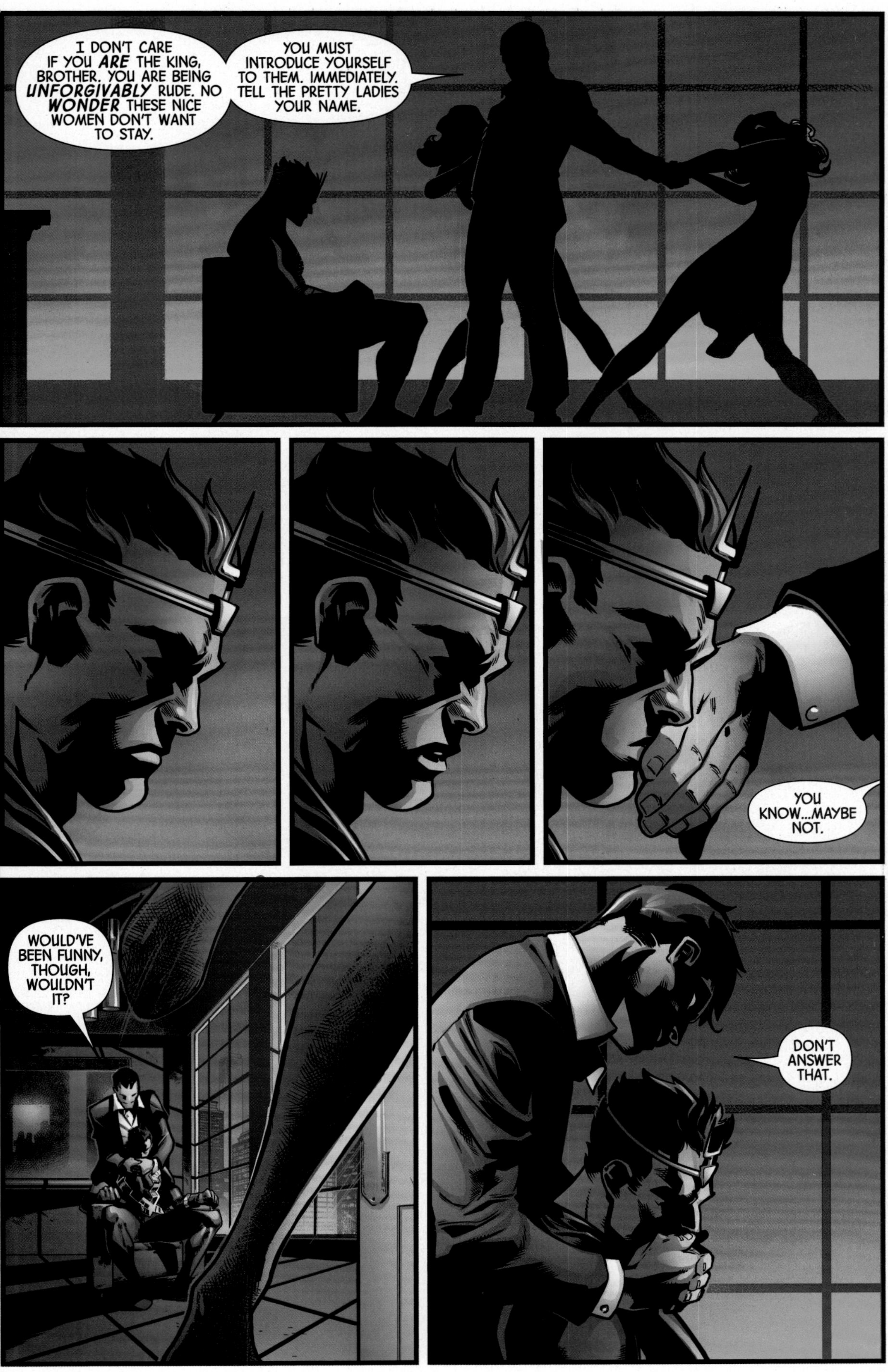

I DON'T CARE IF YOU ARE THE KING, BROTHER. YOU ARE BEING UNFORGIVABLY RUDE. NO WONDER THESE NICE WOMEN DON'T WANT TO STAY.
YOU MUST INTRODUCE YOURSELF TO THEM. IMMEDIATELY. TELL THE PRETTY LADIES YOUR NAME.
YOU KNOW...MAYBE NOT.
WOULD'VE BEEN FUNNY, THOUGH, WOULDN'T IT?
DON'T ANSWER THAT.

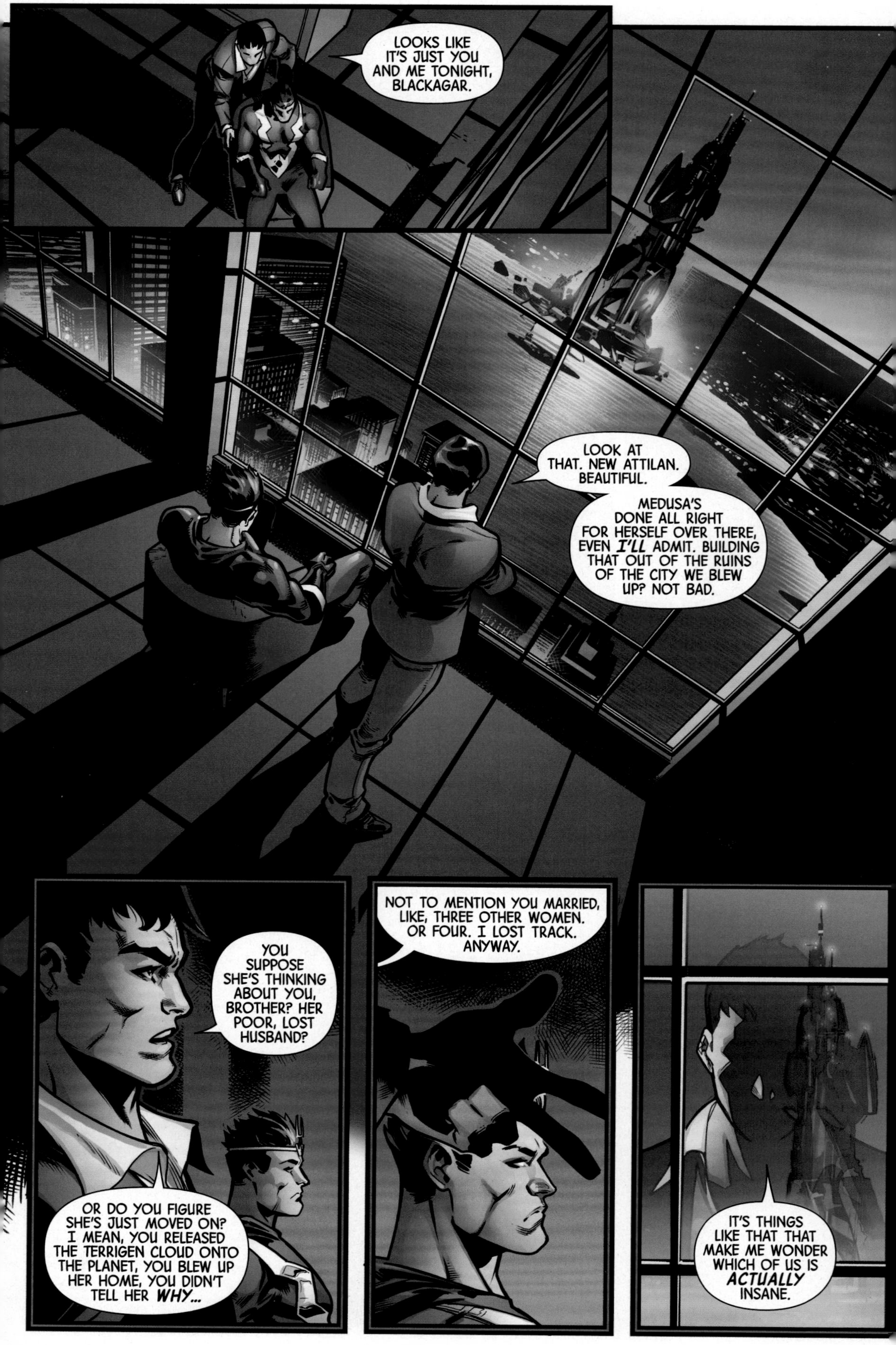

LOOKS LIKE IT'S JUST YOU AND ME TONIGHT, BLACKAGAR.
LOOK AT THAT. NEW ATTILAN. BEAUTIFUL.
MEDUSA'S DONE ALL RIGHT FOR HERSELF OVER THERE, EVEN *I'LL* ADMIT. BUILDING THAT OUT OF THE RUINS OF THE CITY WE BLEW UP? NOT BAD.
YOU SUPPOSE SHE'S THINKING ABOUT YOU, BROTHER? HER POOR, LOST HUSBAND?
OR DO YOU FIGURE SHE'S JUST MOVED ON? I MEAN, YOU RELEASED THE TERRIGEN CLOUD ONTO THE PLANET, YOU BLEW UP HER HOME, YOU DIDN'T TELL HER *WHY...*
NOT TO MENTION YOU MARRIED, LIKE, THREE OTHER WOMEN. OR FOUR. I LOST TRACK. ANYWAY.
IT'S THINGS LIKE THAT THAT MAKE ME WONDER WHICH OF US IS *ACTUALLY* INSANE.

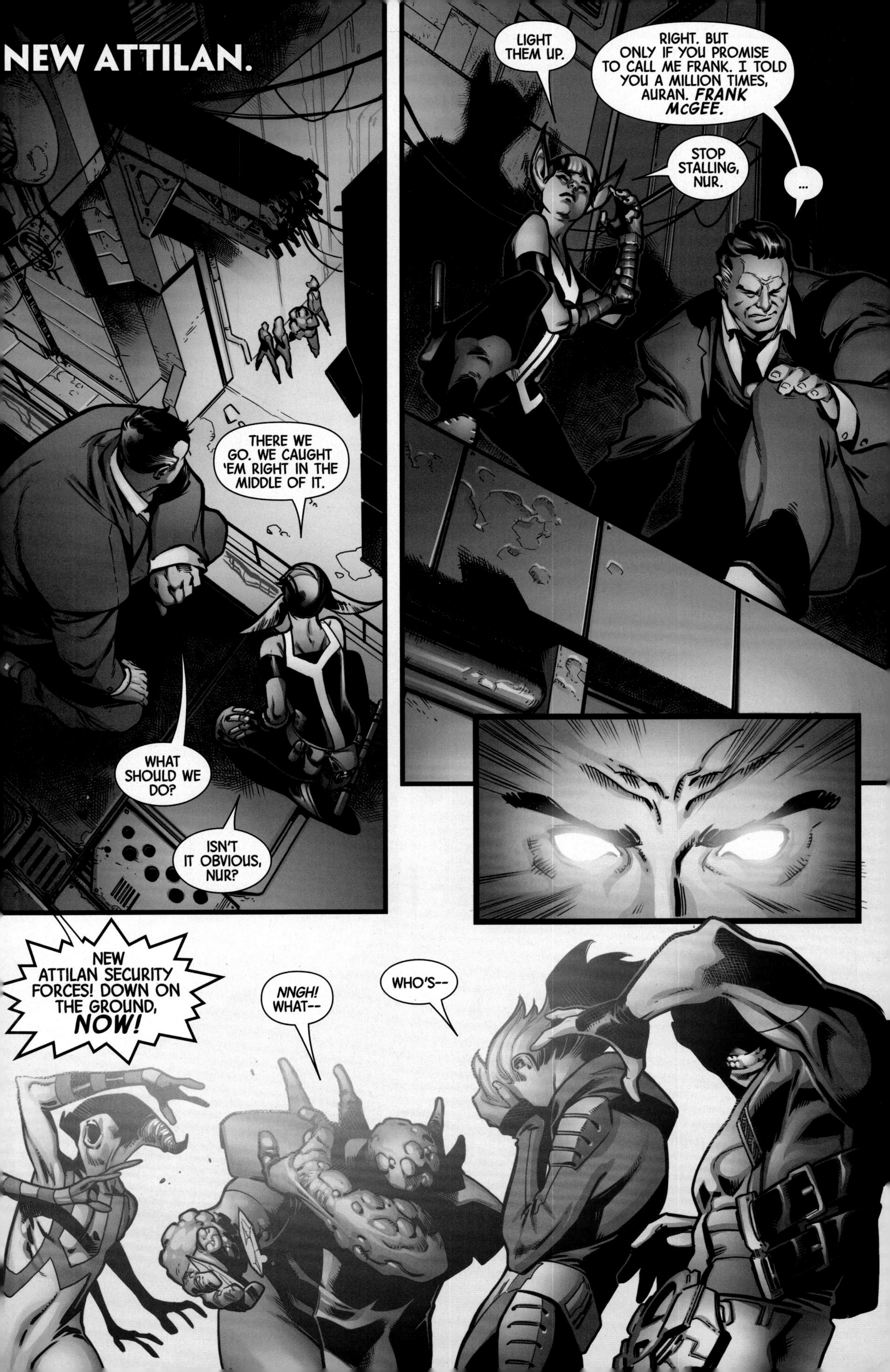

NEW ATTILAN.
THERE WE GO. WE CAUGHT 'EM RIGHT IN THE MIDDLE OF IT.
WHAT SHOULD WE DO?
ISN'T IT OBVIOUS, NUR?
LIGHT THEM UP.
RIGHT. BUT ONLY IF YOU PROMISE TO CALL ME FRANK. I TOLD YOU A MILLION TIMES, AURAN. FRANK McGEE.
STOP STALLING, NUR.
...
NEW ATTILAN SECURITY FORCES! DOWN ON THE GROUND, NOW!
NNGH! WHAT--
WHO'S--

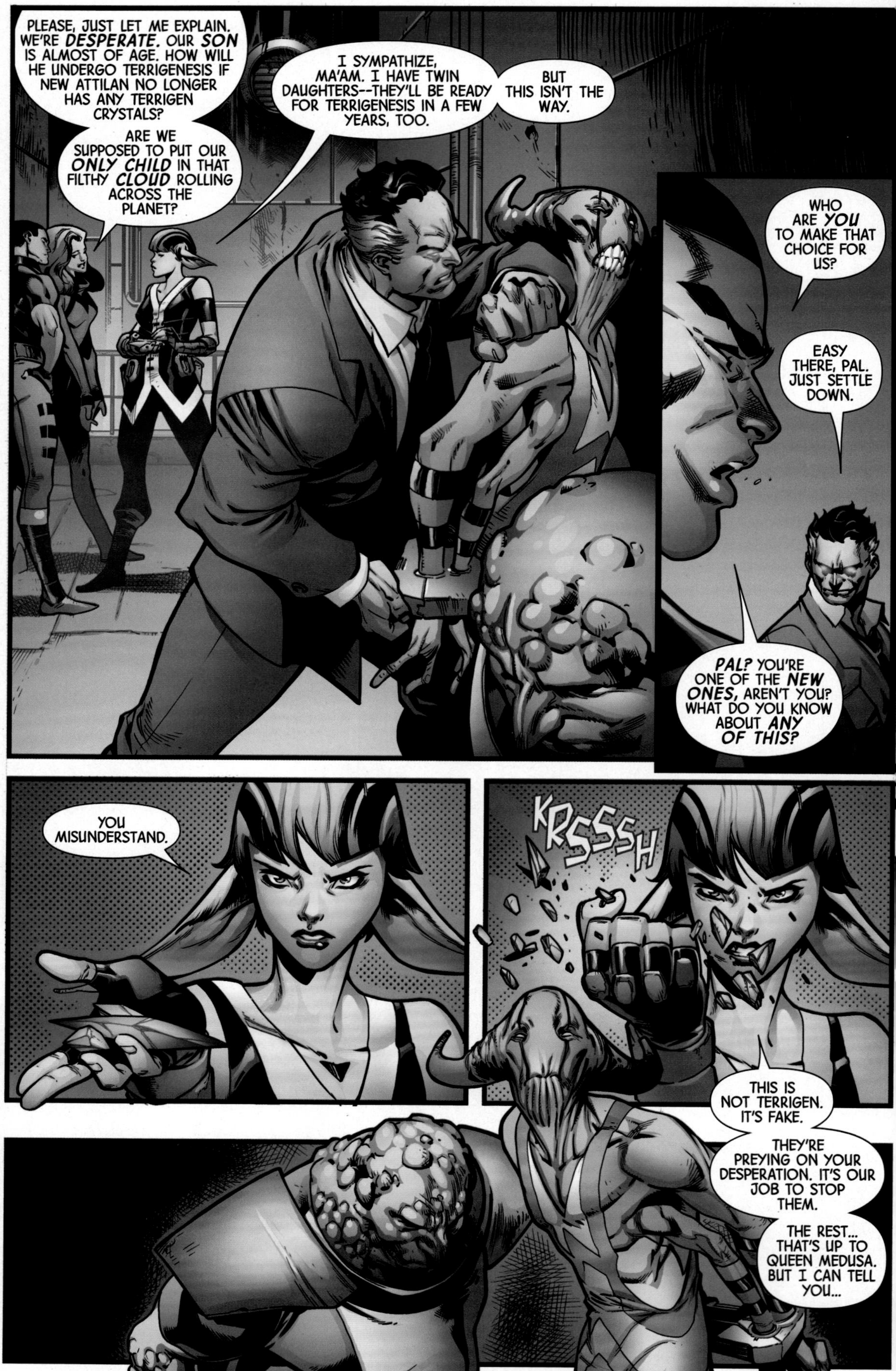
PLEASE, JUST LET ME EXPLAIN. WE'RE DESPERATE. OUR SON IS ALMOST OF AGE. HOW WILL HE UNDERGO TERRIGENESIS IF NEW ATTILAN NO LONGER HAS ANY TERRIGEN CRYSTALS?
ARE WE SUPPOSED TO PUT OUR ONLY CHILD IN THAT FILTHY CLOUD ROLLING ACROSS THE PLANET?
I SYMPATHIZE, MA'AM. I HAVE TWIN DAUGHTERS--THEY'LL BE READY FOR TERRIGENESIS IN A FEW YEARS, TOO.
BUT THIS ISN'T THE WAY.
WHO ARE YOU TO MAKE THAT CHOICE FOR US?
EASY THERE, PAL. JUST SETTLE DOWN.
PAL? YOU'RE ONE OF THE NEW ONES, AREN'T YOU? WHAT DO YOU KNOW ABOUT ANY OF THIS?
YOU MISUNDERSTAND.
KRSSSH
THIS IS NOT TERRIGEN. IT'S FAKE.
THEY'RE PREYING ON YOUR DESPERATION. IT'S OUR JOB TO STOP THEM.
THE REST... THAT'S UP TO QUEEN MEDUSA. BUT I CAN TELL YOU...

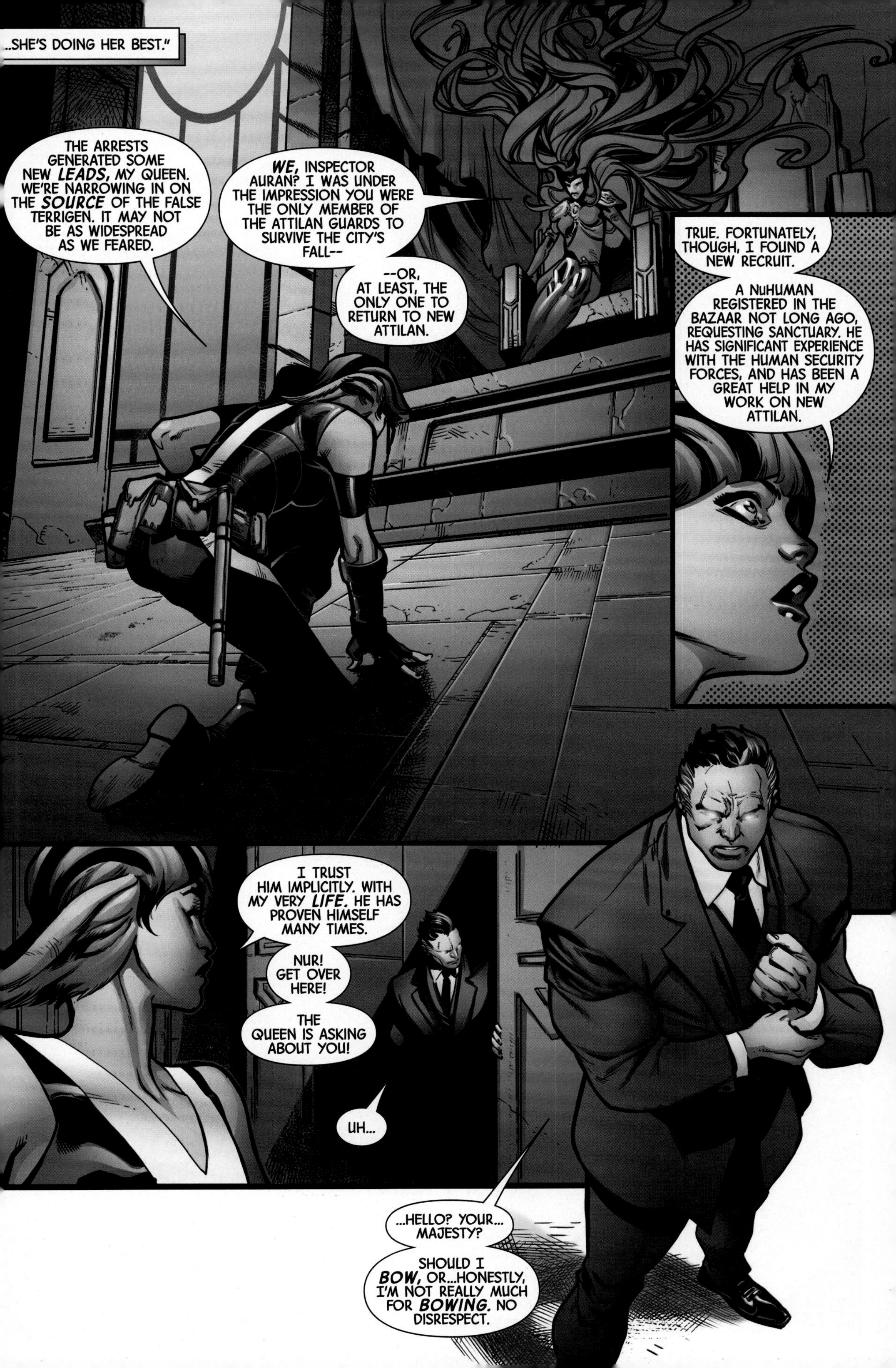

...SHE'S DOING HER BEST."
THE ARRESTS GENERATED SOME NEW LEADS, MY QUEEN. WE'RE NARROWING IN ON THE SOURCE OF THE FALSE TERRIGEN. IT MAY NOT BE AS WIDESPREAD AS WE FEARED.
WE, INSPECTOR AURAN? I WAS UNDER THE IMPRESSION YOU WERE THE ONLY MEMBER OF THE ATTILAN GUARDS TO SURVIVE THE CITY'S FALL--
--OR, AT LEAST, THE ONLY ONE TO RETURN TO NEW ATTILAN.
TRUE. FORTUNATELY, THOUGH, I FOUND A NEW RECRUIT.
A NuHUMAN REGISTERED IN THE BAZAAR NOT LONG AGO, REQUESTING SANCTUARY. HE HAS SIGNIFICANT EXPERIENCE WITH THE HUMAN SECURITY FORCES, AND HAS BEEN A GREAT HELP IN MY WORK ON NEW ATTILAN.
I TRUST HIM IMPLICITLY. WITH MY VERY LIFE. HE HAS PROVEN HIMSELF MANY TIMES.
NUR! GET OVER HERE!
THE QUEEN IS ASKING ABOUT YOU!
UH...
...HELLO? YOUR... MAJESTY?
SHOULD I BOW, OR...HONESTLY, I'M NOT REALLY MUCH FOR BOWING. NO DISRESPECT.

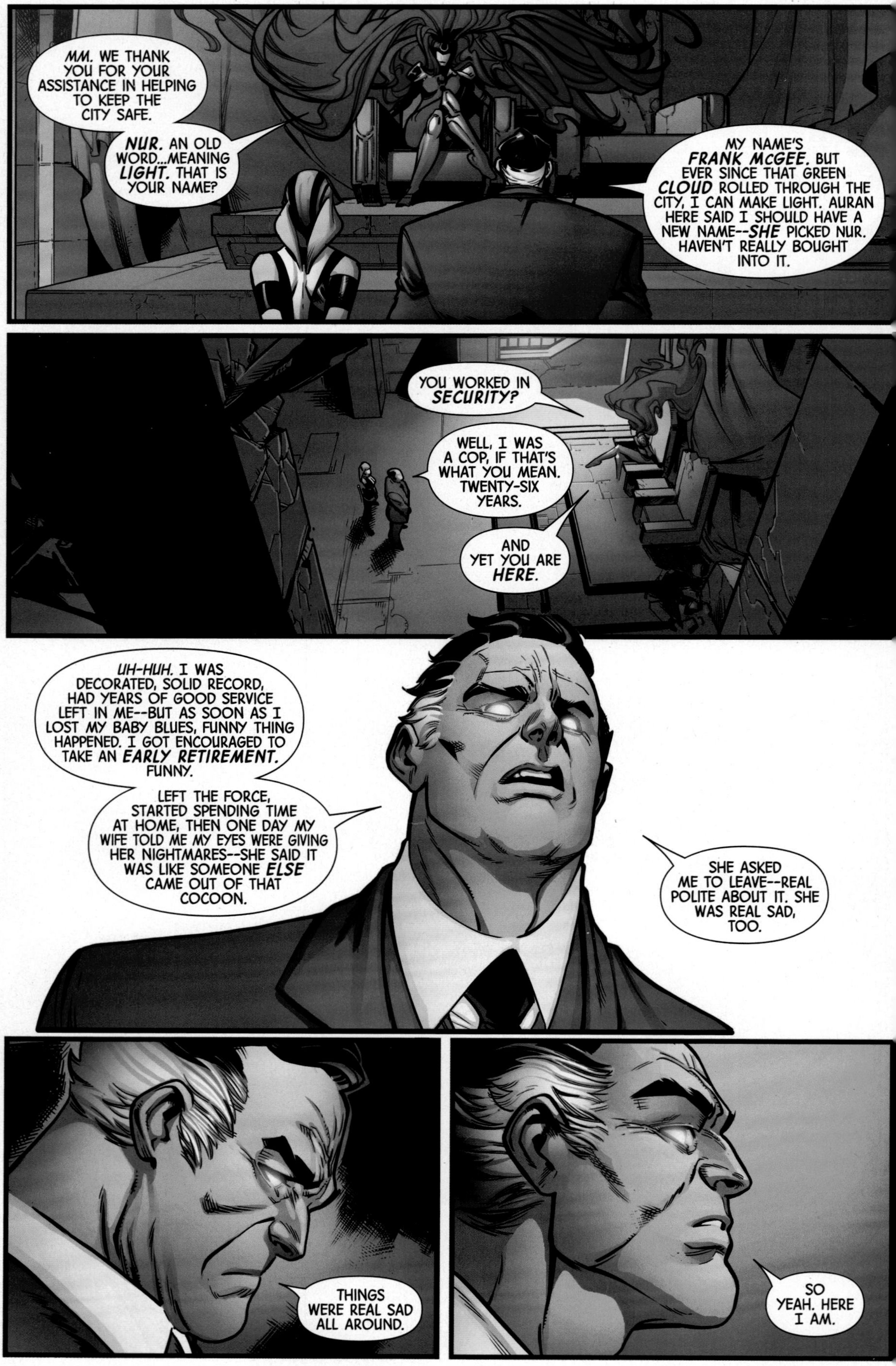
MM. WE THANK YOU FOR YOUR ASSISTANCE IN HELPING TO KEEP THE CITY SAFE.
NUR. AN OLD WORD...MEANING LIGHT. THAT IS YOUR NAME?
MY NAME'S FRANK McGEE. BUT EVER SINCE THAT GREEN CLOUD ROLLED THROUGH THE CITY, I CAN MAKE LIGHT. AURAN HERE SAID I SHOULD HAVE A NEW NAME--SHE PICKED NUR. HAVEN'T REALLY BOUGHT INTO IT.
YOU WORKED IN SECURITY?
WELL, I WAS A COP, IF THAT'S WHAT YOU MEAN. TWENTY-SIX YEARS.
AND YET YOU ARE HERE.
UH-HUH. I WAS DECORATED, SOLID RECORD, HAD YEARS OF GOOD SERVICE LEFT IN ME--BUT AS SOON AS I LOST MY BABY BLUES, FUNNY THING HAPPENED. I GOT ENCOURAGED TO TAKE AN EARLY RETIREMENT. FUNNY.
LEFT THE FORCE, STARTED SPENDING TIME AT HOME, THEN ONE DAY MY WIFE TOLD ME MY EYES WERE GIVING HER NIGHTMARES--SHE SAID IT WAS LIKE SOMEONE ELSE CAME OUT OF THAT COCOON.
SHE ASKED ME TO LEAVE--REAL POLITE ABOUT IT. SHE WAS REAL SAD, TOO.
THINGS WERE REAL SAD ALL AROUND.
SO YEAH. HERE I AM.

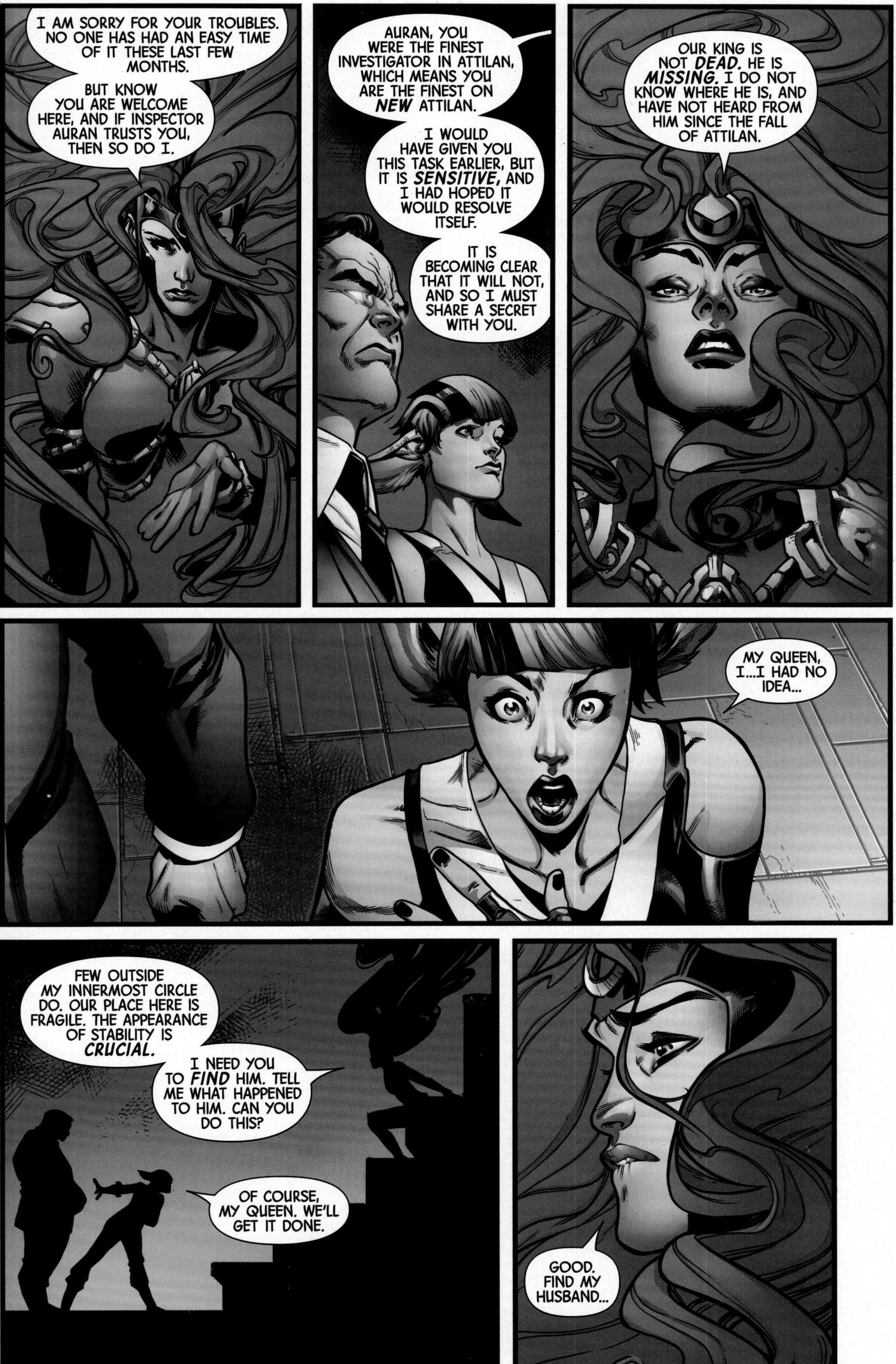
I AM SORRY FOR YOUR TROUBLES. NO ONE HAS HAD AN EASY TIME OF IT THESE LAST FEW MONTHS.
BUT KNOW YOU ARE WELCOME HERE, AND IF INSPECTOR AURAN TRUSTS YOU, THEN SO DO I.
AURAN, YOU WERE THE FINEST INVESTIGATOR IN ATTILAN, WHICH MEANS YOU ARE THE FINEST ON NEW ATTILAN.
I WOULD HAVE GIVEN YOU THIS TASK EARLIER, BUT IT IS SENSITIVE, AND I HAD HOPED IT WOULD RESOLVE ITSELF.
IT IS BECOMING CLEAR THAT IT WILL NOT, AND SO I MUST SHARE A SECRET WITH YOU.
OUR KING IS NOT DEAD. HE IS MISSING. I DO NOT KNOW WHERE HE IS, AND HAVE NOT HEARD FROM HIM SINCE THE FALL OF ATTILAN.
MY QUEEN, I...I HAD NO IDEA...
FEW OUTSIDE MY INNERMOST CIRCLE DO. OUR PLACE HERE IS FRAGILE. THE APPEARANCE OF STABILITY IS CRUCIAL.
I NEED YOU TO FIND HIM. TELL ME WHAT HAPPENED TO HIM. CAN YOU DO THIS?
OF COURSE, MY QUEEN. WE'LL GET IT DONE.
GOOD. FIND MY HUSBAND...

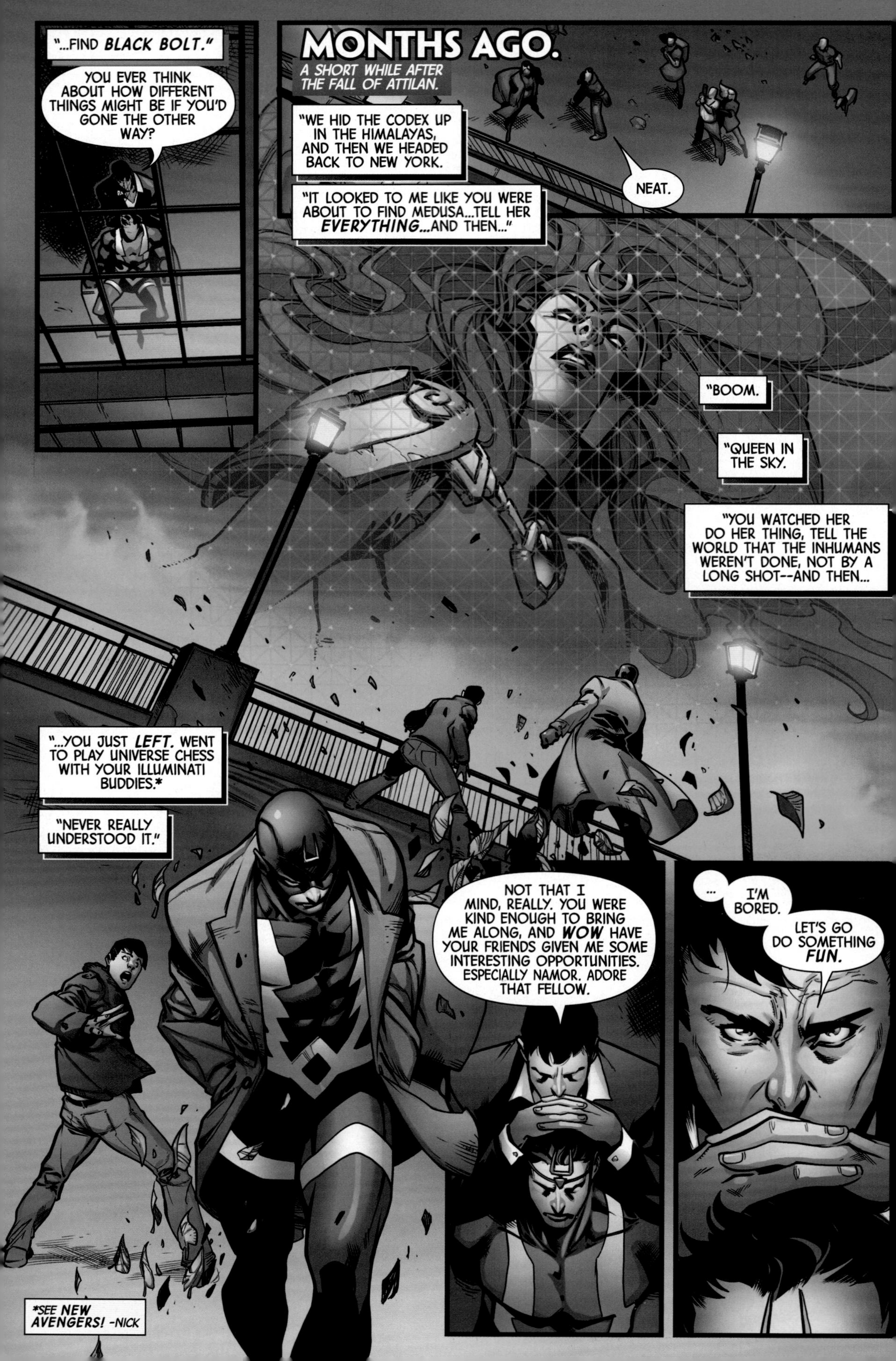
"...FIND BLACK BOLT."
YOU EVER THINK ABOUT HOW DIFFERENT THINGS MIGHT BE IF YOU'D GONE THE OTHER WAY?
MONTHS AGO.
A SHORT WHILE AFTER THE FALL OF ATTILAN.
"WE HID THE CODEX UP IN THE HIMALAYAS, AND THEN WE HEADED BACK TO NEW YORK.
NEAT.
"IT LOOKED TO ME LIKE YOU WERE ABOUT TO FIND MEDUSA...TELL HER EVERYTHING...AND THEN..."
"BOOM.
"QUEEN IN THE SKY.
"YOU WATCHED HER DO HER THING, TELL THE WORLD THAT THE INHUMANS WEREN'T DONE, NOT BY A LONG SHOT--AND THEN...
"...YOU JUST LEFT. WENT TO PLAY UNIVERSE CHESS WITH YOUR ILLUMINATI BUDDIES.*
"NEVER REALLY UNDERSTOOD IT."
NOT THAT I MIND, REALLY. YOU WERE KIND ENOUGH TO BRING ME ALONG, AND WOW HAVE YOUR FRIENDS GIVEN ME SOME INTERESTING OPPORTUNITIES. ESPECIALLY NAMOR. ADORE THAT FELLOW.
...
I'M BORED.
LET'S GO DO SOMETHING FUN.
*SEE NEW AVENGERS! -NICK

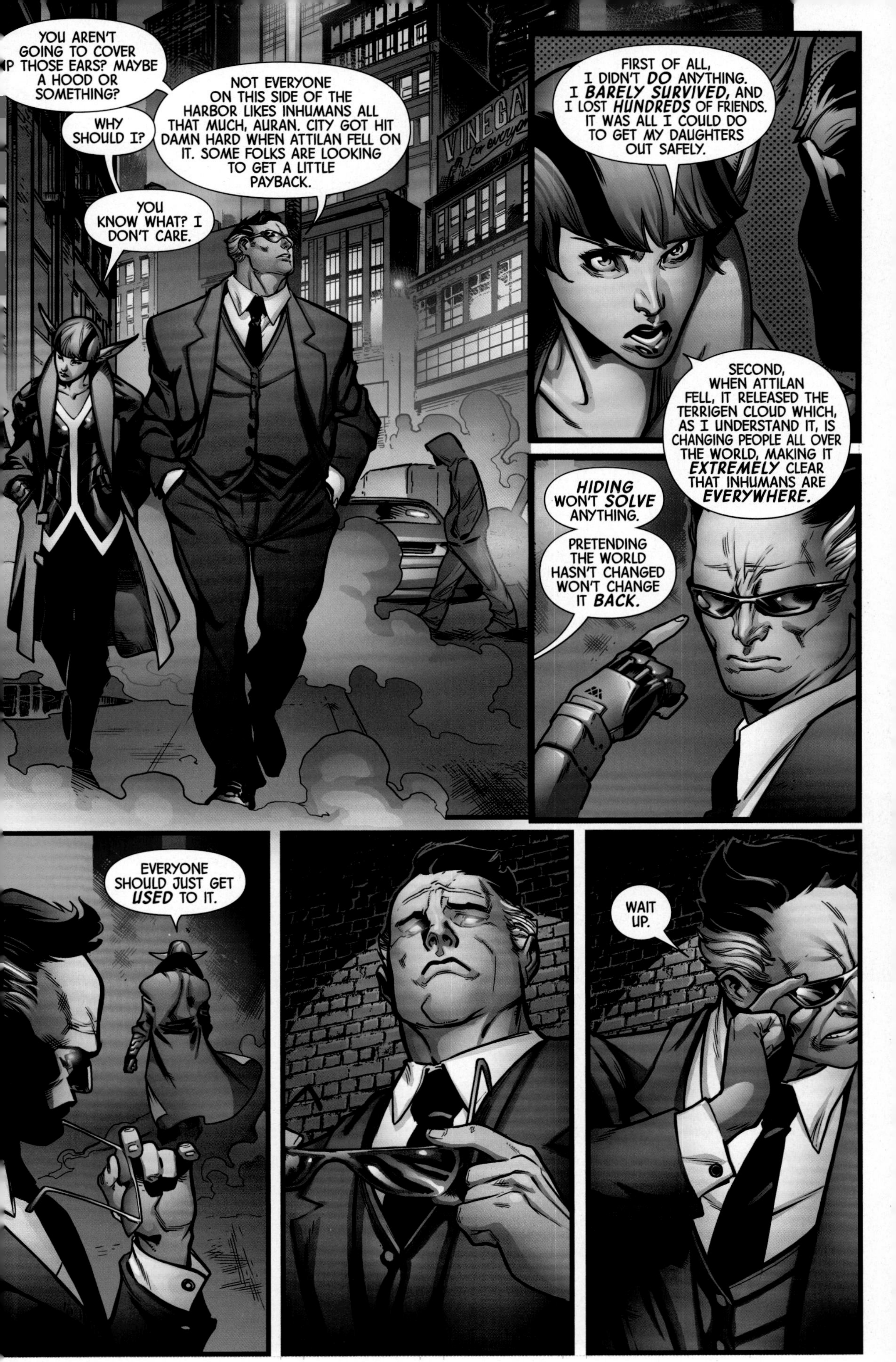

YOU AREN'T GOING TO COVER UP THOSE EARS? MAYBE A HOOD OR SOMETHING?
WHY SHOULD I?
NOT EVERYONE ON THIS SIDE OF THE HARBOR LIKES INHUMANS ALL THAT MUCH, AURAN. CITY GOT HIT DAMN HARD WHEN ATTILAN FELL ON IT. SOME FOLKS ARE LOOKING TO GET A LITTLE PAYBACK.
YOU KNOW WHAT? I DON'T CARE.
VINEGA
FIRST OF ALL, I DIDN'T DO ANYTHING. I BARELY SURVIVED, AND I LOST HUNDREDS OF FRIENDS. IT WAS ALL I COULD DO TO GET MY DAUGHTERS OUT SAFELY.
SECOND, WHEN ATTILAN FELL, IT RELEASED THE TERRIGEN CLOUD WHICH, AS I UNDERSTAND IT, IS CHANGING PEOPLE ALL OVER THE WORLD, MAKING IT EXTREMELY CLEAR THAT INHUMANS ARE EVERYWHERE.
HIDING WON'T SOLVE ANYTHING.
PRETENDING THE WORLD HASN'T CHANGED WON'T CHANGE IT BACK.
EVERYONE SHOULD JUST GET USED TO IT.
WAIT UP.

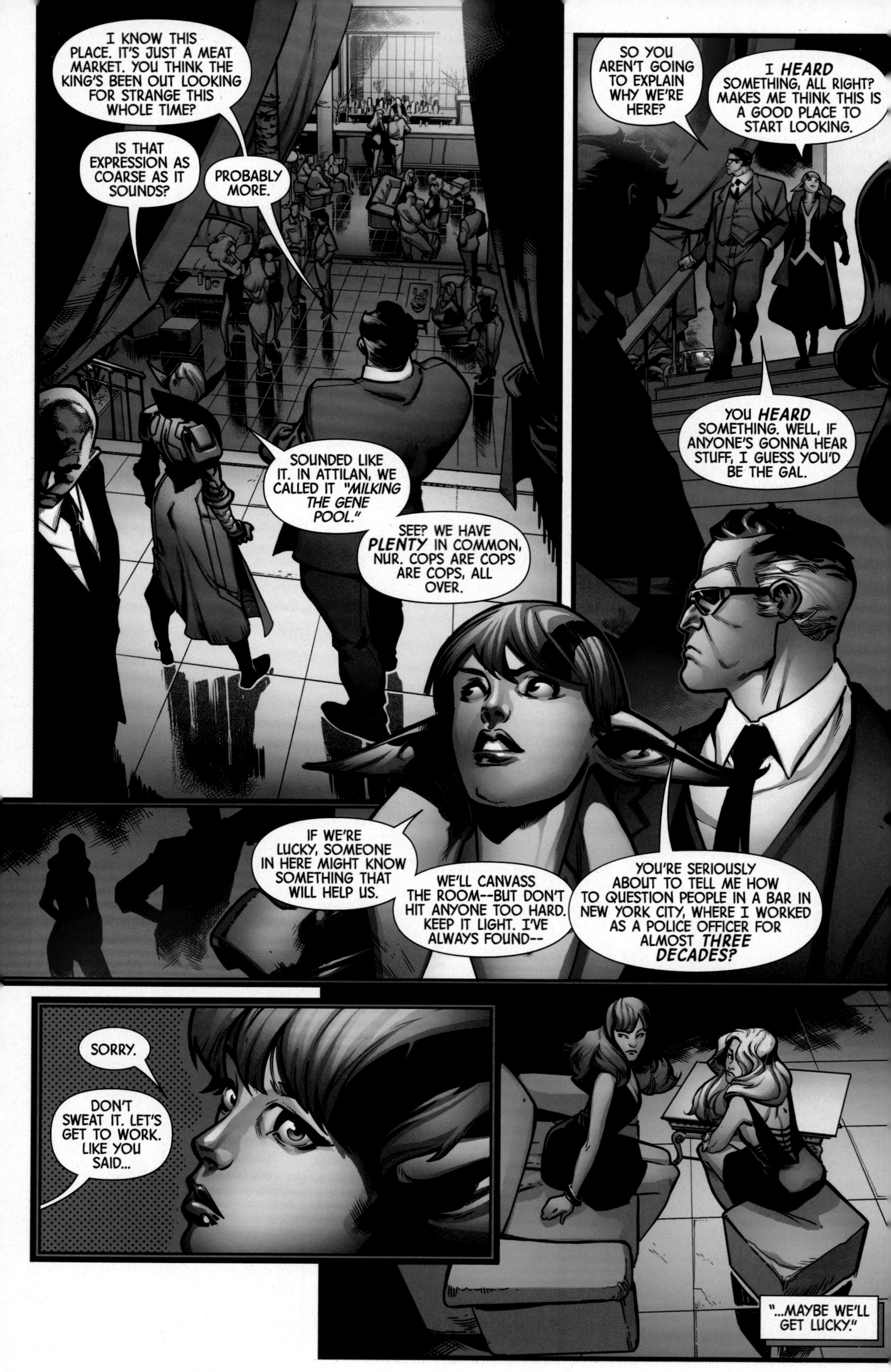
I KNOW THIS PLACE. IT'S JUST A MEAT MARKET. YOU THINK THE KING'S BEEN OUT LOOKING FOR STRANGE THIS WHOLE TIME?
IS THAT EXPRESSION AS COARSE AS IT SOUNDS?
PROBABLY MORE.
SOUNDED LIKE IT. IN ATTILAN, WE CALLED IT "MILKING THE GENE POOL."
SEE? WE HAVE PLENTY IN COMMON, NUR. COPS ARE COPS ARE COPS, ALL OVER.
SO YOU AREN'T GOING TO EXPLAIN WHY WE'RE HERE?
I HEARD SOMETHING, ALL RIGHT? MAKES ME THINK THIS IS A GOOD PLACE TO START LOOKING.
YOU HEARD SOMETHING. WELL, IF ANYONE'S GONNA HEAR STUFF, I GUESS YOU'D BE THE GAL.
IF WE'RE LUCKY, SOMEONE IN HERE MIGHT KNOW SOMETHING THAT WILL HELP US.
WE'LL CANVASS THE ROOM--BUT DON'T HIT ANYONE TOO HARD. KEEP IT LIGHT. I'VE ALWAYS FOUND--
YOU'RE SERIOUSLY ABOUT TO TELL ME HOW TO QUESTION PEOPLE IN A BAR IN NEW YORK CITY, WHERE I WORKED AS A POLICE OFFICER FOR ALMOST THREE DECADES?
SORRY.
DON'T SWEAT IT. LET'S GET TO WORK. LIKE YOU SAID...
"...MAYBE WE'LL GET LUCKY."

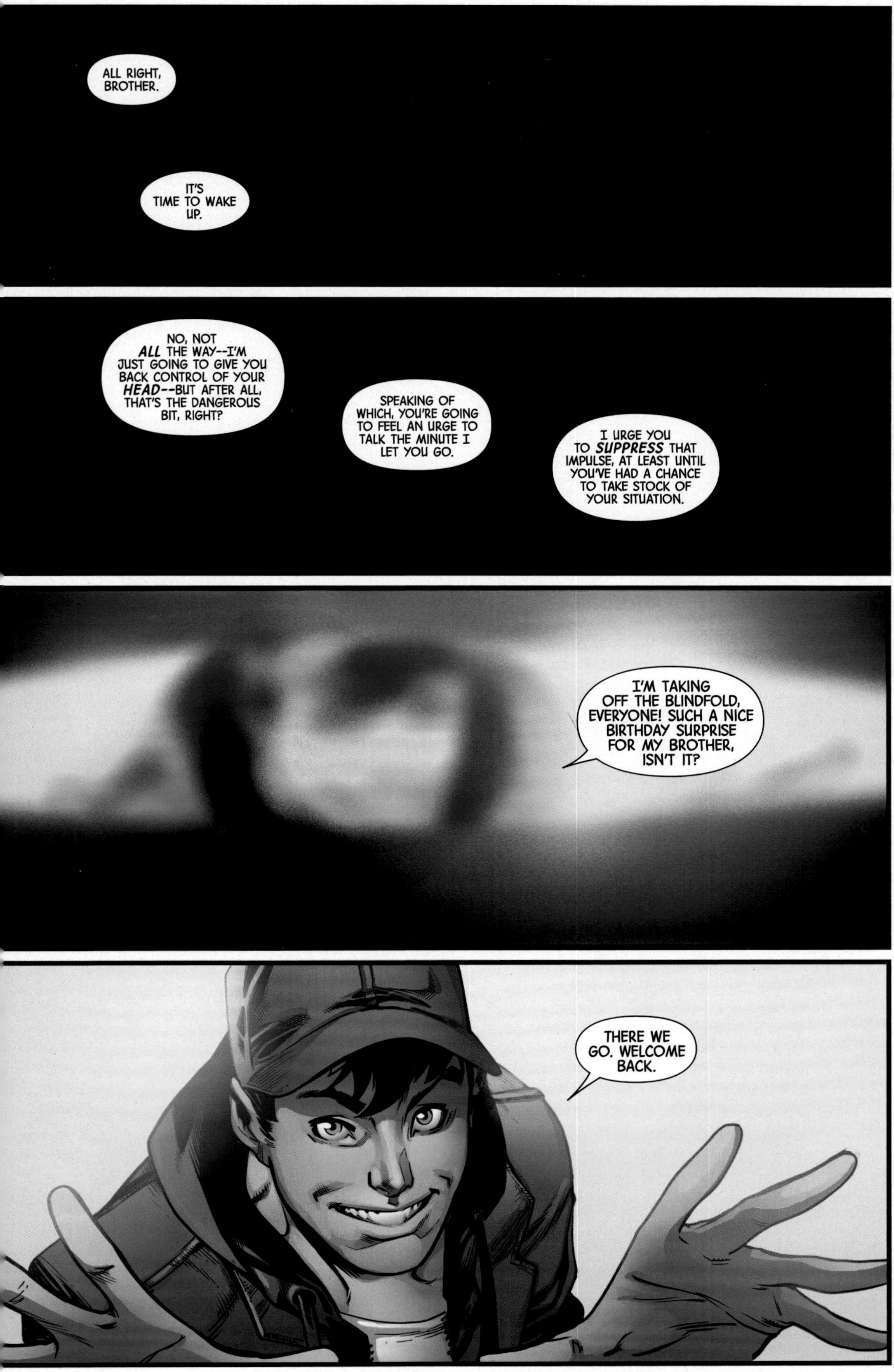
ALL RIGHT, BROTHER.
IT'S TIME TO WAKE UP.
NO, NOT ALL THE WAY--I'M JUST GOING TO GIVE YOU BACK CONTROL OF YOUR HEAD--BUT AFTER ALL, THAT'S THE DANGEROUS BIT, RIGHT?
SPEAKING OF WHICH, YOU'RE GOING TO FEEL AN URGE TO TALK THE MINUTE I LET YOU GO.
I URGE YOU TO SUPPRESS THAT IMPULSE, AT LEAST UNTIL YOU'VE HAD A CHANCE TO TAKE STOCK OF YOUR SITUATION.
I'M TAKING OFF THE BLINDFOLD, EVERYONE! SUCH A NICE BIRTHDAY SURPRISE FOR MY BROTHER, ISN'T IT?
THERE WE GO. WELCOME BACK.

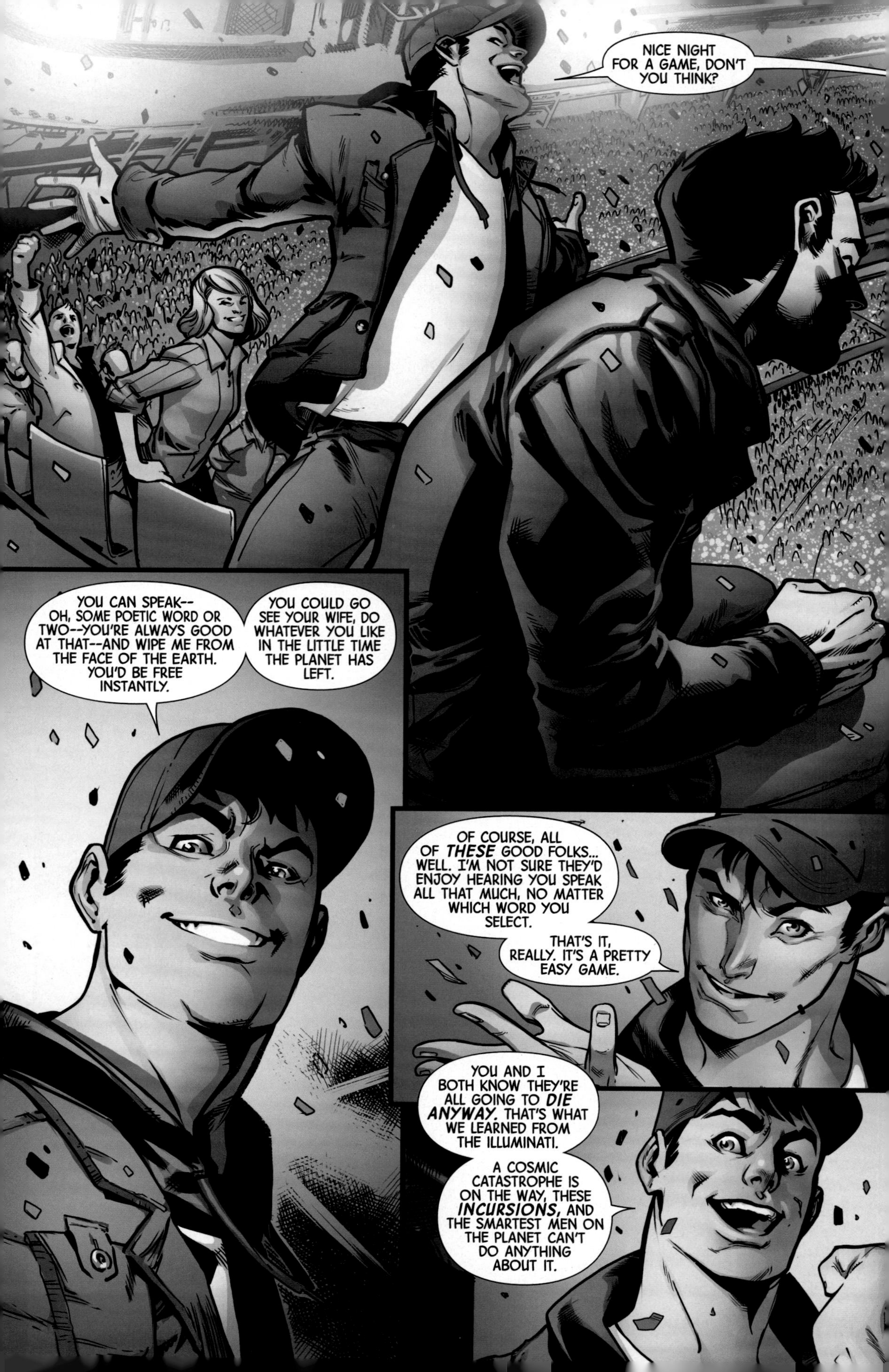
NICE NIGHT FOR A GAME, DON'T YOU THINK?
YOU CAN SPEAK-- OH, SOME POETIC WORD OR TWO--YOU'RE ALWAYS GOOD AT THAT--AND WIPE ME FROM THE FACE OF THE EARTH. YOU'D BE FREE INSTANTLY.
YOU COULD GO SEE YOUR WIFE, DO WHATEVER YOU LIKE IN THE LITTLE TIME THE PLANET HAS LEFT.
OF COURSE, ALL OF THESE GOOD FOLKS... WELL. I'M NOT SURE THEY'D ENJOY HEARING YOU SPEAK ALL THAT MUCH, NO MATTER WHICH WORD YOU SELECT.
THAT'S IT, REALLY. IT'S A PRETTY EASY GAME.
YOU AND I BOTH KNOW THEY'RE ALL GOING TO DIE ANYWAY. THAT'S WHAT WE LEARNED FROM THE ILLUMINATI.
A COSMIC CATASTROPHE IS ON THE WAY, THESE INCURSIONS, AND THE SMARTEST MEN ON THE PLANET CAN'T DO ANYTHING ABOUT IT.

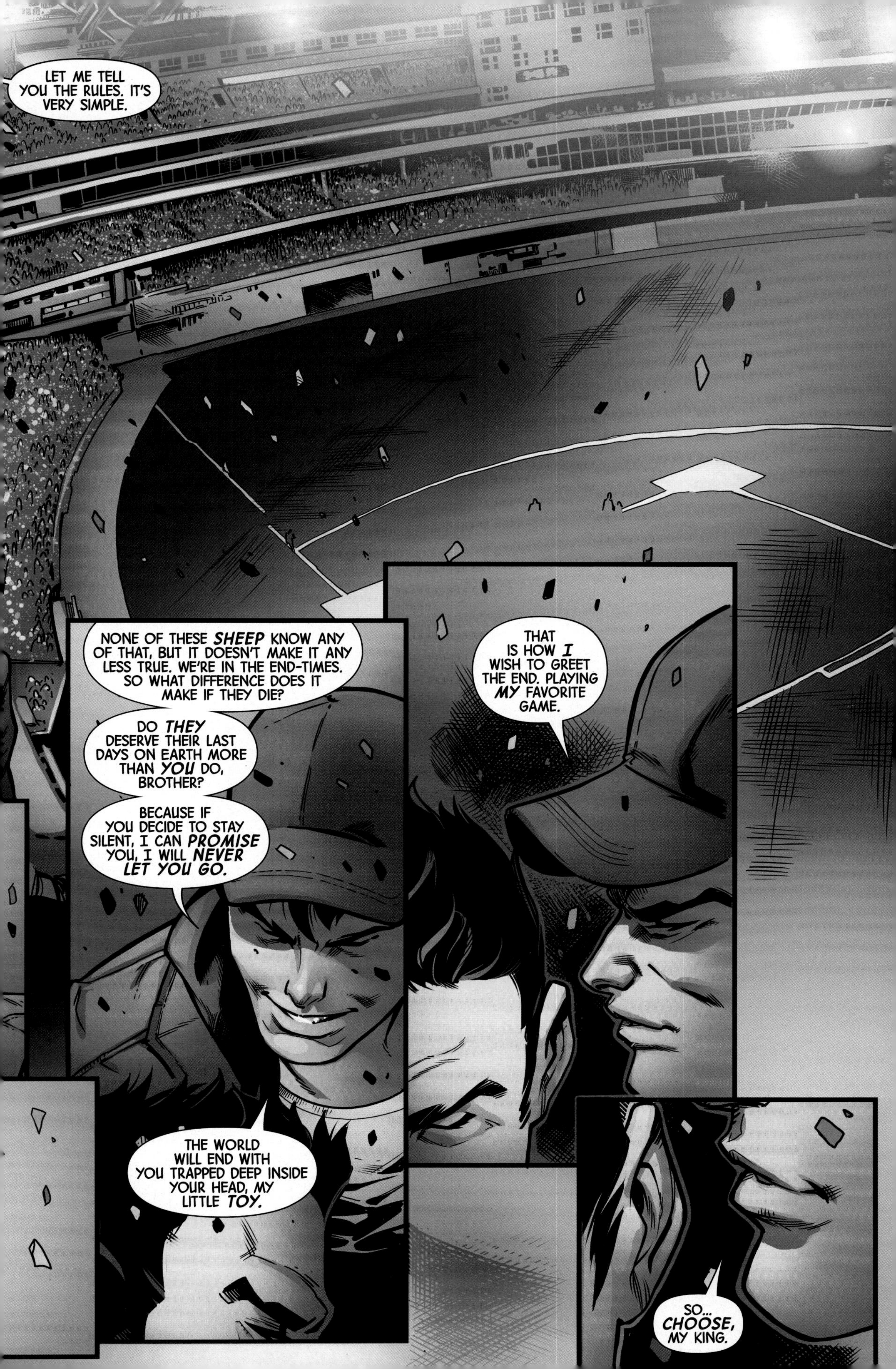
LET ME TELL YOU THE RULES. IT'S VERY SIMPLE.
NONE OF THESE SHEEP KNOW ANY OF THAT, BUT IT DOESN'T MAKE IT ANY LESS TRUE. WE'RE IN THE END-TIMES. SO WHAT DIFFERENCE DOES IT MAKE IF THEY DIE?
DO THEY DESERVE THEIR LAST DAYS ON EARTH MORE THAN YOU DO, BROTHER?
BECAUSE IF YOU DECIDE TO STAY SILENT, I CAN PROMISE YOU, I WILL NEVER LET YOU GO.
THAT IS HOW I WISH TO GREET THE END. PLAYING MY FAVORITE GAME.
THE WORLD WILL END WITH YOU TRAPPED DEEP INSIDE YOUR HEAD, MY LITTLE TOY.
SO... CHOOSE, MY KING.

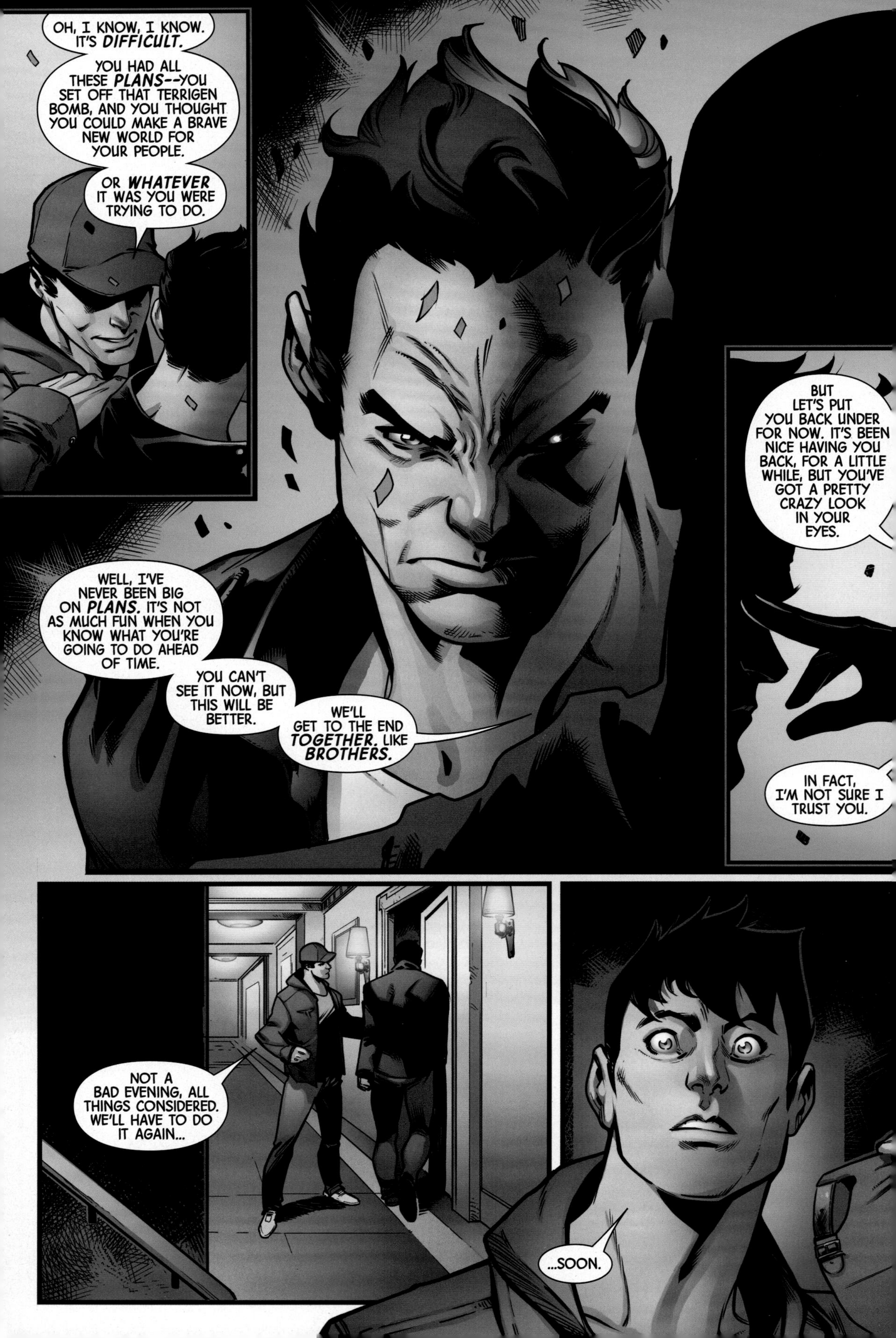

OH, I KNOW, I KNOW. IT'S DIFFICULT.
YOU HAD ALL THESE PLANS--YOU SET OFF THAT TERRIGEN BOMB, AND YOU THOUGHT YOU COULD MAKE A BRAVE NEW WORLD FOR YOUR PEOPLE.
OR WHATEVER IT WAS YOU WERE TRYING TO DO.
BUT LET'S PUT YOU BACK UNDER FOR NOW. IT'S BEEN NICE HAVING YOU BACK, FOR A LITTLE WHILE, BUT YOU'VE GOT A PRETTY CRAZY LOOK IN YOUR EYES.
WELL, I'VE NEVER BEEN BIG ON PLANS. IT'S NOT AS MUCH FUN WHEN YOU KNOW WHAT YOU'RE GOING TO DO AHEAD OF TIME.
YOU CAN'T SEE IT NOW, BUT THIS WILL BE BETTER.
WE'LL GET TO THE END TOGETHER. LIKE BROTHERS.
IN FACT, I'M NOT SURE I TRUST YOU.
NOT A BAD EVENING, ALL THINGS CONSIDERED. WE'LL HAVE TO DO IT AGAIN...
...SOON.

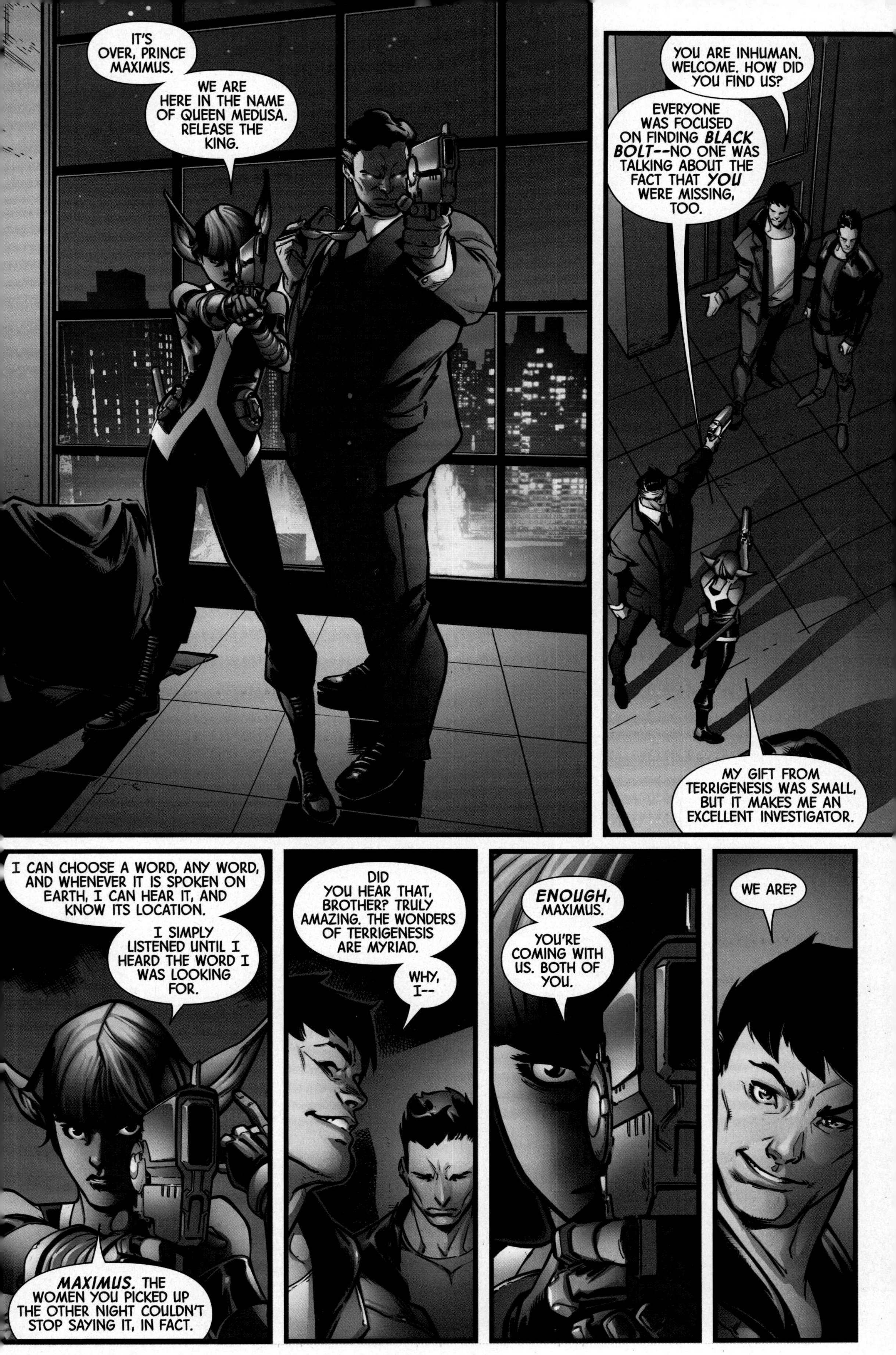
IT'S OVER, PRINCE MAXIMUS.
WE ARE HERE IN THE NAME OF QUEEN MEDUSA. RELEASE THE KING.
YOU ARE INHUMAN. WELCOME. HOW DID YOU FIND US?
EVERYONE WAS FOCUSED ON FINDING BLACK BOLT--NO ONE WAS TALKING ABOUT THE FACT THAT YOU WERE MISSING, TOO.
MY GIFT FROM TERRIGENESIS WAS SMALL, BUT IT MAKES ME AN EXCELLENT INVESTIGATOR.
I CAN CHOOSE A WORD, ANY WORD, AND WHENEVER IT IS SPOKEN ON EARTH, I CAN HEAR IT, AND KNOW ITS LOCATION.
I SIMPLY LISTENED UNTIL I HEARD THE WORD I WAS LOOKING FOR.
MAXIMUS. THE WOMEN YOU PICKED UP THE OTHER NIGHT COULDN'T STOP SAYING IT, IN FACT.
DID YOU HEAR THAT, BROTHER? TRULY AMAZING. THE WONDERS OF TERRIGENESIS ARE MYRIAD.
WHY, I--
ENOUGH, MAXIMUS.
YOU'RE COMING WITH US. BOTH OF YOU.
WE ARE?

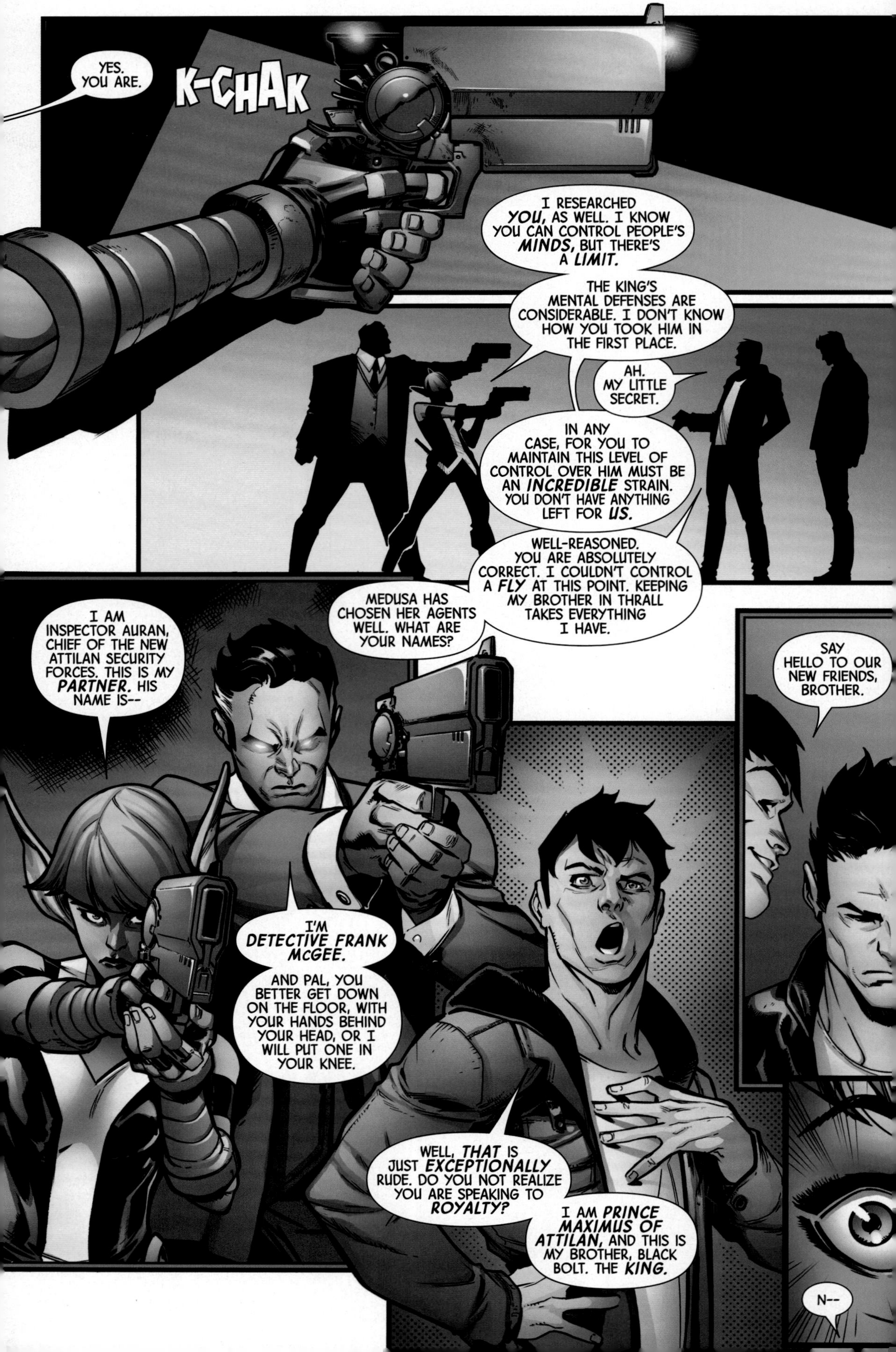

YES. YOU ARE.
K-CHAK
I RESEARCHED YOU, AS WELL. I KNOW YOU CAN CONTROL PEOPLE'S MINDS, BUT THERE'S A LIMIT.
THE KING'S MENTAL DEFENSES ARE CONSIDERABLE. I DON'T KNOW HOW YOU TOOK HIM IN THE FIRST PLACE.
AH. MY LITTLE SECRET.
IN ANY CASE, FOR YOU TO MAINTAIN THIS LEVEL OF CONTROL OVER HIM MUST BE AN INCREDIBLE STRAIN. YOU DON'T HAVE ANYTHING LEFT FOR US.
WELL-REASONED. YOU ARE ABSOLUTELY CORRECT. I COULDN'T CONTROL A FLY AT THIS POINT. KEEPING MY BROTHER IN THRALL TAKES EVERYTHING I HAVE.
MEDUSA HAS CHOSEN HER AGENTS WELL. WHAT ARE YOUR NAMES?
I AM INSPECTOR AURAN, CHIEF OF THE NEW ATTILAN SECURITY FORCES. THIS IS MY PARTNER. HIS NAME IS--
I'M DETECTIVE FRANK McGEE.
AND PAL, YOU BETTER GET DOWN ON THE FLOOR, WITH YOUR HANDS BEHIND YOUR HEAD, OR I WILL PUT ONE IN YOUR KNEE.
WELL, THAT IS JUST EXCEPTIONALLY RUDE. DO YOU NOT REALIZE YOU ARE SPEAKING TO ROYALTY?
I AM PRINCE MAXIMUS OF ATTILAN, AND THIS IS MY BROTHER, BLACK BOLT. THE KING.
SAY HELLO TO OUR NEW FRIENDS, BROTHER.
N--

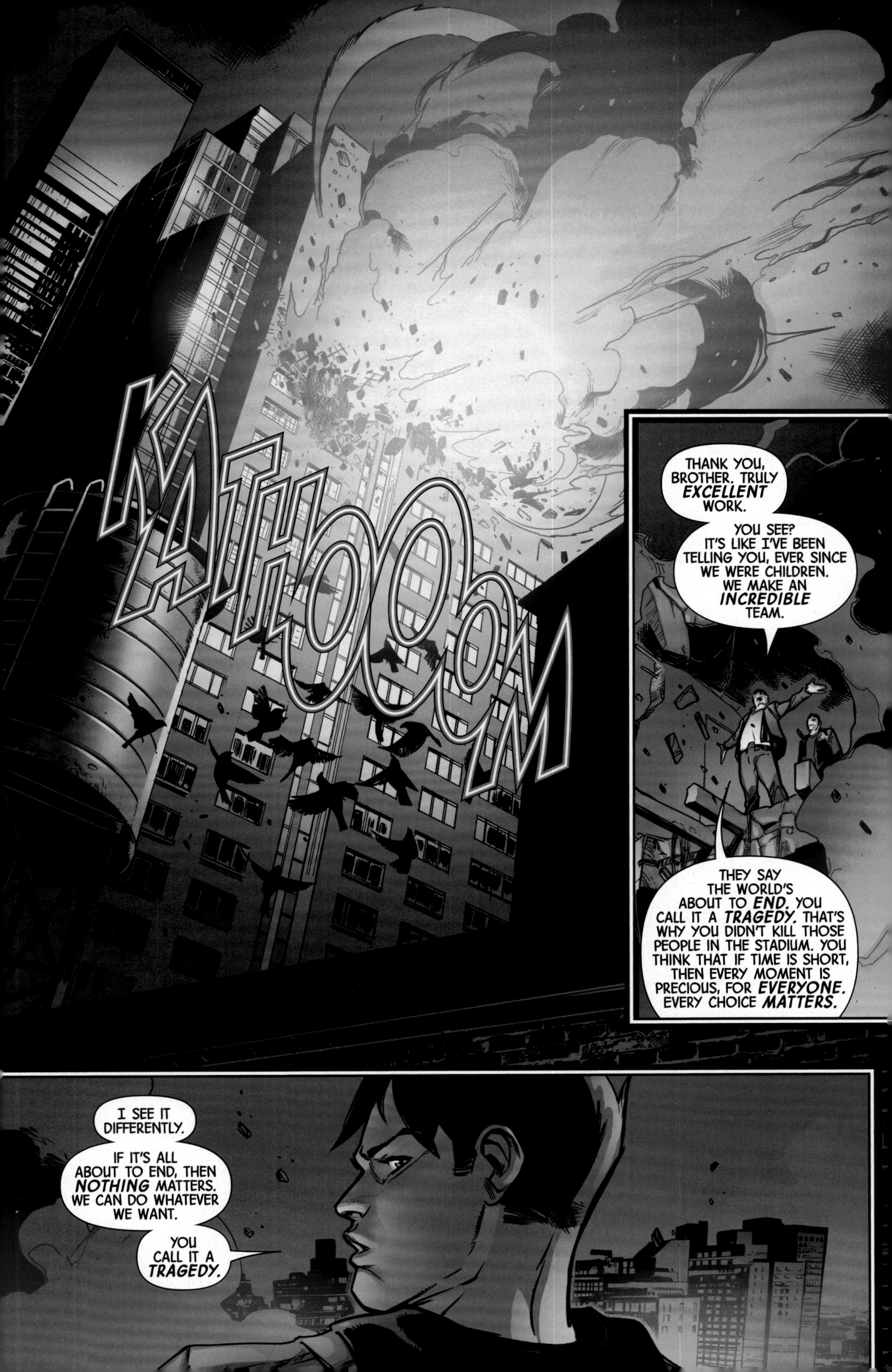
KATHOOOOM
THANK YOU, BROTHER. TRULY *EXCELLENT* WORK.
YOU SEE? IT'S LIKE I'VE BEEN TELLING YOU, EVER SINCE WE WERE CHILDREN. WE MAKE AN *INCREDIBLE* TEAM.
THEY SAY THE WORLD'S ABOUT TO *END.* YOU CALL IT A *TRAGEDY.* THAT'S WHY YOU DIDN'T KILL THOSE PEOPLE IN THE STADIUM. YOU THINK THAT IF TIME IS SHORT, THEN EVERY MOMENT IS PRECIOUS, FOR *EVERYONE.* EVERY CHOICE *MATTERS.*
I SEE IT DIFFERENTLY.
IF IT'S ALL ABOUT TO END, THEN *NOTHING* MATTERS. WE CAN DO WHATEVER WE WANT.
YOU CALL IT A *TRAGEDY.*

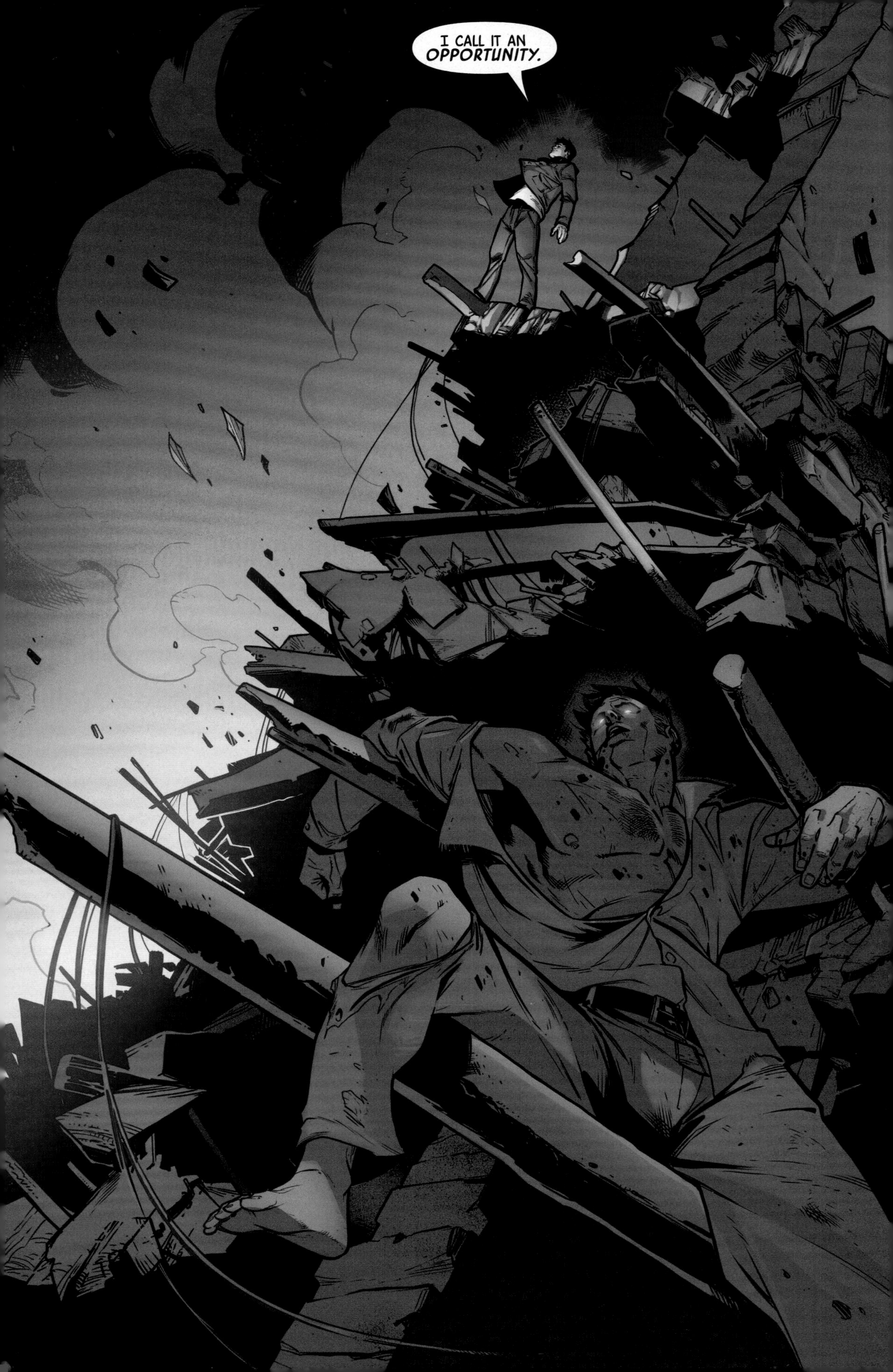
I CALL IT AN OPPORTUNITY.

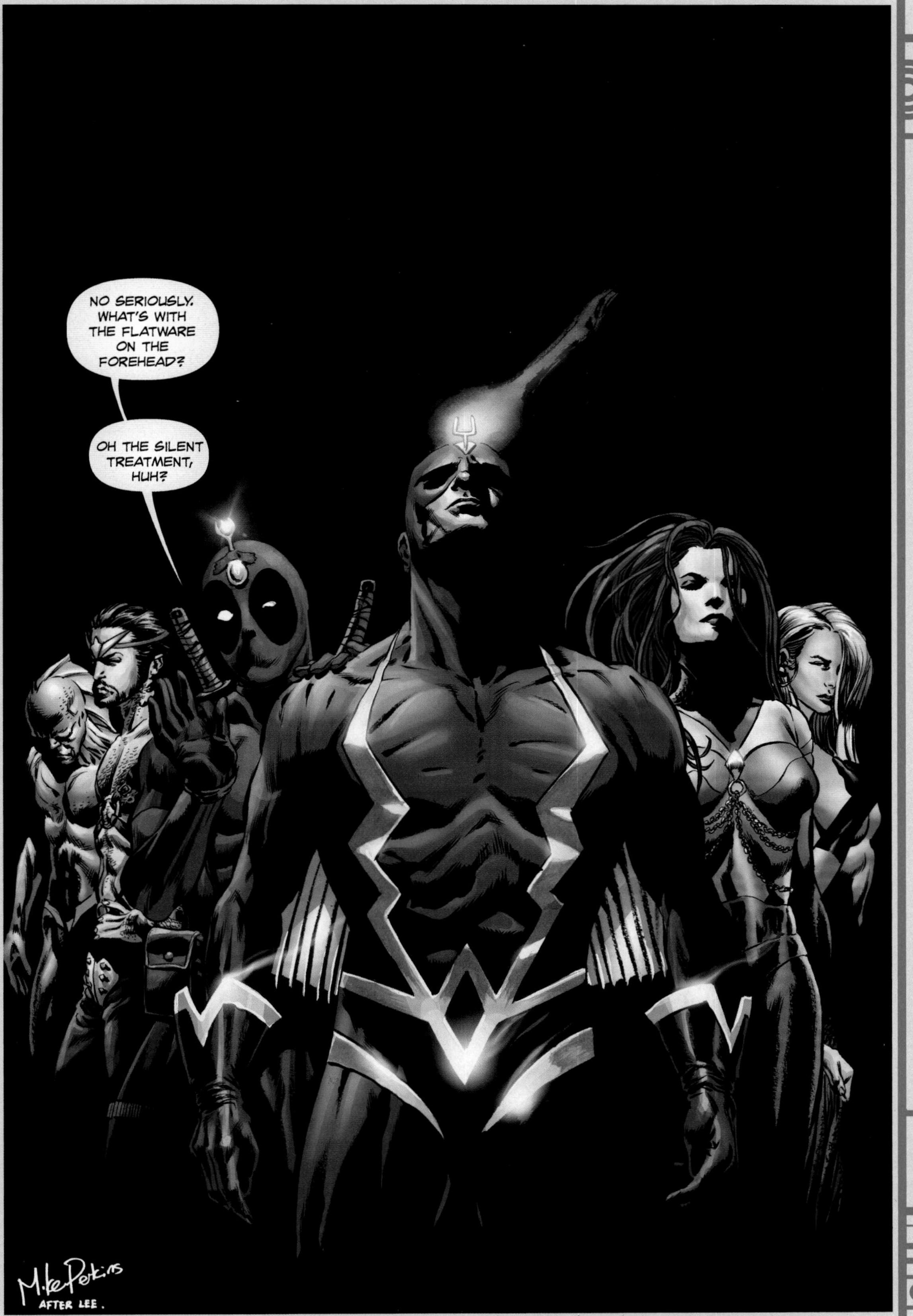
NO SERIOUSLY. WHAT'S WITH THE FLATWARE ON THE FOREHEAD?
OH THE SILENT TREATMENT, HUH?
Mike Perkins
AFTER LEE.

DEADPOOL 75TH ANNIVERSARY VARIANT
BY MIKE PERKINS & ANDY TROY

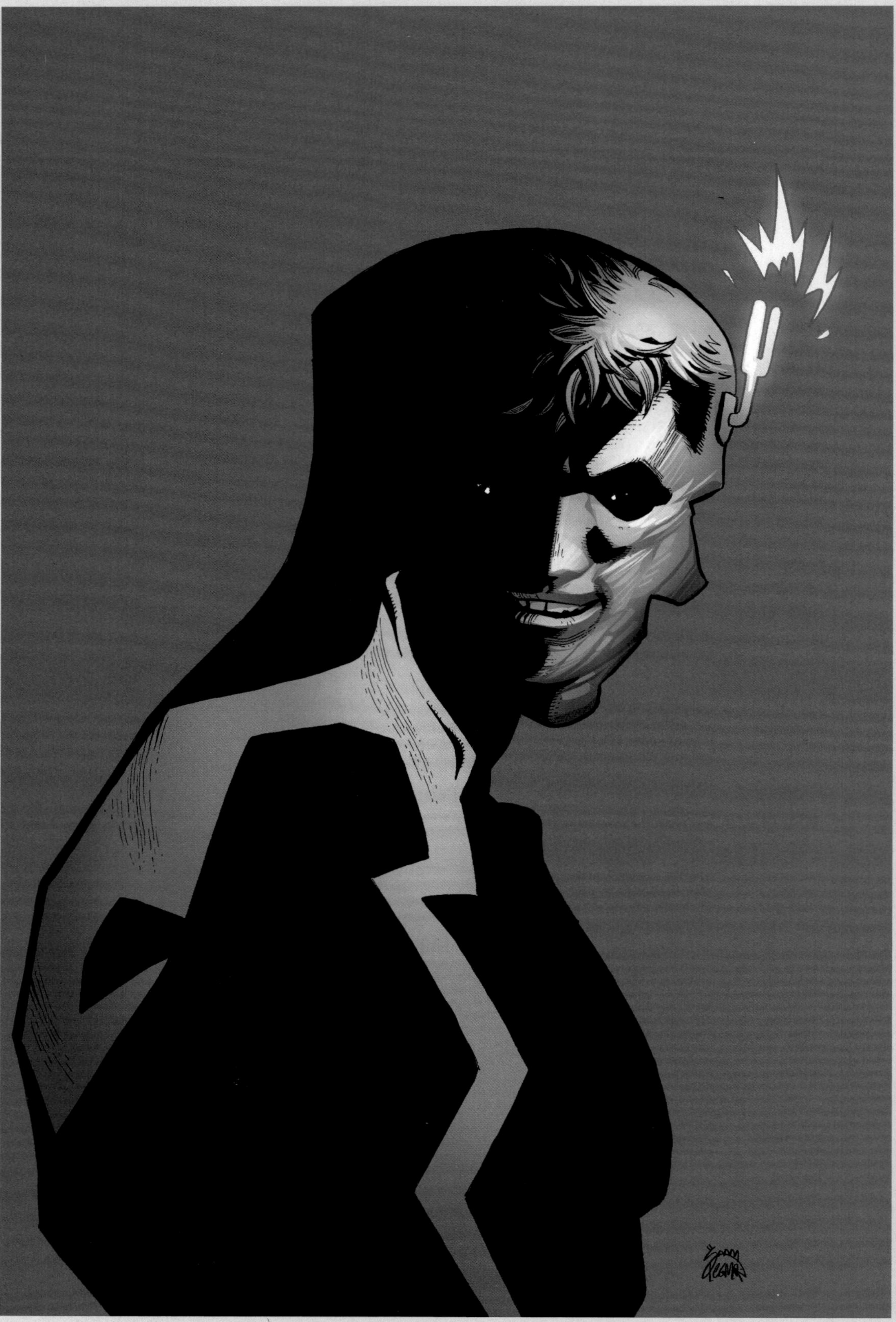

8 PART EIGHT: COMES THE LIGHT

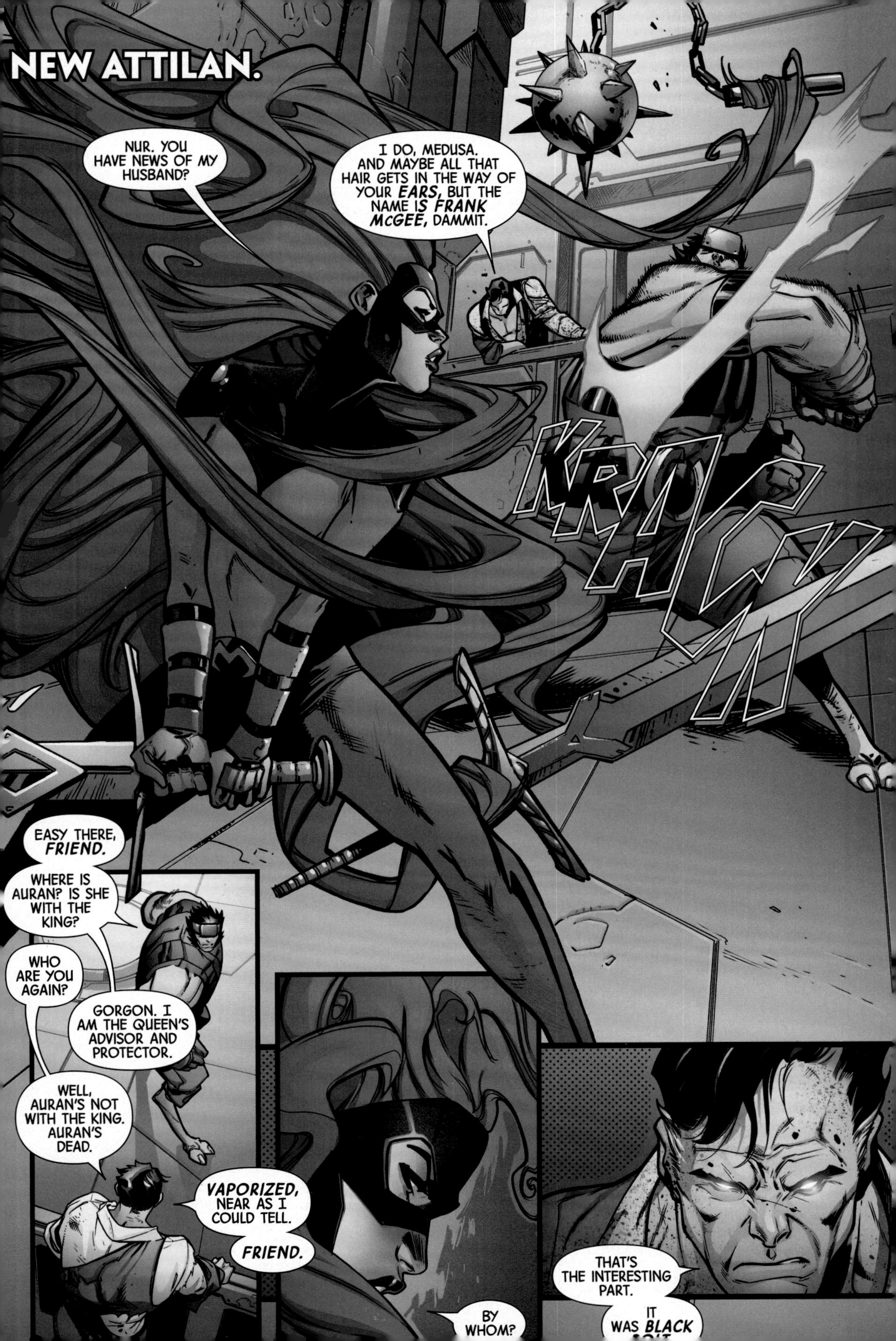
NEW ATTILAN.
NUR. YOU HAVE NEWS OF MY HUSBAND?
I DO, MEDUSA. AND MAYBE ALL THAT HAIR GETS IN THE WAY OF YOUR *EARS*, BUT THE NAME IS *FRANK McGEE*, DAMMIT.
KRACK
EASY THERE, *FRIEND.*
WHERE IS AURAN? IS SHE WITH THE KING?
WHO ARE YOU AGAIN?
GORGON. I AM THE QUEEN'S ADVISOR AND PROTECTOR.
WELL, AURAN'S NOT WITH THE KING. AURAN'S DEAD.
VAPORIZED, NEAR AS I COULD TELL.
FRIEND.
BY WHOM?
THAT'S THE INTERESTING PART.
IT WAS *BLACK*

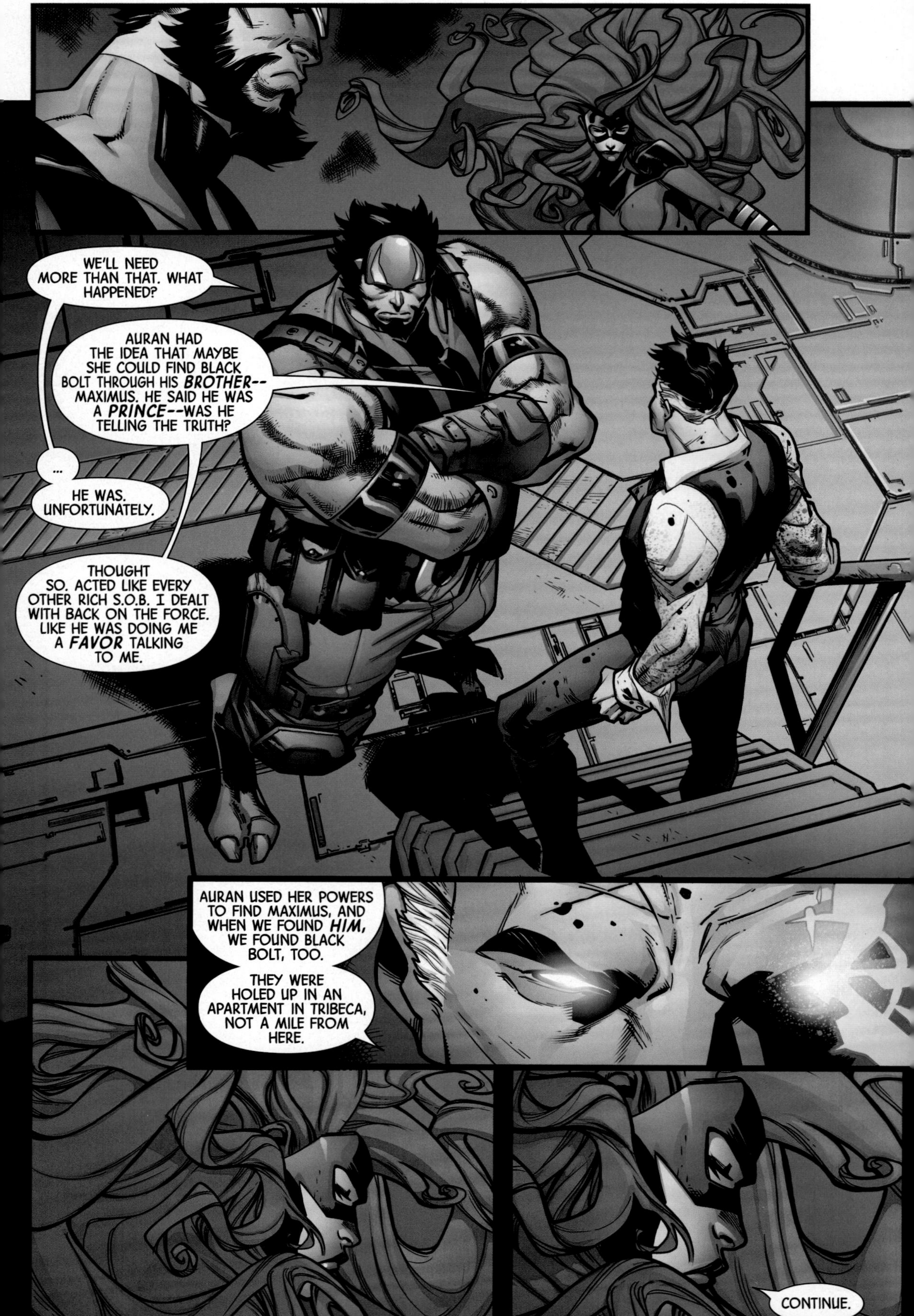
WE'LL NEED MORE THAN THAT. WHAT HAPPENED?
AURAN HAD THE IDEA THAT MAYBE SHE COULD FIND BLACK BOLT THROUGH HIS BROTHER--MAXIMUS. HE SAID HE WAS A PRINCE--WAS HE TELLING THE TRUTH?
...
HE WAS. UNFORTUNATELY.
THOUGHT SO. ACTED LIKE EVERY OTHER RICH S.O.B. I DEALT WITH BACK ON THE FORCE. LIKE HE WAS DOING ME A FAVOR TALKING TO ME.
AURAN USED HER POWERS TO FIND MAXIMUS, AND WHEN WE FOUND HIM, WE FOUND BLACK BOLT, TOO.
THEY WERE HOLED UP IN AN APARTMENT IN TRIBECA, NOT A MILE FROM HERE.
CONTINUE.

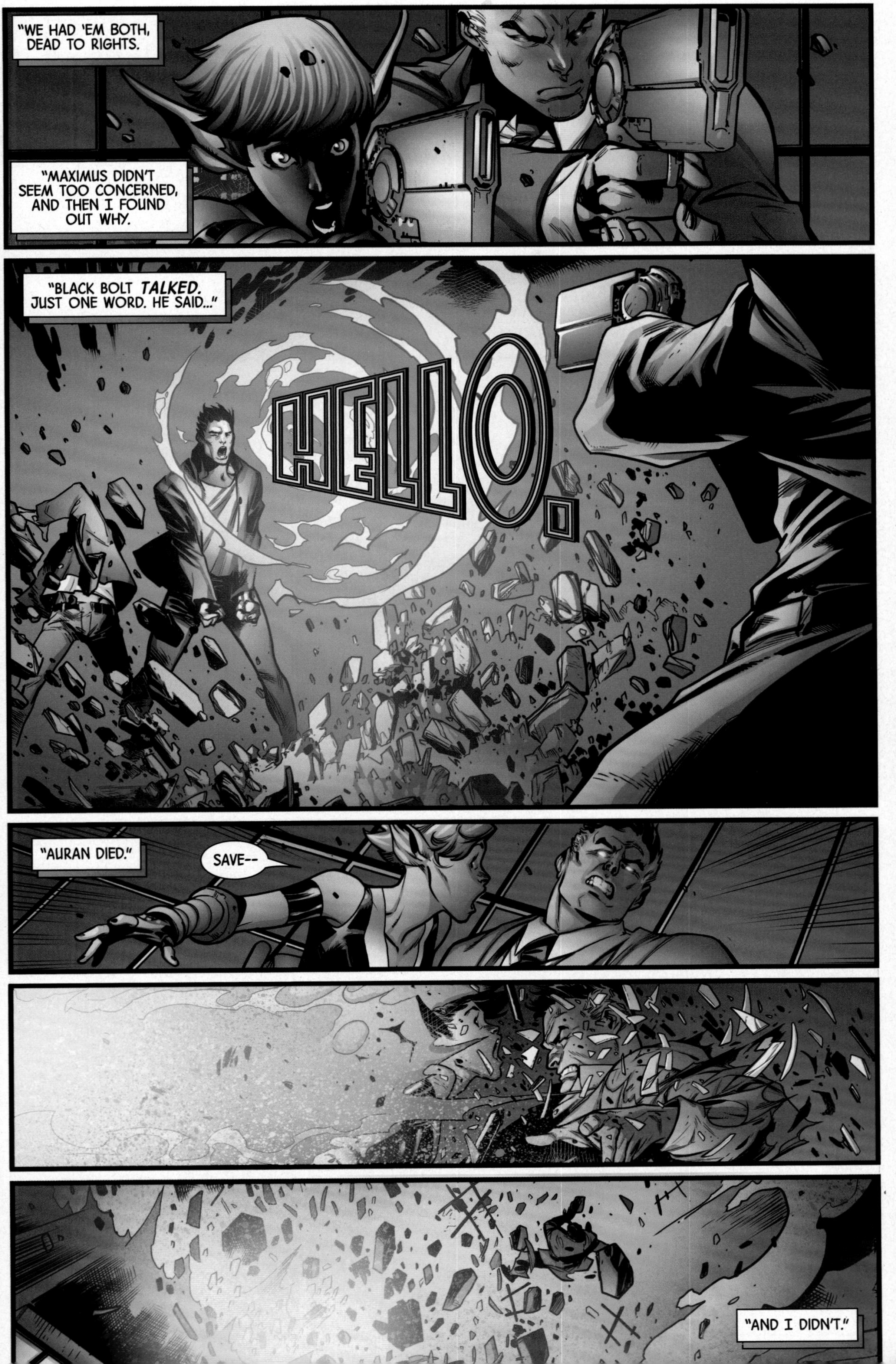
"WE HAD 'EM BOTH, DEAD TO RIGHTS.
"MAXIMUS DIDN'T SEEM TOO CONCERNED, AND THEN I FOUND OUT WHY.
"BLACK BOLT TALKED. JUST ONE WORD. HE SAID..."
HELLO.
"AURAN DIED."
SAVE--
"AND I DIDN'T."

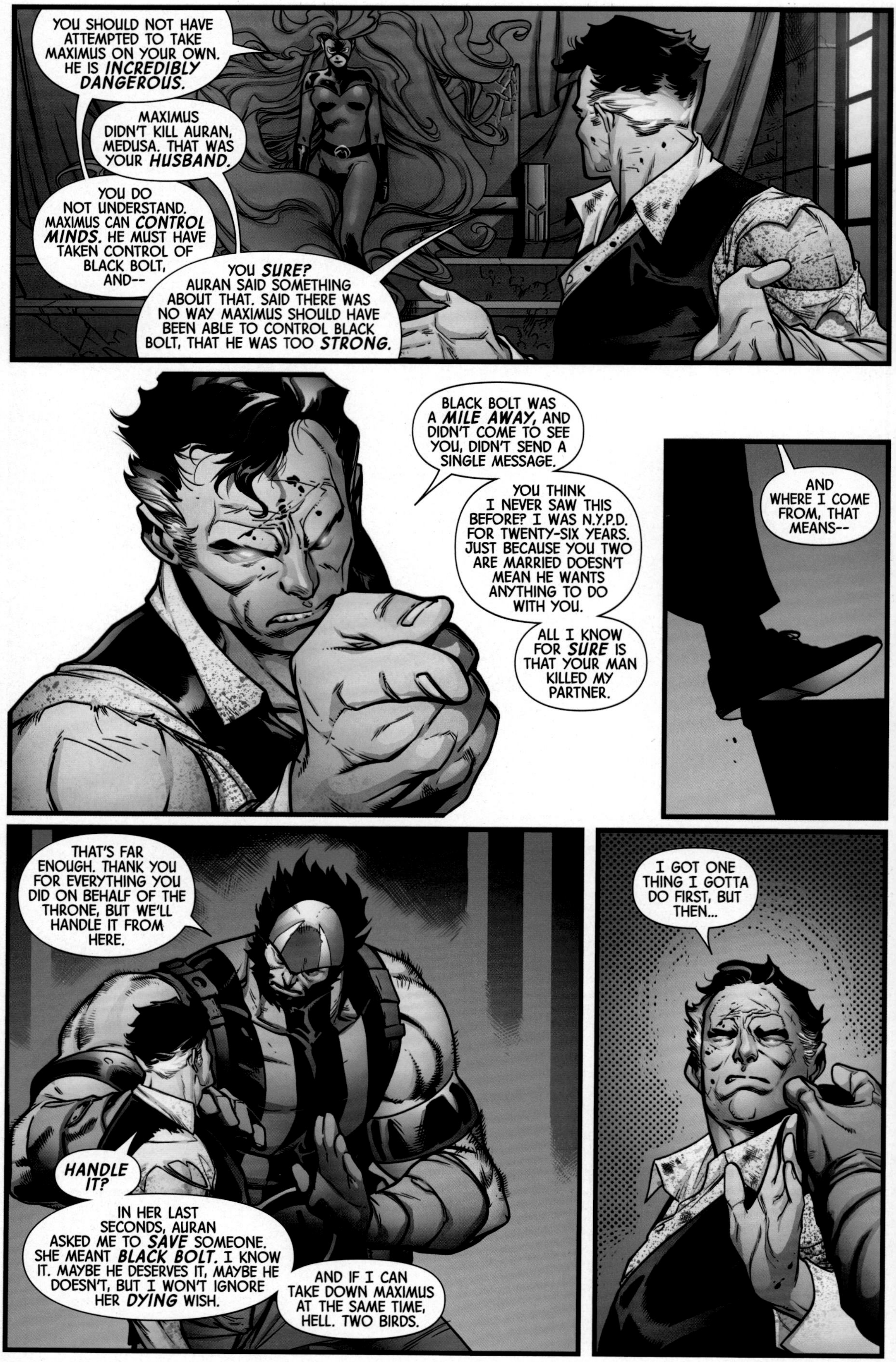
YOU SHOULD NOT HAVE ATTEMPTED TO TAKE MAXIMUS ON YOUR OWN. HE IS INCREDIBLY DANGEROUS.
MAXIMUS DIDN'T KILL AURAN, MEDUSA. THAT WAS YOUR HUSBAND.
YOU DO NOT UNDERSTAND. MAXIMUS CAN CONTROL MINDS. HE MUST HAVE TAKEN CONTROL OF BLACK BOLT, AND--
YOU SURE? AURAN SAID SOMETHING ABOUT THAT. SAID THERE WAS NO WAY MAXIMUS SHOULD HAVE BEEN ABLE TO CONTROL BLACK BOLT, THAT HE WAS TOO STRONG.
BLACK BOLT WAS A MILE AWAY, AND DIDN'T COME TO SEE YOU, DIDN'T SEND A SINGLE MESSAGE.
YOU THINK I NEVER SAW THIS BEFORE? I WAS N.Y.P.D. FOR TWENTY-SIX YEARS. JUST BECAUSE YOU TWO ARE MARRIED DOESN'T MEAN HE WANTS ANYTHING TO DO WITH YOU.
ALL I KNOW FOR SURE IS THAT YOUR MAN KILLED MY PARTNER.
AND WHERE I COME FROM, THAT MEANS--
THAT'S FAR ENOUGH. THANK YOU FOR EVERYTHING YOU DID ON BEHALF OF THE THRONE, BUT WE'LL HANDLE IT FROM HERE.
HANDLE IT?
IN HER LAST SECONDS, AURAN ASKED ME TO SAVE SOMEONE. SHE MEANT BLACK BOLT. I KNOW IT. MAYBE HE DESERVES IT, MAYBE HE DOESN'T, BUT I WON'T IGNORE HER DYING WISH.
AND IF I CAN TAKE DOWN MAXIMUS AT THE SAME TIME, HELL. TWO BIRDS.
I GOT ONE THING I GOTTA DO FIRST, BUT THEN...

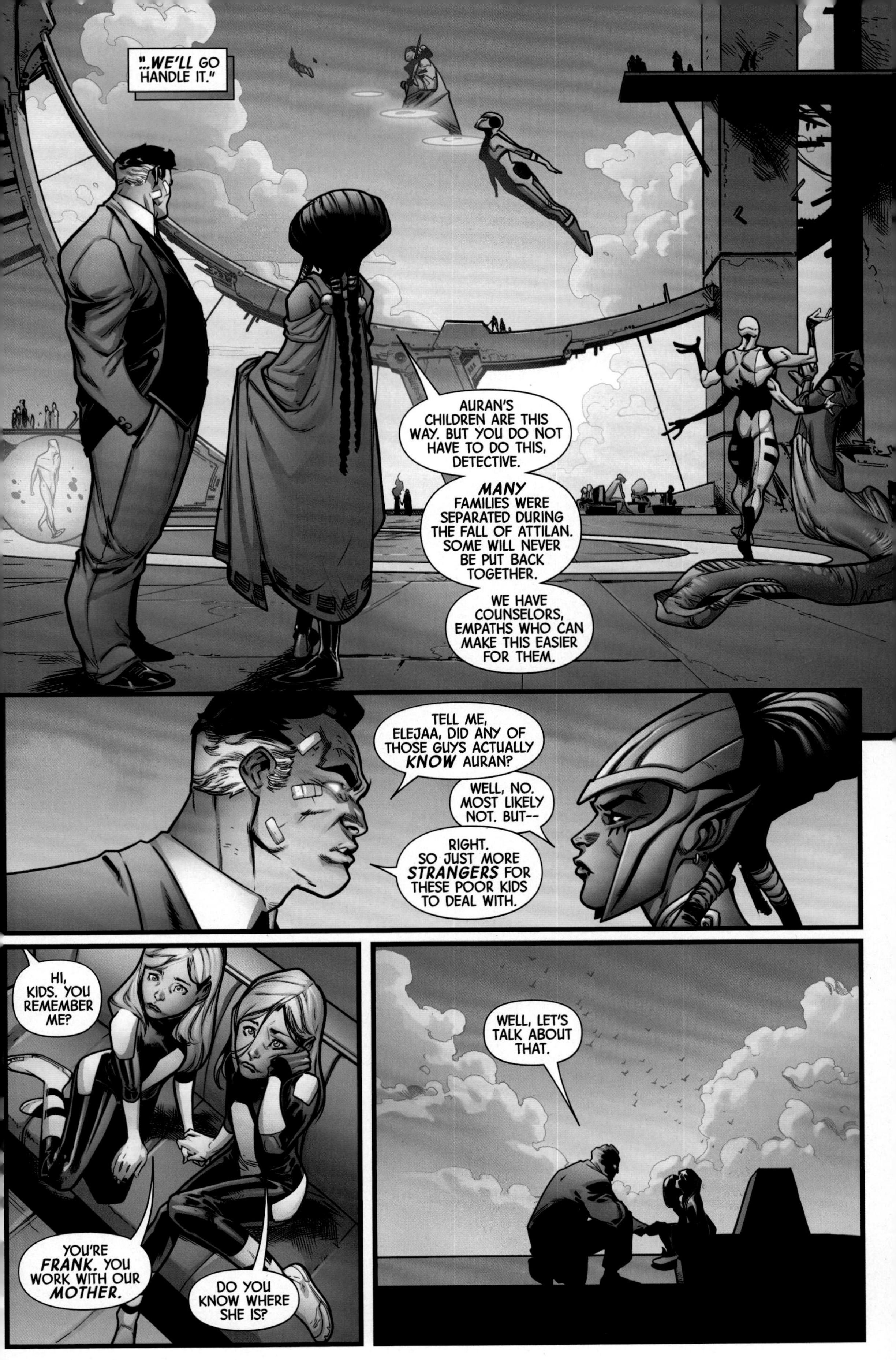

"...WE'LL GO HANDLE IT."
AURAN'S CHILDREN ARE THIS WAY. BUT YOU DO NOT HAVE TO DO THIS, DETECTIVE.
MANY FAMILIES WERE SEPARATED DURING THE FALL OF ATTILAN. SOME WILL NEVER BE PUT BACK TOGETHER.
WE HAVE COUNSELORS, EMPATHS WHO CAN MAKE THIS EASIER FOR THEM.
TELL ME, ELEJAA, DID ANY OF THOSE GUYS ACTUALLY KNOW AURAN?
WELL, NO. MOST LIKELY NOT. BUT--
RIGHT. SO JUST MORE STRANGERS FOR THESE POOR KIDS TO DEAL WITH.
HI, KIDS. YOU REMEMBER ME?
YOU'RE FRANK. YOU WORK WITH OUR MOTHER.
DO YOU KNOW WHERE SHE IS?
WELL, LET'S TALK ABOUT THAT.

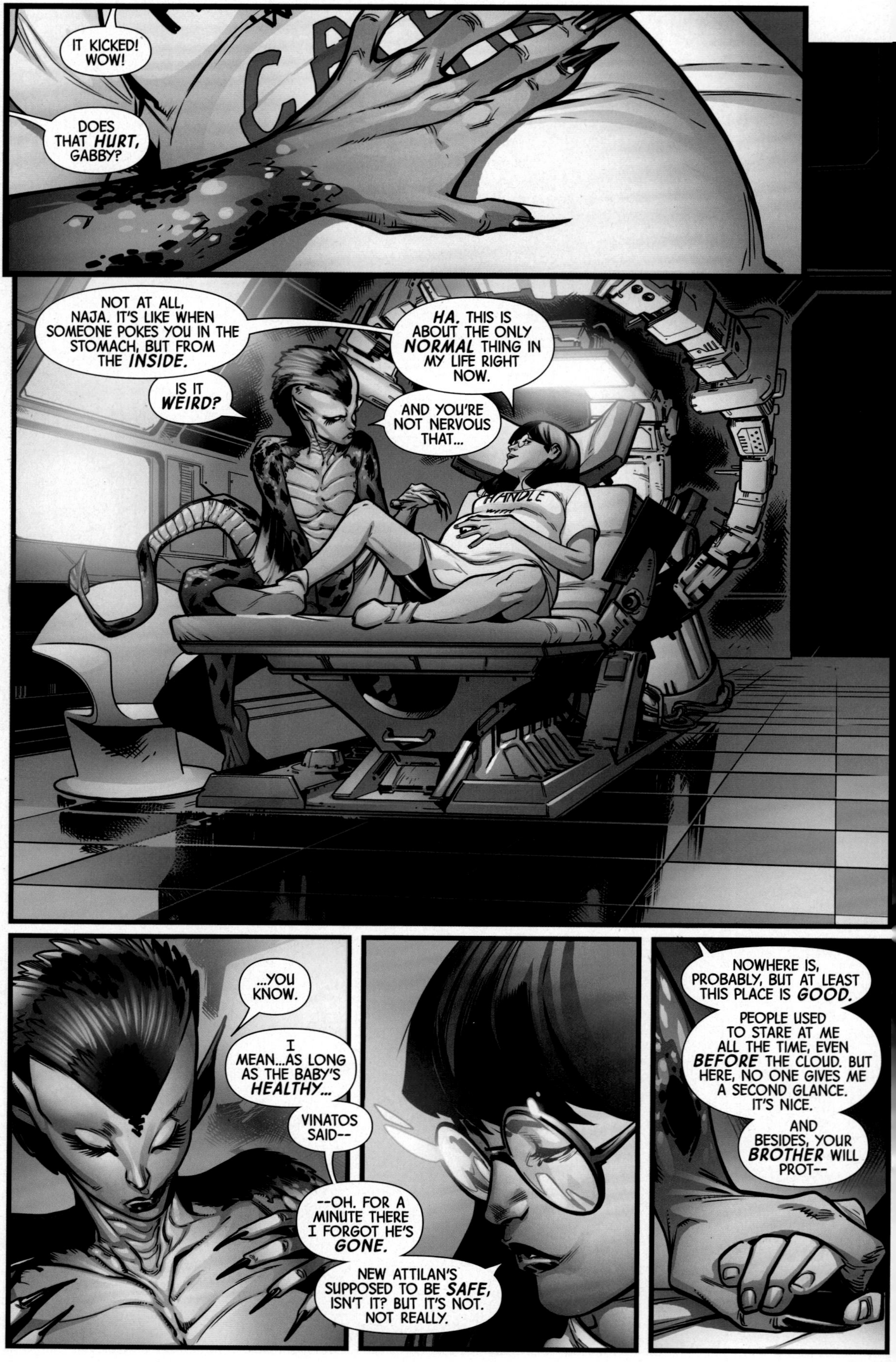
IT KICKED! WOW!
DOES THAT HURT, GABBY?
NOT AT ALL, NAJA. IT'S LIKE WHEN SOMEONE POKES YOU IN THE STOMACH, BUT FROM THE INSIDE.
IS IT WEIRD?
HA. THIS IS ABOUT THE ONLY NORMAL THING IN MY LIFE RIGHT NOW.
AND YOU'RE NOT NERVOUS THAT...
HANDLE
...YOU KNOW.
I MEAN...AS LONG AS THE BABY'S HEALTHY...
VINATOS SAID--
--OH. FOR A MINUTE THERE I FORGOT HE'S GONE.
NEW ATTILAN'S SUPPOSED TO BE SAFE, ISN'T IT? BUT IT'S NOT. NOT REALLY.
NOWHERE IS, PROBABLY, BUT AT LEAST THIS PLACE IS GOOD.
PEOPLE USED TO STARE AT ME ALL THE TIME, EVEN BEFORE THE CLOUD. BUT HERE, NO ONE GIVES ME A SECOND GLANCE. IT'S NICE.
AND BESIDES, YOUR BROTHER WILL PROT--

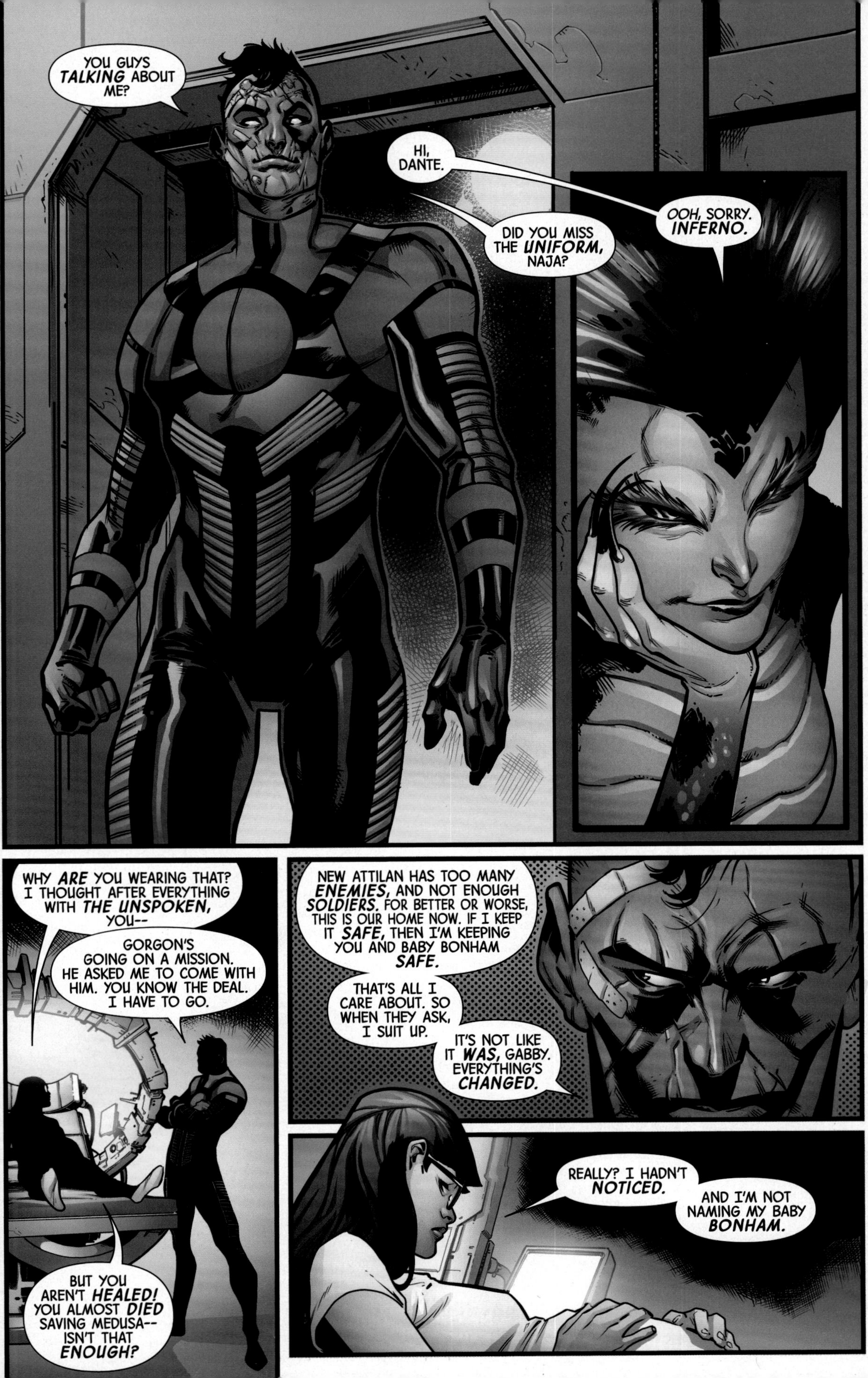
YOU GUYS TALKING ABOUT ME?
HI, DANTE.
OOH, SORRY. INFERNO.
DID YOU MISS THE UNIFORM, NAJA?
WHY ARE YOU WEARING THAT? I THOUGHT AFTER EVERYTHING WITH THE UNSPOKEN, YOU--
GORGON'S GOING ON A MISSION. HE ASKED ME TO COME WITH HIM. YOU KNOW THE DEAL. I HAVE TO GO.
BUT YOU AREN'T HEALED! YOU ALMOST DIED SAVING MEDUSA-- ISN'T THAT ENOUGH?
NEW ATTILAN HAS TOO MANY ENEMIES, AND NOT ENOUGH SOLDIERS. FOR BETTER OR WORSE, THIS IS OUR HOME NOW. IF I KEEP IT SAFE, THEN I'M KEEPING YOU AND BABY BONHAM SAFE.
THAT'S ALL I CARE ABOUT. SO WHEN THEY ASK, I SUIT UP.
IT'S NOT LIKE IT WAS, GABBY. EVERYTHING'S CHANGED.
REALLY? I HADN'T NOTICED.
AND I'M NOT NAMING MY BABY BONHAM.

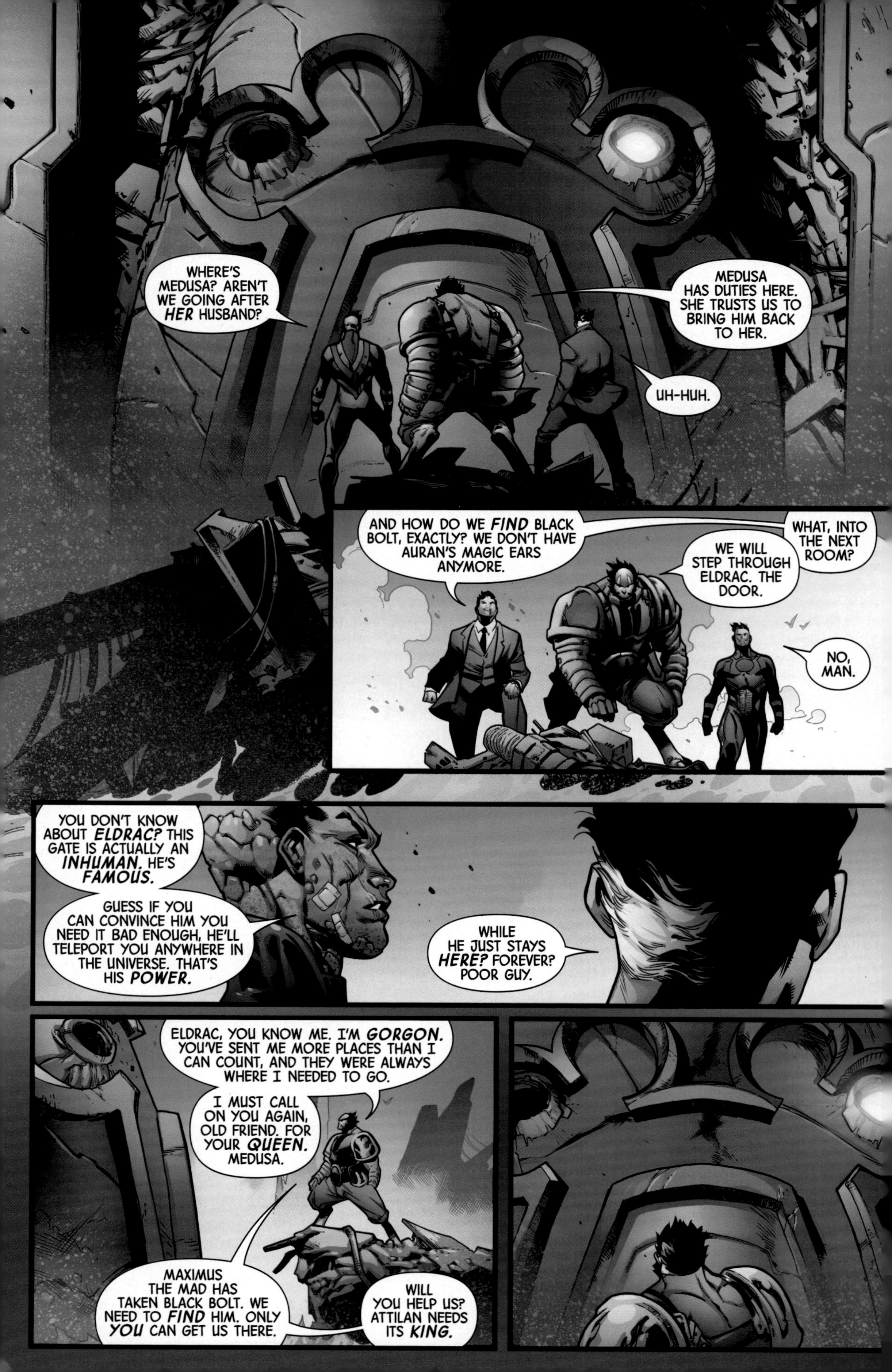
WHERE'S MEDUSA? AREN'T WE GOING AFTER HER HUSBAND?
MEDUSA HAS DUTIES HERE. SHE TRUSTS US TO BRING HIM BACK TO HER.
UH-HUH.
AND HOW DO WE FIND BLACK BOLT, EXACTLY? WE DON'T HAVE AURAN'S MAGIC EARS ANYMORE.
WE WILL STEP THROUGH ELDRAC. THE DOOR.
WHAT, INTO THE NEXT ROOM?
NO, MAN.
YOU DON'T KNOW ABOUT ELDRAC? THIS GATE IS ACTUALLY AN INHUMAN. HE'S FAMOUS.
GUESS IF YOU CAN CONVINCE HIM YOU NEED IT BAD ENOUGH, HE'LL TELEPORT YOU ANYWHERE IN THE UNIVERSE. THAT'S HIS POWER.
WHILE HE JUST STAYS HERE? FOREVER? POOR GUY.
ELDRAC, YOU KNOW ME. I'M GORGON. YOU'VE SENT ME MORE PLACES THAN I CAN COUNT, AND THEY WERE ALWAYS WHERE I NEEDED TO GO.
I MUST CALL ON YOU AGAIN, OLD FRIEND. FOR YOUR QUEEN. MEDUSA.
MAXIMUS THE MAD HAS TAKEN BLACK BOLT. WE NEED TO FIND HIM. ONLY YOU CAN GET US THERE.
WILL YOU HELP US? ATTILAN NEEDS ITS KING.

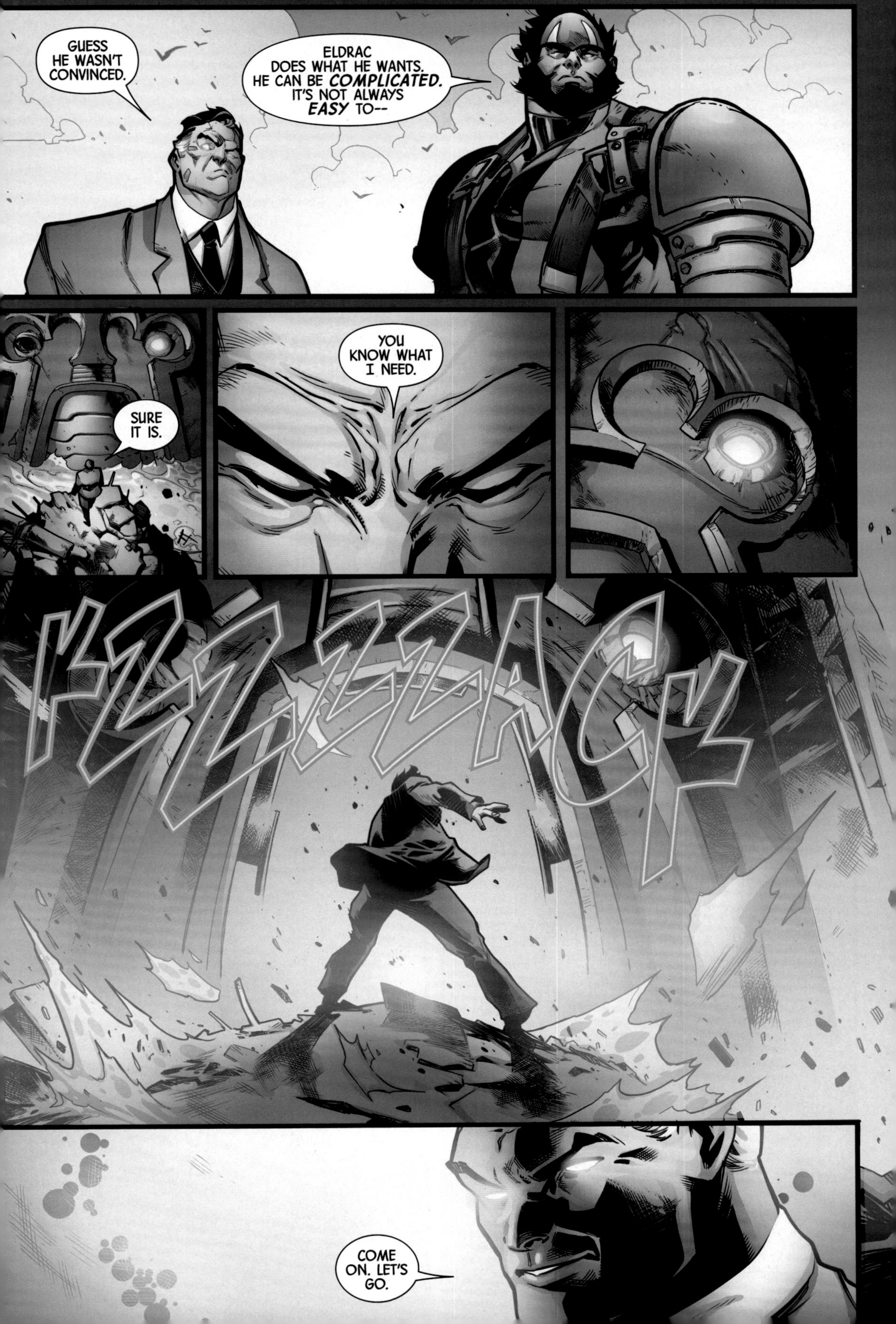
GUESS HE WASN'T CONVINCED.
ELDRAC DOES WHAT HE WANTS. HE CAN BE *COMPLICATED.* IT'S NOT ALWAYS *EASY* TO--
SURE IT IS.
YOU KNOW WHAT I NEED.
KZZZZACK
COME ON. LET'S GO.

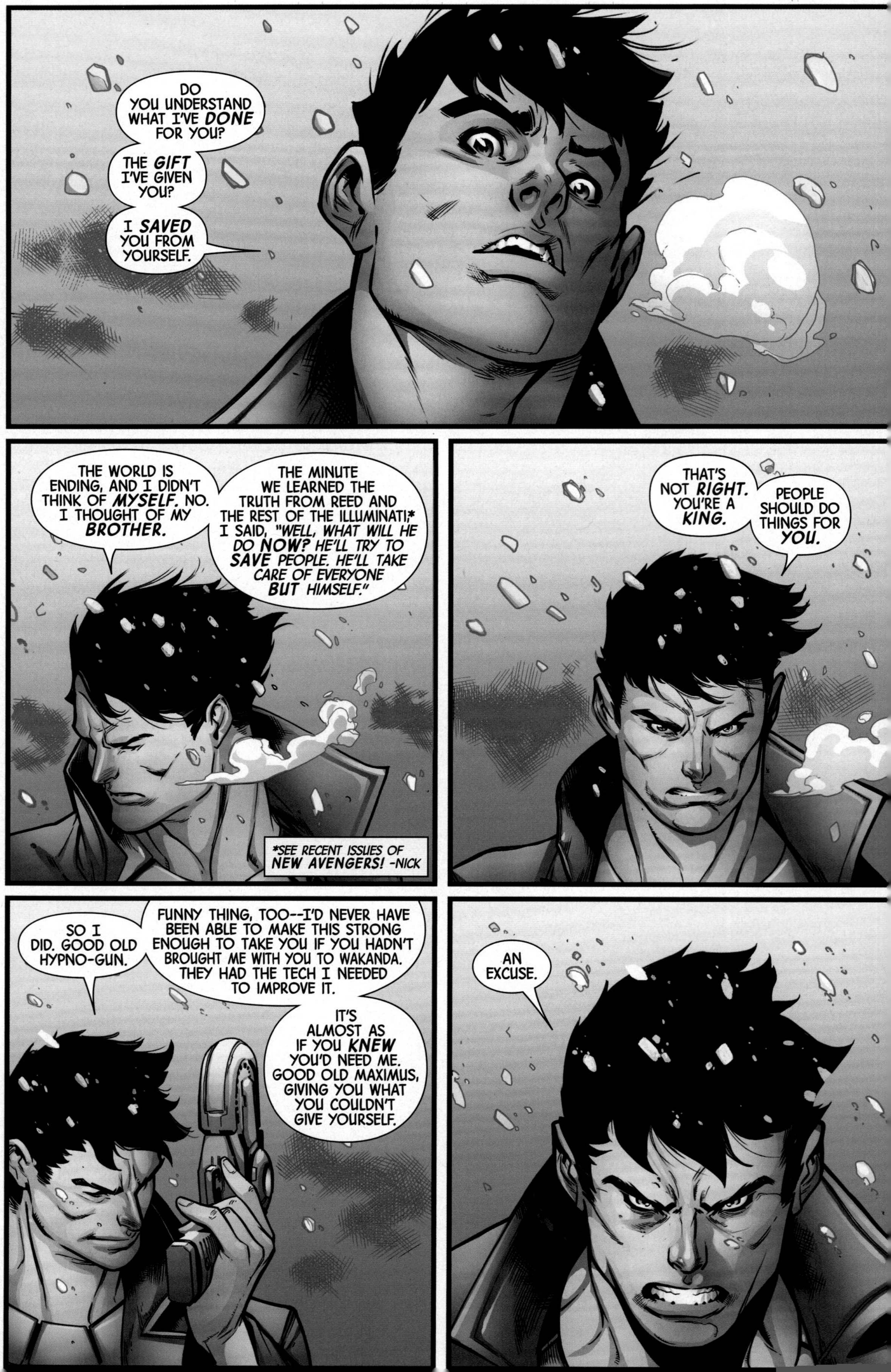
DO YOU UNDERSTAND WHAT I'VE DONE FOR YOU?
THE GIFT I'VE GIVEN YOU?
I SAVED YOU FROM YOURSELF.
THE WORLD IS ENDING, AND I DIDN'T THINK OF MYSELF. NO. I THOUGHT OF MY BROTHER.
THE MINUTE WE LEARNED THE TRUTH FROM REED AND THE REST OF THE ILLUMINATI,* I SAID, "WELL, WHAT WILL HE DO NOW? HE'LL TRY TO SAVE PEOPLE. HE'LL TAKE CARE OF EVERYONE BUT HIMSELF."
*SEE RECENT ISSUES OF NEW AVENGERS! -NICK
THAT'S NOT RIGHT. YOU'RE A KING.
PEOPLE SHOULD DO THINGS FOR YOU.
SO I DID. GOOD OLD HYPNO-GUN.
FUNNY THING, TOO--I'D NEVER HAVE BEEN ABLE TO MAKE THIS STRONG ENOUGH TO TAKE YOU IF YOU HADN'T BROUGHT ME WITH YOU TO WAKANDA. THEY HAD THE TECH I NEEDED TO IMPROVE IT.
IT'S ALMOST AS IF YOU KNEW YOU'D NEED ME. GOOD OLD MAXIMUS, GIVING YOU WHAT YOU COULDN'T GIVE YOURSELF.
AN EXCUSE.

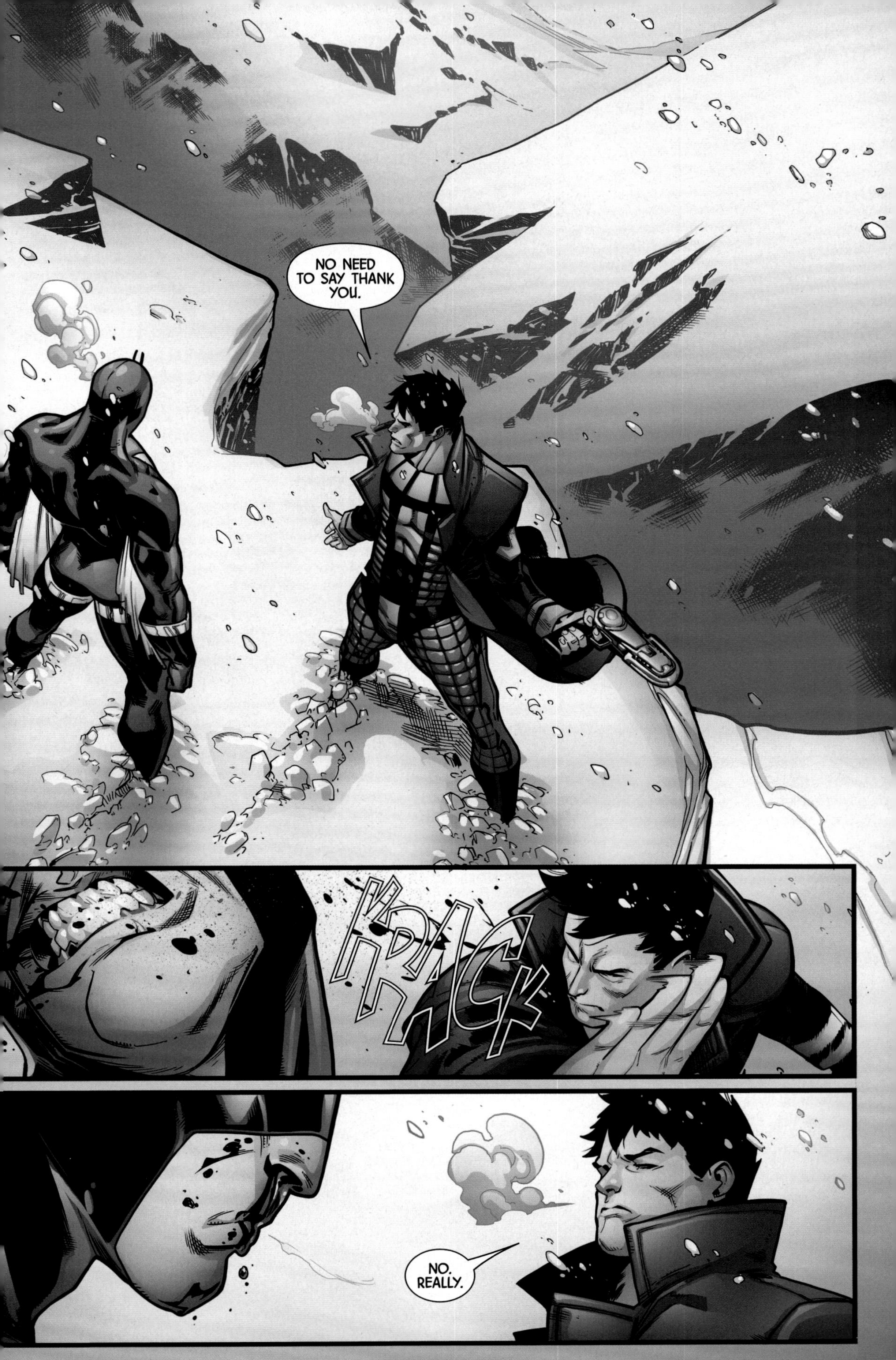
NO NEED TO SAY THANK YOU.
KRACK
NO. REALLY.

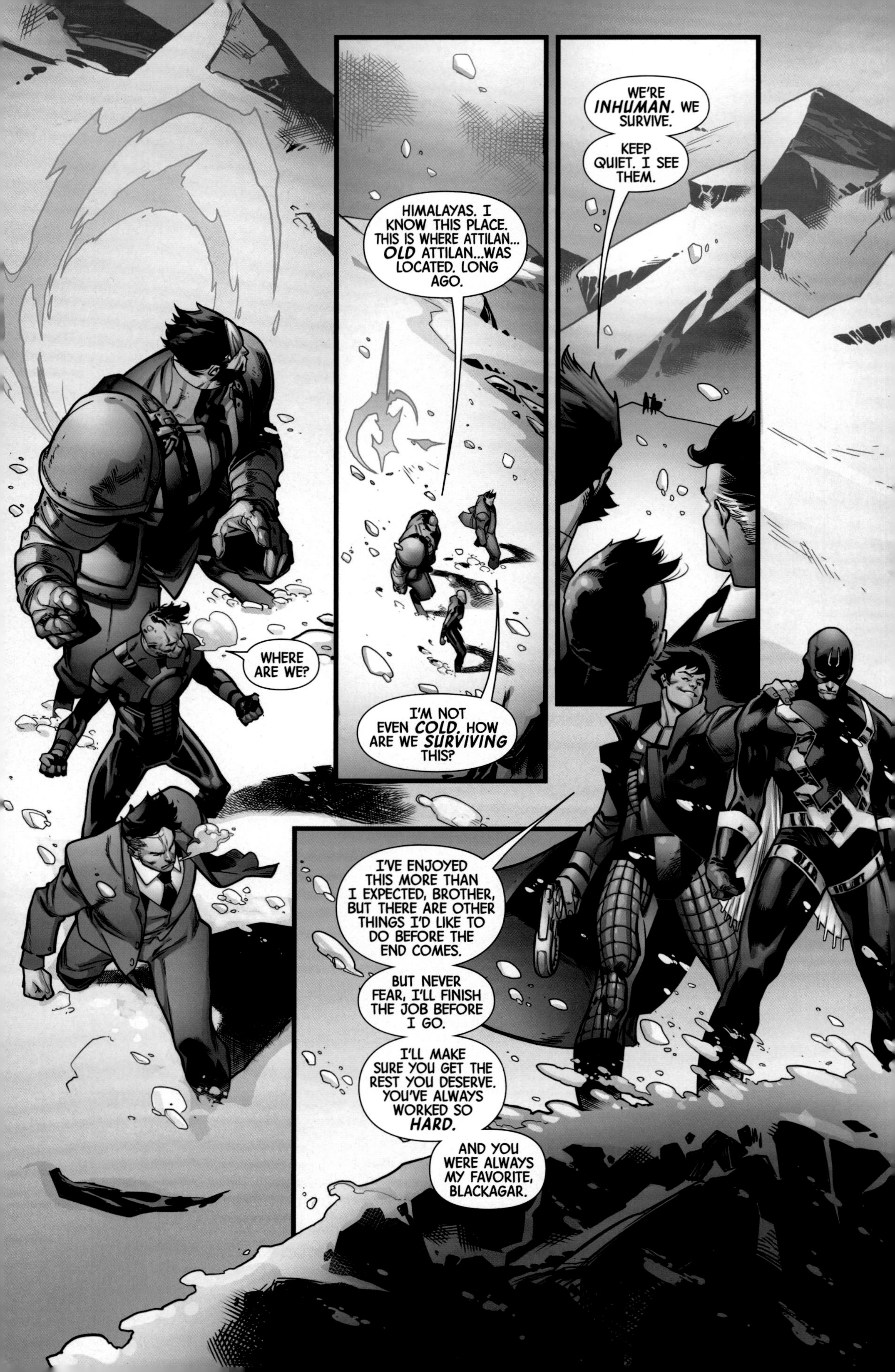
WHERE ARE WE?
HIMALAYAS. I KNOW THIS PLACE. THIS IS WHERE ATTILAN... OLD ATTILAN...WAS LOCATED. LONG AGO.
I'M NOT EVEN COLD. HOW ARE WE SURVIVING THIS?
WE'RE INHUMAN. WE SURVIVE.
KEEP QUIET. I SEE THEM.
I'VE ENJOYED THIS MORE THAN I EXPECTED, BROTHER, BUT THERE ARE OTHER THINGS I'D LIKE TO DO BEFORE THE END COMES.
BUT NEVER FEAR, I'LL FINISH THE JOB BEFORE I GO.
I'LL MAKE SURE YOU GET THE REST YOU DESERVE. YOU'VE ALWAYS WORKED SO HARD.
AND YOU WERE ALWAYS MY FAVORITE, BLACKAGAR.

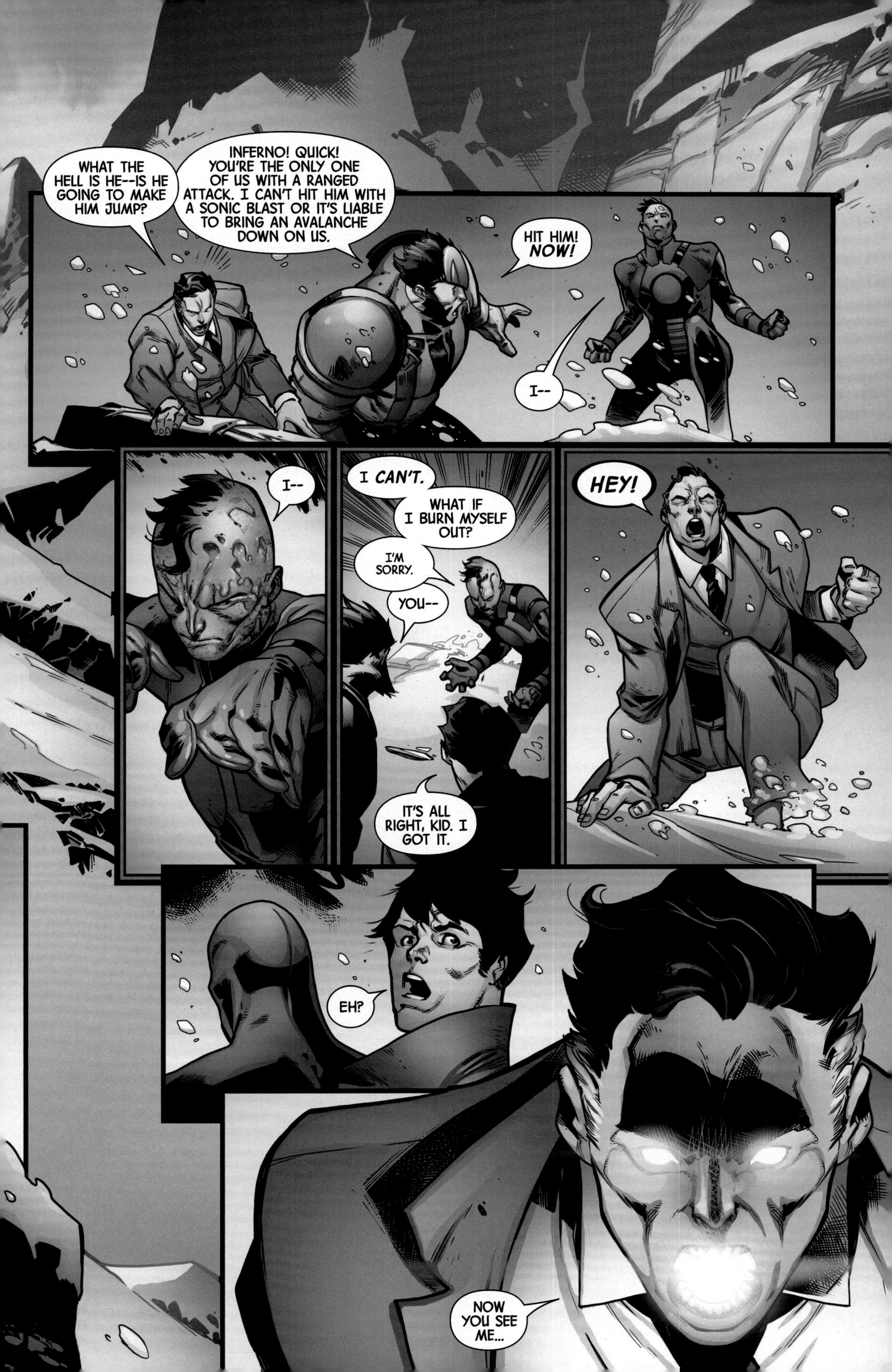
WHAT THE HELL IS HE--IS HE GOING TO MAKE HIM JUMP?
INFERNO! QUICK! YOU'RE THE ONLY ONE OF US WITH A RANGED ATTACK. I CAN'T HIT HIM WITH A SONIC BLAST OR IT'S LIABLE TO BRING AN AVALANCHE DOWN ON US.
HIT HIM! NOW!
I--
I--
I CAN'T.
WHAT IF I BURN MYSELF OUT?
I'M SORRY.
YOU--
IT'S ALL RIGHT, KID. I GOT IT.
HEY!
EH?
NOW YOU SEE ME...

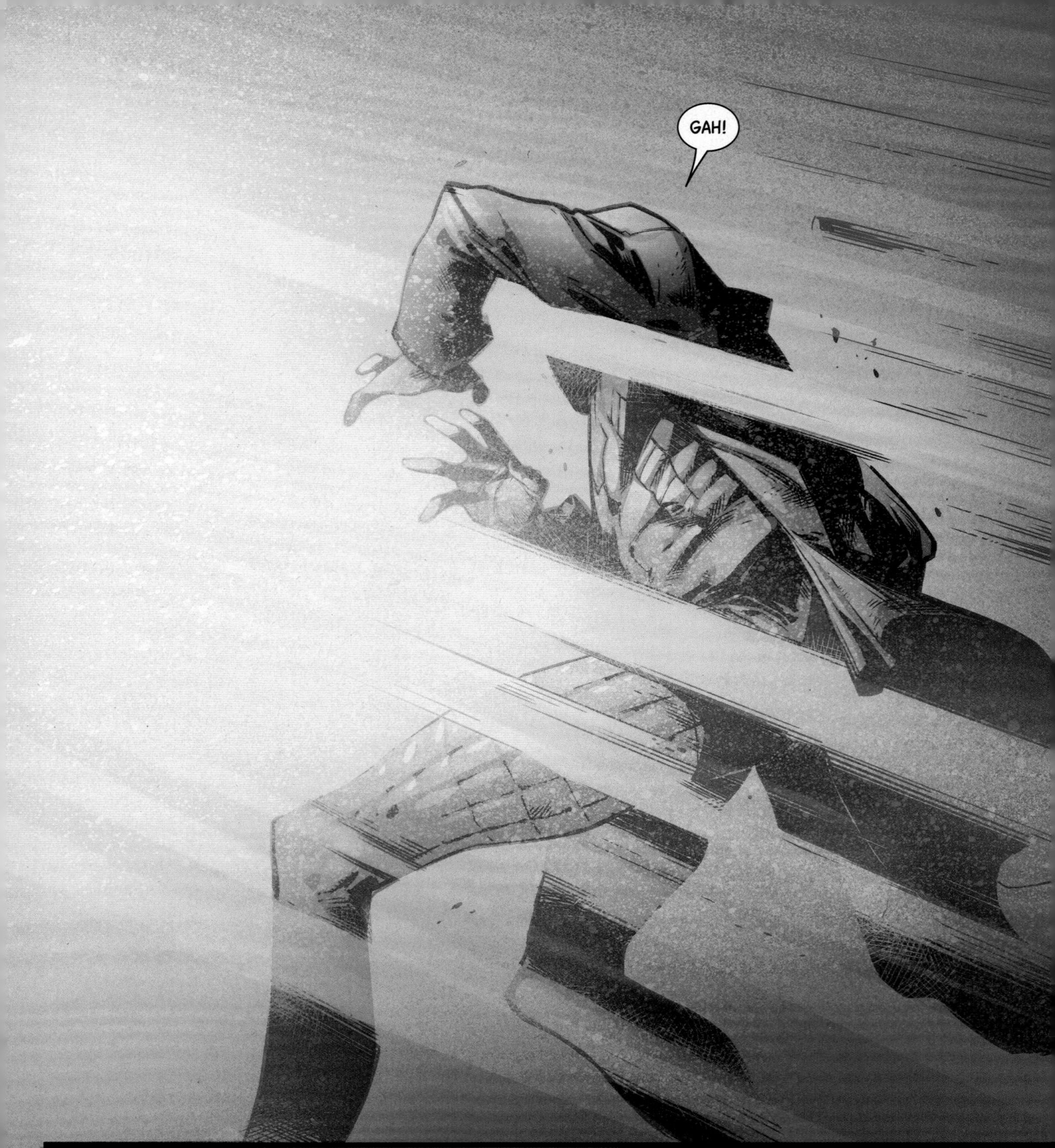
GAH!

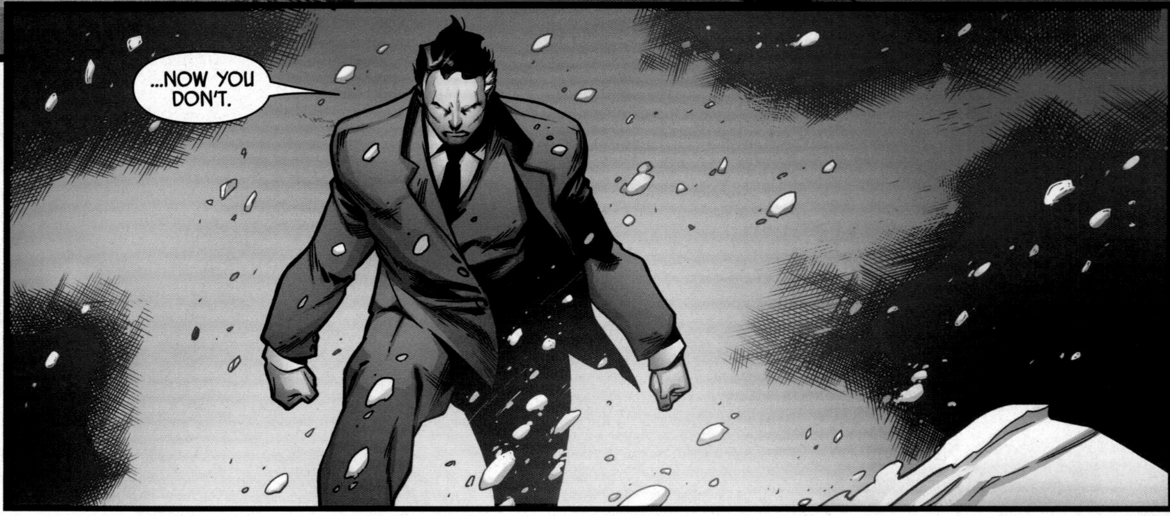
...NOW YOU DON'T.

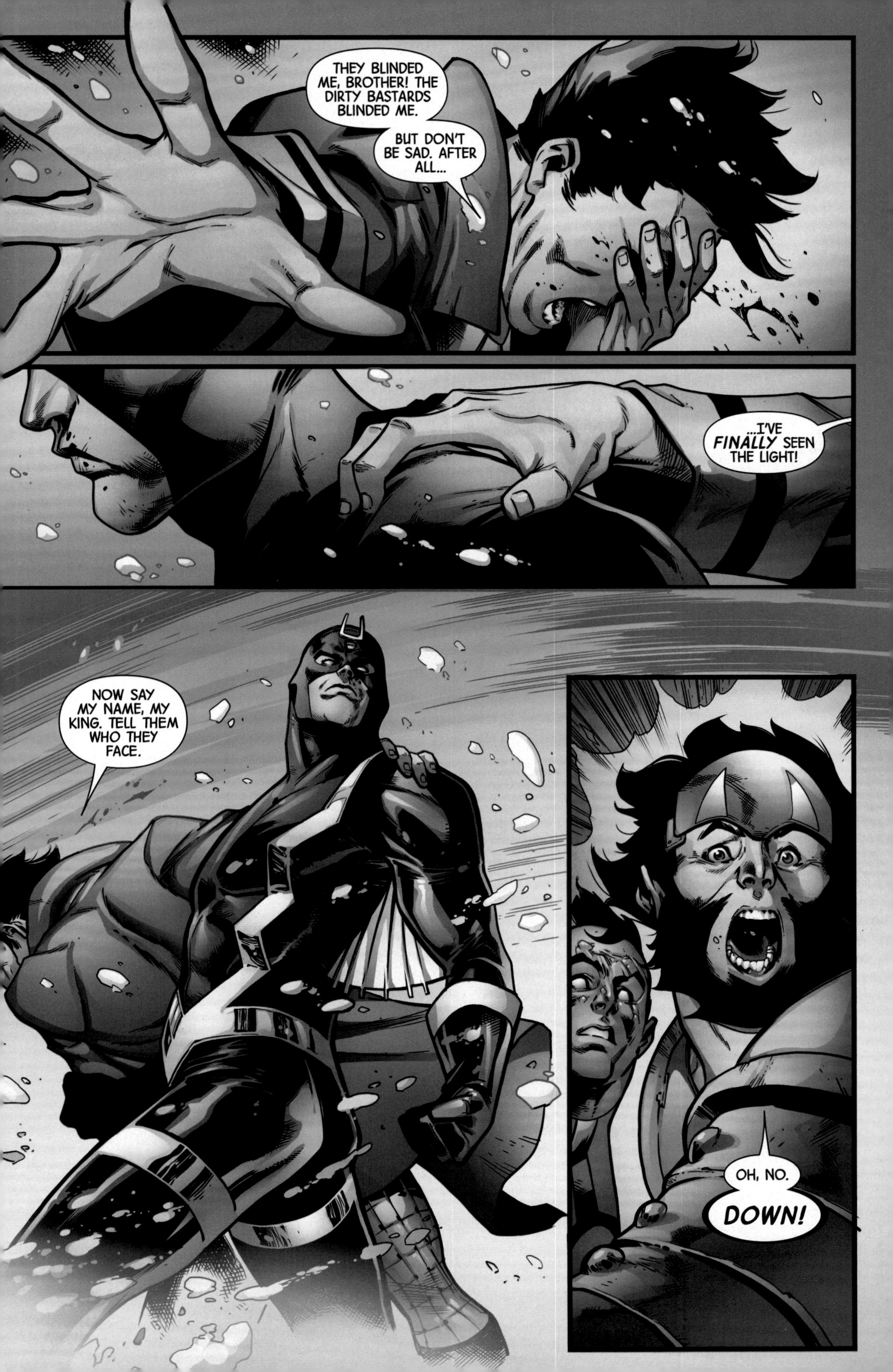
THEY BLINDED ME, BROTHER! THE DIRTY BASTARDS BLINDED ME.
BUT DON'T BE SAD. AFTER ALL...
...I'VE FINALLY SEEN THE LIGHT!
NOW SAY MY NAME, MY KING. TELL THEM WHO THEY FACE.
OH, NO.
DOWN!

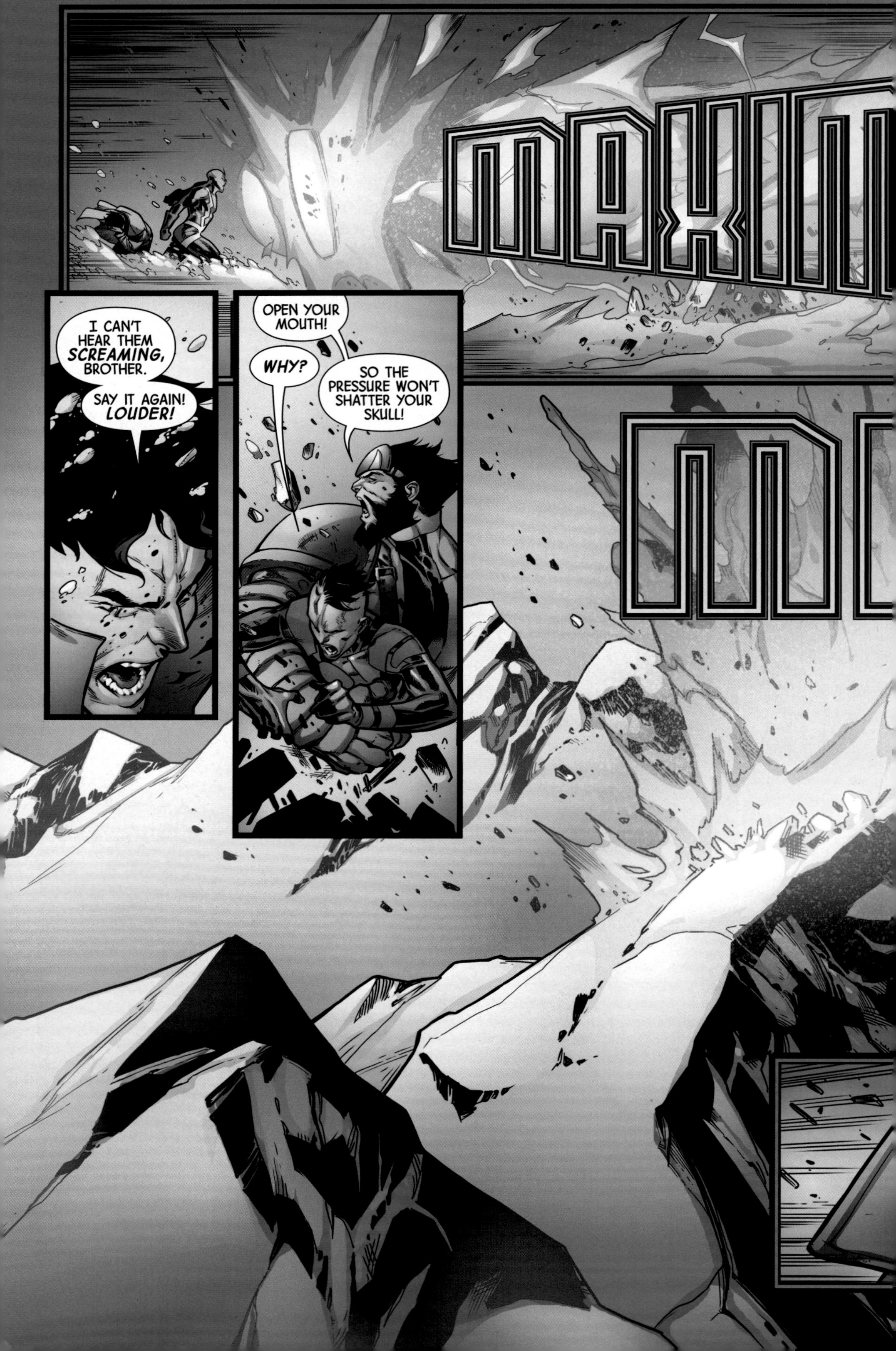
MAXIMU
I CAN'T HEAR THEM SCREAMING, BROTHER.
SAY IT AGAIN! LOUDER!
OPEN YOUR MOUTH!
WHY?
SO THE PRESSURE WON'T SHATTER YOUR SKULL!
MU

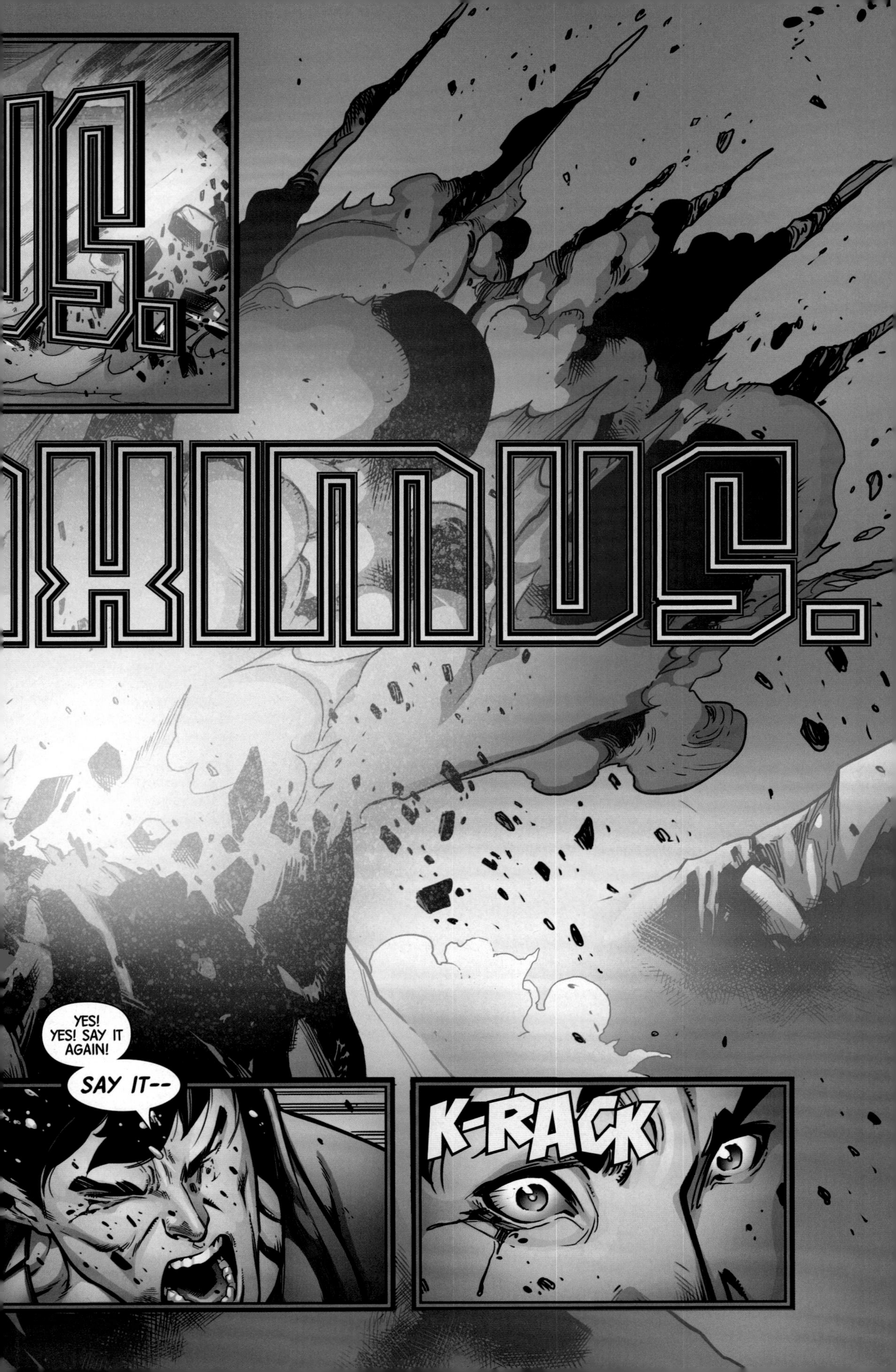
XIMUS.
YES! YES! SAY IT AGAIN!
SAY IT--
K-RACK

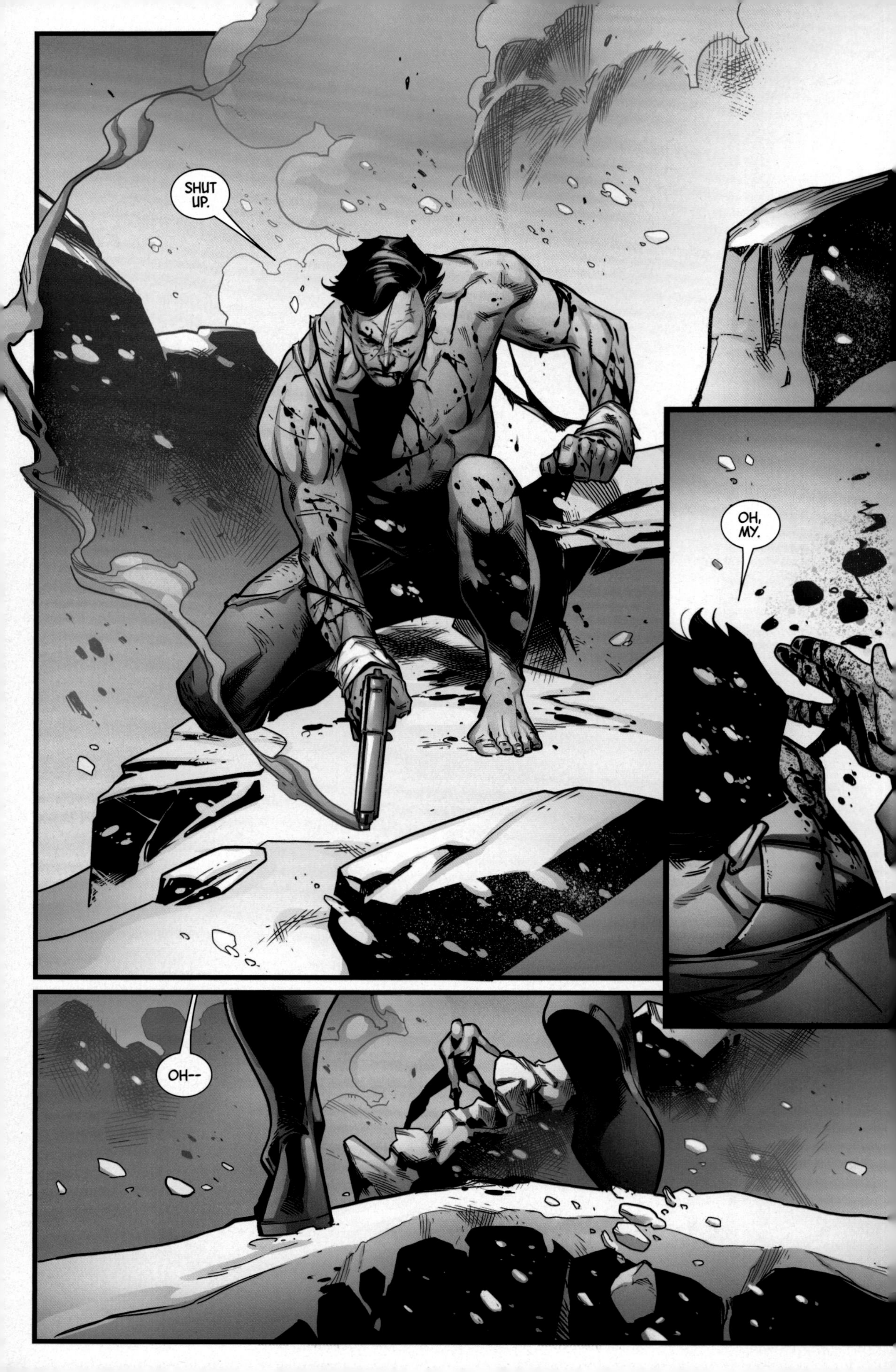
SHUT UP.
OH, MY.
OH--

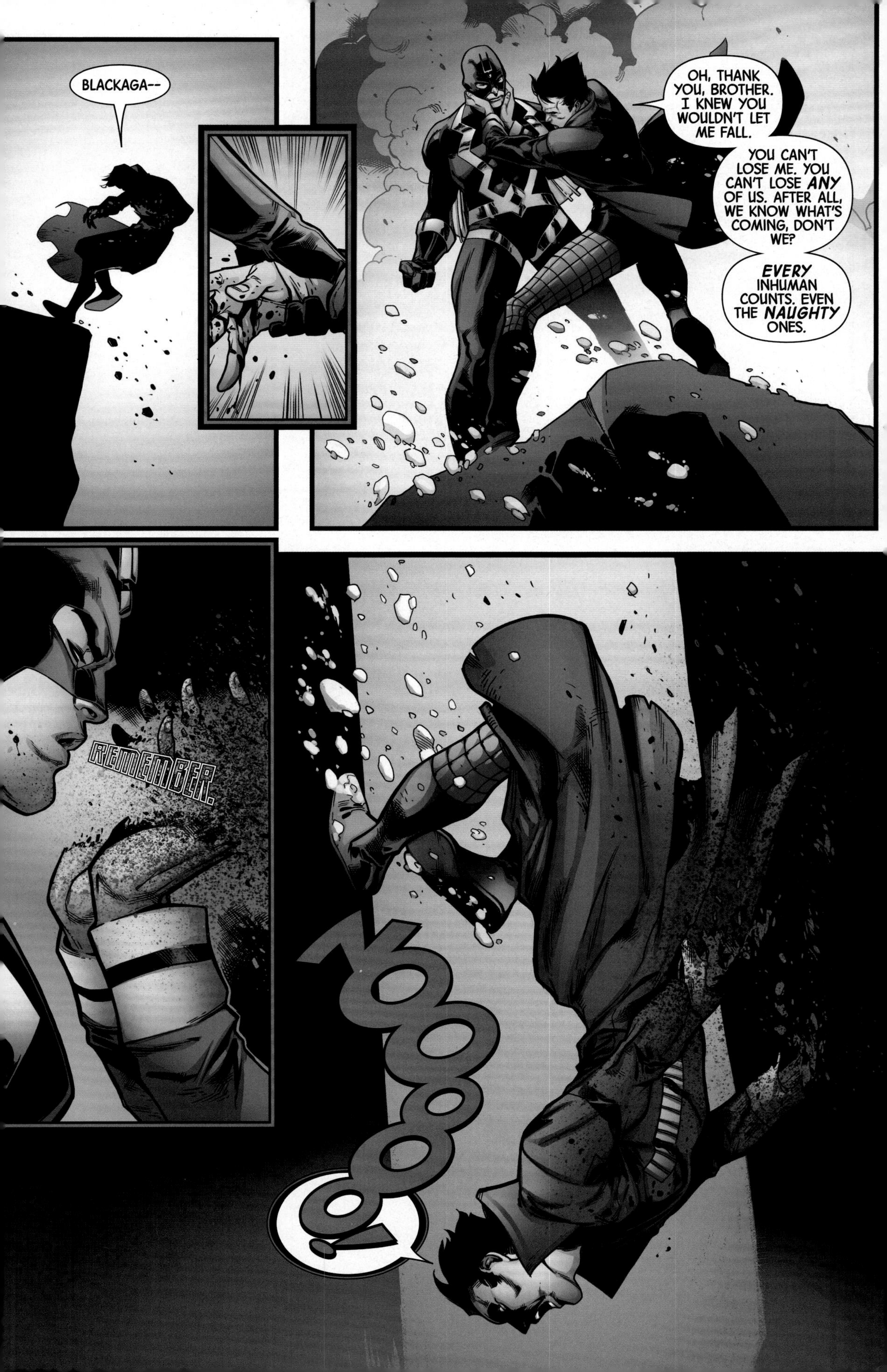
BLACKAGA--
OH, THANK YOU, BROTHER. I KNEW YOU WOULDN'T LET ME FALL.
YOU CAN'T LOSE ME. YOU CAN'T LOSE ANY OF US. AFTER ALL, WE KNOW WHAT'S COMING, DON'T WE?
EVERY INHUMAN COUNTS. EVEN THE NAUGHTY ONES.
REMEMBER.
NOOOO!

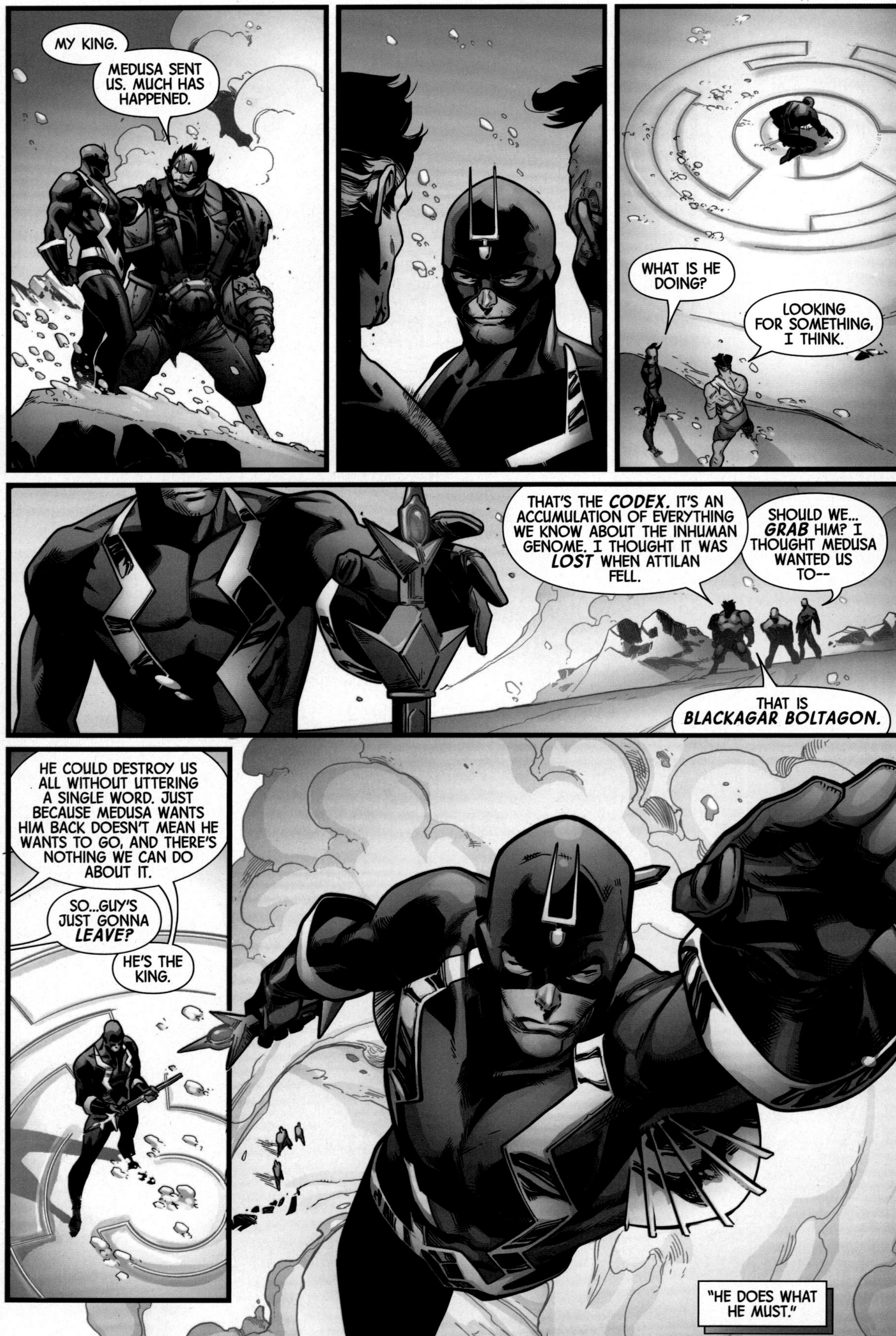
MY KING.
MEDUSA SENT US. MUCH HAS HAPPENED.
WHAT IS HE DOING?
LOOKING FOR SOMETHING, I THINK.
THAT'S THE CODEX. IT'S AN ACCUMULATION OF EVERYTHING WE KNOW ABOUT THE INHUMAN GENOME. I THOUGHT IT WAS LOST WHEN ATTILAN FELL.
SHOULD WE... GRAB HIM? I THOUGHT MEDUSA WANTED US TO--
THAT IS BLACKAGAR BOLTAGON.
HE COULD DESTROY US ALL WITHOUT UTTERING A SINGLE WORD. JUST BECAUSE MEDUSA WANTS HIM BACK DOESN'T MEAN HE WANTS TO GO, AND THERE'S NOTHING WE CAN DO ABOUT IT.
SO...GUY'S JUST GONNA LEAVE?
HE'S THE KING.
"HE DOES WHAT HE MUST."

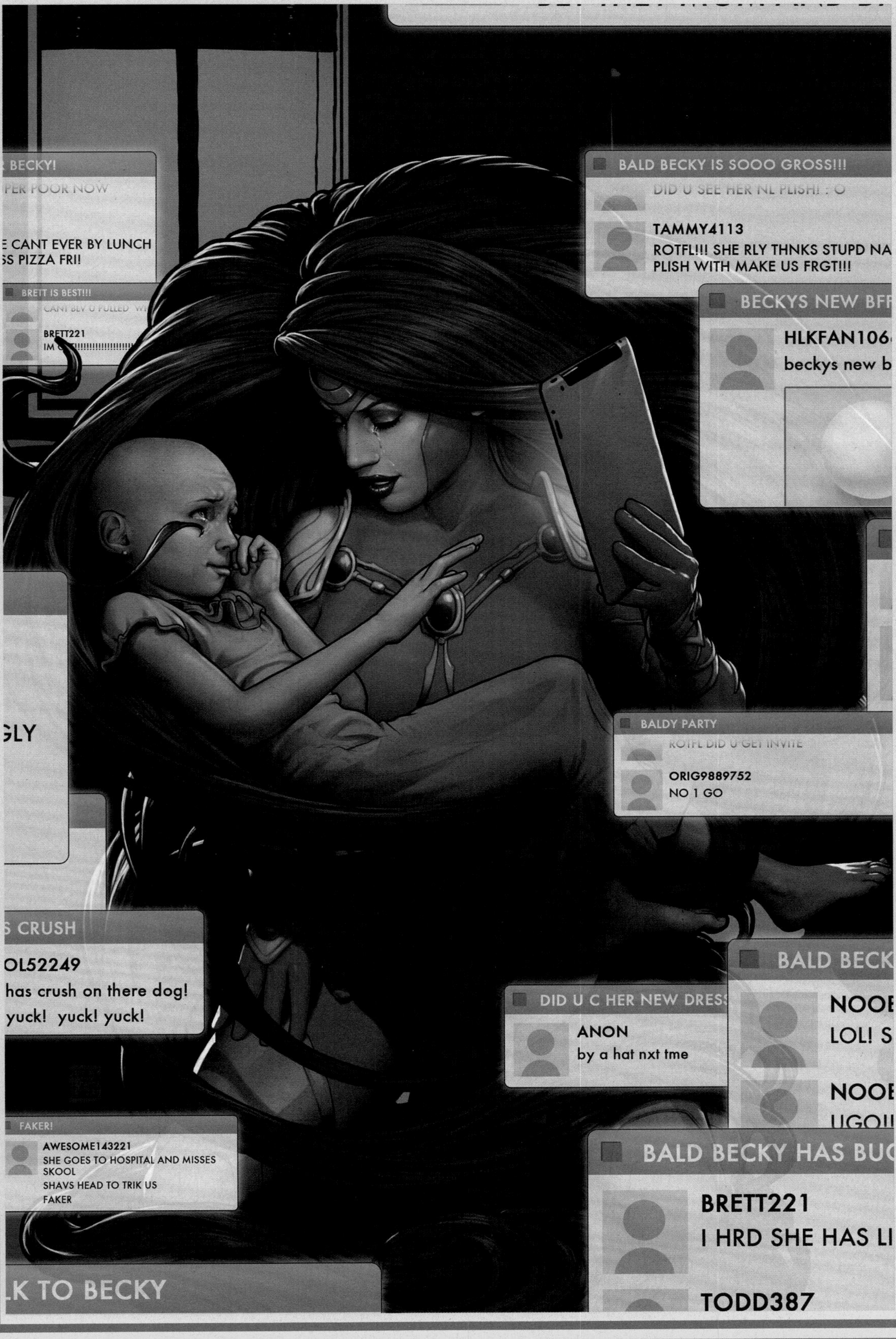
BECKY!
E CANT EVER BY LUNCH
SS PIZZA FRI!
BRETT IS BEST!!!
BRETT221
BALD BECKY IS SOOO GROSS!!!
DID U SEE HER NL PLISH! : O
TAMMY4113
ROTFL!!! SHE RLY THNKS STUPD NA
PLISH WITH MAKE US FRGT!!!
BECKYS NEW BF
HLKFAN106
beckys new b
GLY
BALDY PARTY
ROTFL DID U GET INVITE
ORIG9889752
NO 1 GO
S CRUSH
OL52249
has crush on there dog!
yuck! yuck! yuck!
DID U C HER NEW DRESS
ANON
by a hat nxt tme
BALD BECK
NOOB
LOL! S
NOOB
UGO!!
FAKER!
AWESOME143221
SHE GOES TO HOSPITAL AND MISSES SKOOL
SHAVS HEAD TO TRIK US
FAKER
BALD BECKY HAS BU
BRETT221
I HRD SHE HAS LI
TODD387
LK TO BECKY

STOMP OUT BULLYING VARIANT
BY JOHN TYLER CHRISTOPHER

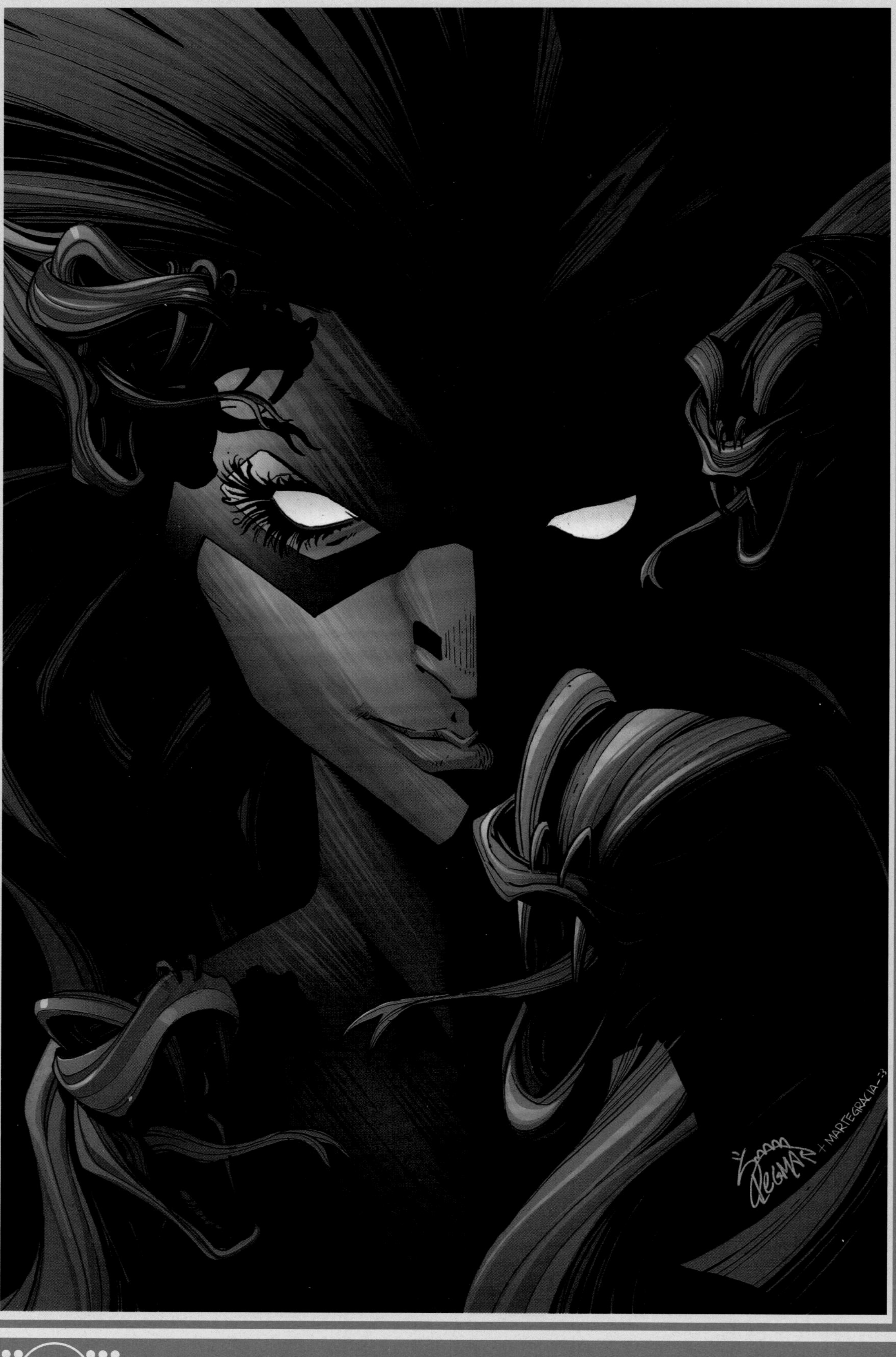
+ MARTEGRACIA-13

9 PART NINE: ENNILUX

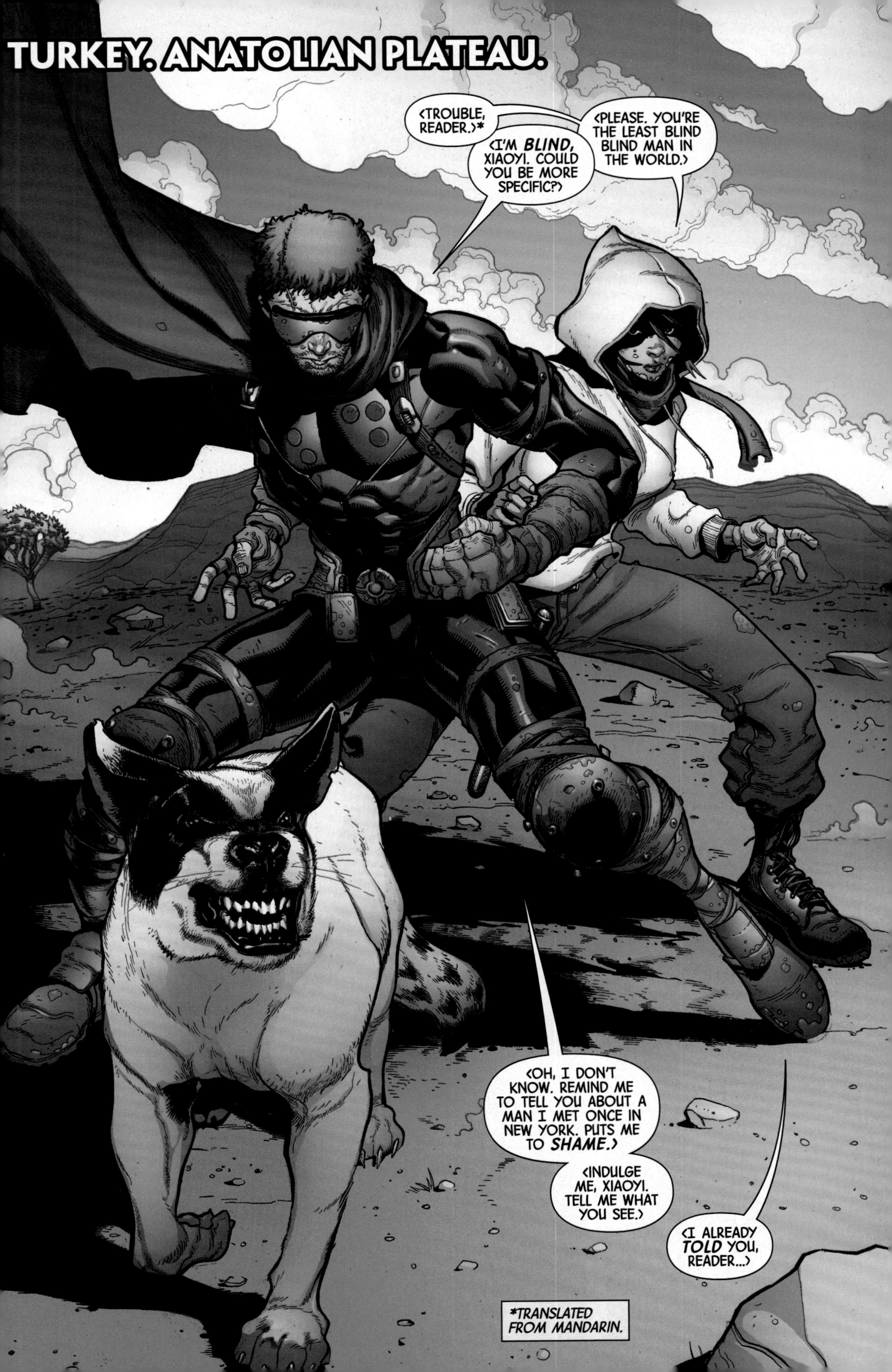
TURKEY. ANATOLIAN PLATEAU.
<TROUBLE, READER.>*
<I'M BLIND, XIAOYI. COULD YOU BE MORE SPECIFIC?>
<PLEASE. YOU'RE THE LEAST BLIND BLIND MAN IN THE WORLD.>
<OH, I DON'T KNOW. REMIND ME TO TELL YOU ABOUT A MAN I MET ONCE IN NEW YORK. PUTS ME TO SHAME.>
<INDULGE ME, XIAOYI. TELL ME WHAT YOU SEE.>
<I ALREADY TOLD YOU, READER...>
*TRANSLATED FROM MANDARIN.

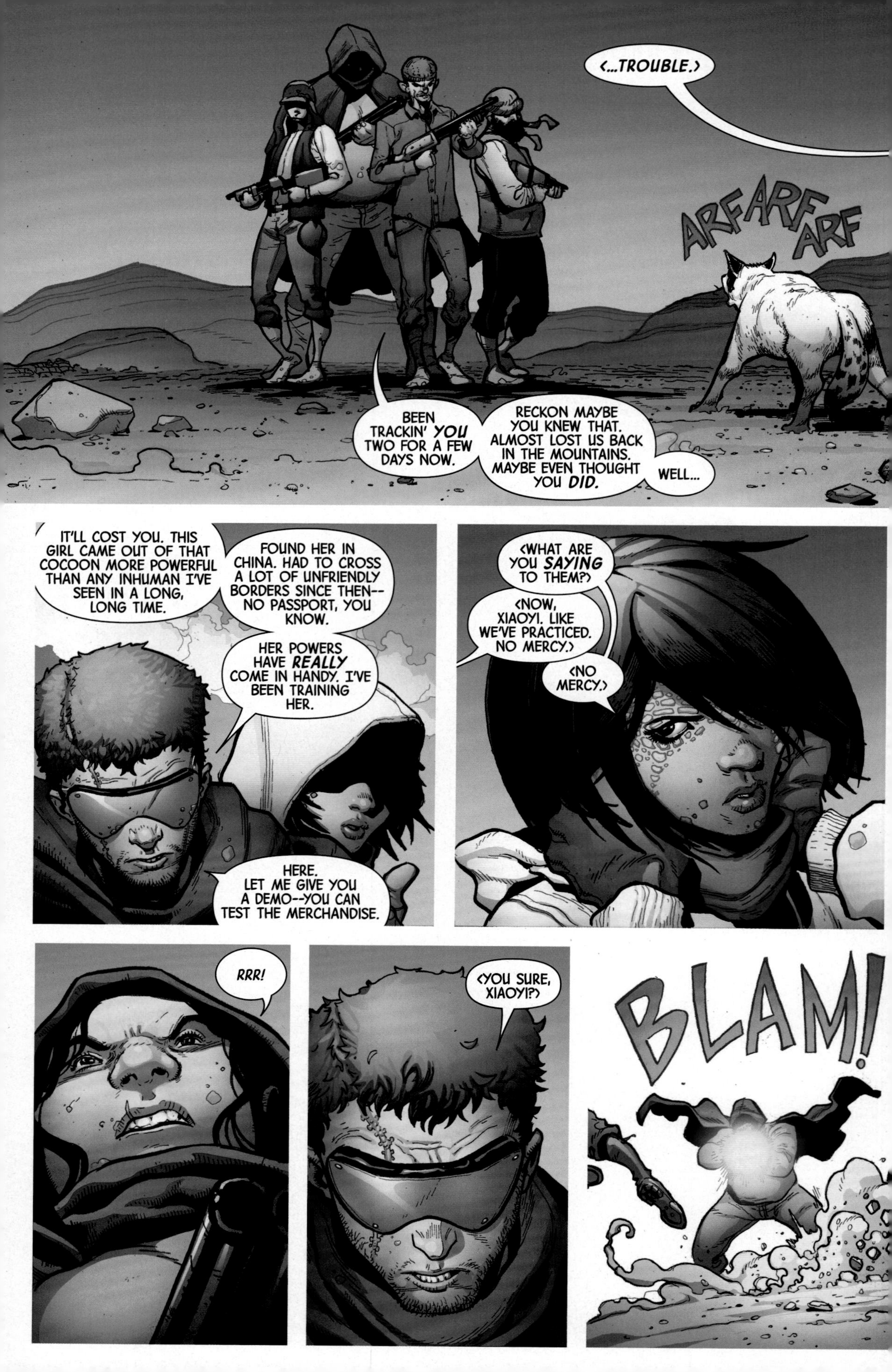

<...TROUBLE.>
ARF ARF ARF ARF
BEEN TRACKIN' YOU TWO FOR A FEW DAYS NOW.
RECKON MAYBE YOU KNEW THAT. ALMOST LOST US BACK IN THE MOUNTAINS. MAYBE EVEN THOUGHT YOU DID.
WELL...
IT'LL COST YOU. THIS GIRL CAME OUT OF THAT COCOON MORE POWERFUL THAN ANY INHUMAN I'VE SEEN IN A LONG, LONG TIME.
FOUND HER IN CHINA. HAD TO CROSS A LOT OF UNFRIENDLY BORDERS SINCE THEN-- NO PASSPORT, YOU KNOW.
HER POWERS HAVE REALLY COME IN HANDY. I'VE BEEN TRAINING HER.
HERE. LET ME GIVE YOU A DEMO--YOU CAN TEST THE MERCHANDISE.
<WHAT ARE YOU SAYING TO THEM?>
<NOW, XIAOYI. LIKE WE'VE PRACTICED. NO MERCY.>
<NO MERCY.>
RRR!
<YOU SURE, XIAOYI?>
BLAM!

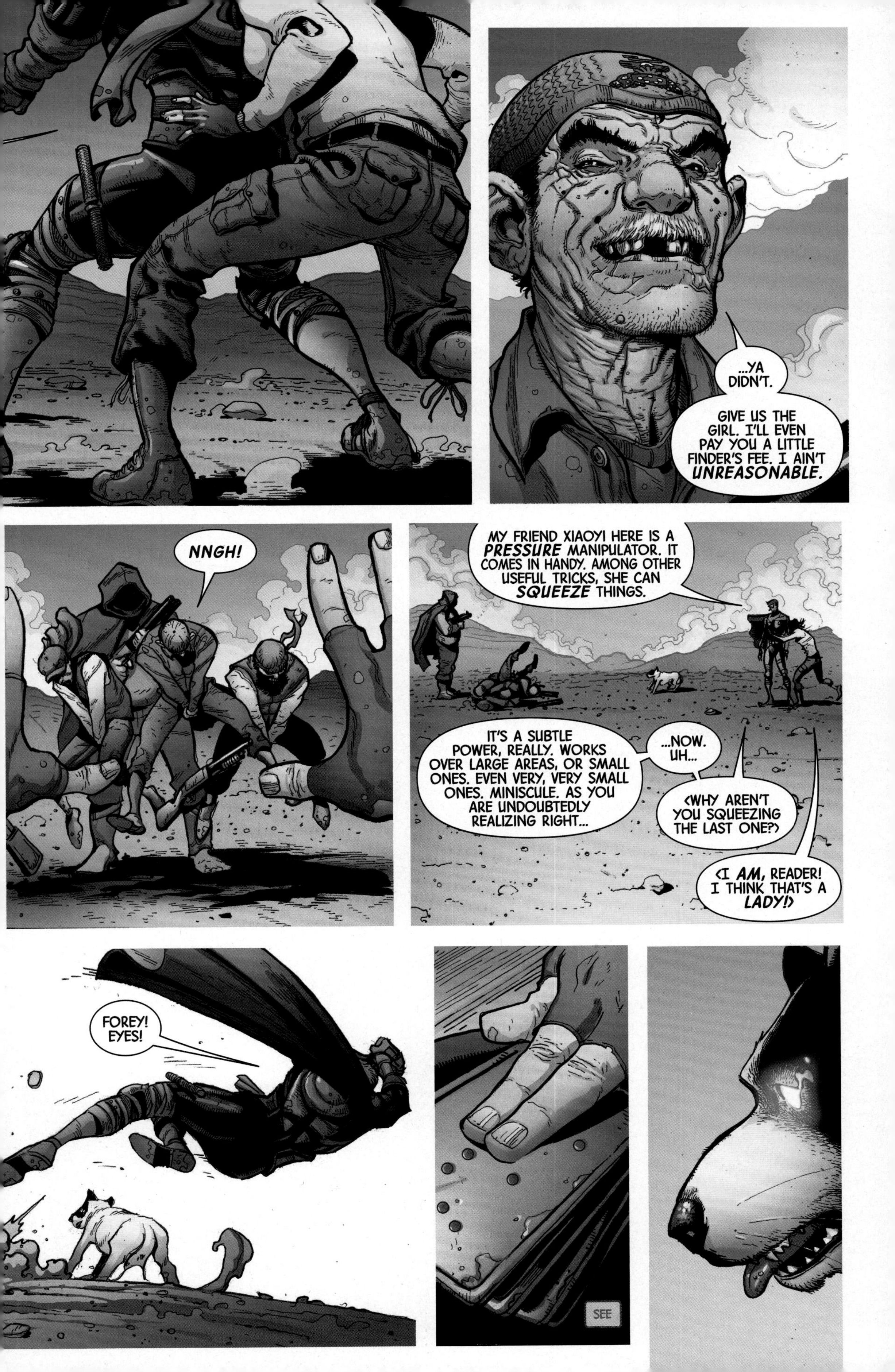
...YA DIDN'T.
GIVE US THE GIRL. I'LL EVEN PAY YOU A LITTLE FINDER'S FEE. I AIN'T UNREASONABLE.
NNGH!
MY FRIEND XIAOYI HERE IS A PRESSURE MANIPULATOR. IT COMES IN HANDY. AMONG OTHER USEFUL TRICKS, SHE CAN SQUEEZE THINGS.
IT'S A SUBTLE POWER, REALLY. WORKS OVER LARGE AREAS, OR SMALL ONES. EVEN VERY, VERY SMALL ONES. MINISCULE. AS YOU ARE UNDOUBTEDLY REALIZING RIGHT...
...NOW. UH...
<WHY AREN'T YOU SQUEEZING THE LAST ONE?>
<I AM, READER! I THINK THAT'S A LADY!>
FOREY! EYES!
SEE

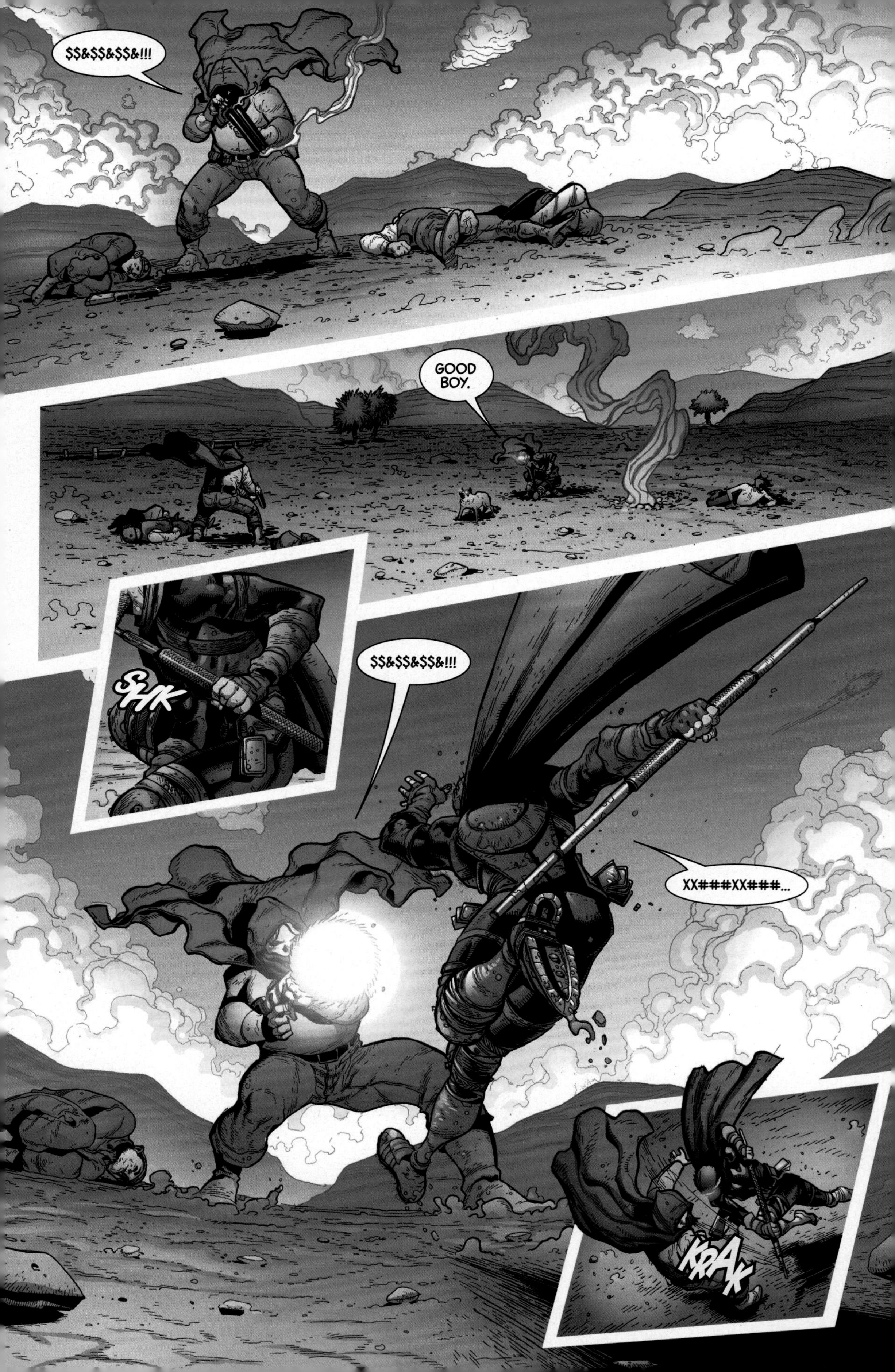
$$&$$&$$&!!!
GOOD BOY.
SHK
$$&$$&$$&!!!
XX###XX###...
KRAK

<THANK YOU, READER.>

<WHAT ARE YOU THANKING *ME* FOR? YOU GOT *FOUR* OF THEM, XIAOYI. I ONLY GOT *ONE*. I THANK *YOU*.>

WHO'S A GOOD BOY, FOREY?

RFF!

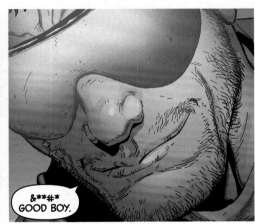

&***#* GOOD BOY.

<THESE PROBABLY AREN'T THE ONLY PEOPLE TRACKING US. LET'S GET GOING.>

<TO ENNILUX? IS IT FAR? WE'VE BEEN TRAVELING *FOREVER*.>

<NOT FAR. A WEEK OR TWO, IF WE CAN BUY PASSAGE ACROSS THE AEGEAN.>

<GOOD WORK, XIAOYI.>

<THANKS, READER.>

NEW ATTILAN.

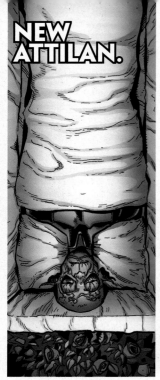

PLEASE, ALLOW ME TO MAKE INTRODUCTIONS--I DON'T BELIEVE YOU HAVE ALL MET EACH OTHER.

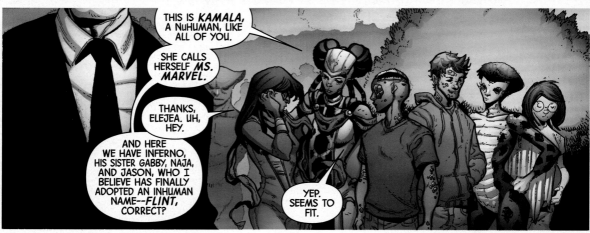

THIS IS KAMALA, A NuHUMAN, LIKE ALL OF YOU.

SHE CALLS HERSELF MS. MARVEL.

THANKS, ELEJEA. UH, HEY.

AND HERE WE HAVE INFERNO, HIS SISTER GABBY, NAJA, AND JASON, WHO I BELIEVE HAS FINALLY ADOPTED AN INHUMAN NAME--FLINT, CORRECT?

YEP. SEEMS TO FIT.

DID YOU KNOW VINATOS? I HAVEN'T SEEN YOU AROUND NEW ATTILAN BEFORE.

I ONLY MET HIM ONCE, WHEN I WAS SICK. BUT HE HELPED ME--TOLD ME SOME THINGS ABOUT MY POWERS.*

HE WAS NICE TO ME. I'M SORRY HE... I'M SORRY HE'S GONE. I WANTED TO PAY MY RESPECTS.

*DIDN'T YOU READ MS. MARVEL #9? -NEEDY NICK

GLAD YOU SEE YOU'RE FEELING BETTER, ELEJEA.

IT WILL TAKE MORE THAN A BULLET TO KILL ME. HOW DOES YOUR HEALING PROGRESS, DANTE?

I'M GETTING BETTER. I HAVEN'T BEEN ABLE TO, UH...LIGHT UP SINCE IT HAPPENED, THOUGH. GORGON'S HELPING ME.

ANYWAY, I WANTED TO ASK-- ISN'T MEDUSA GOING TO COME? I WOULD HAVE THOUGHT--

QUEEN MEDUSA WILL BE HERE SHORTLY.

IN FACT...

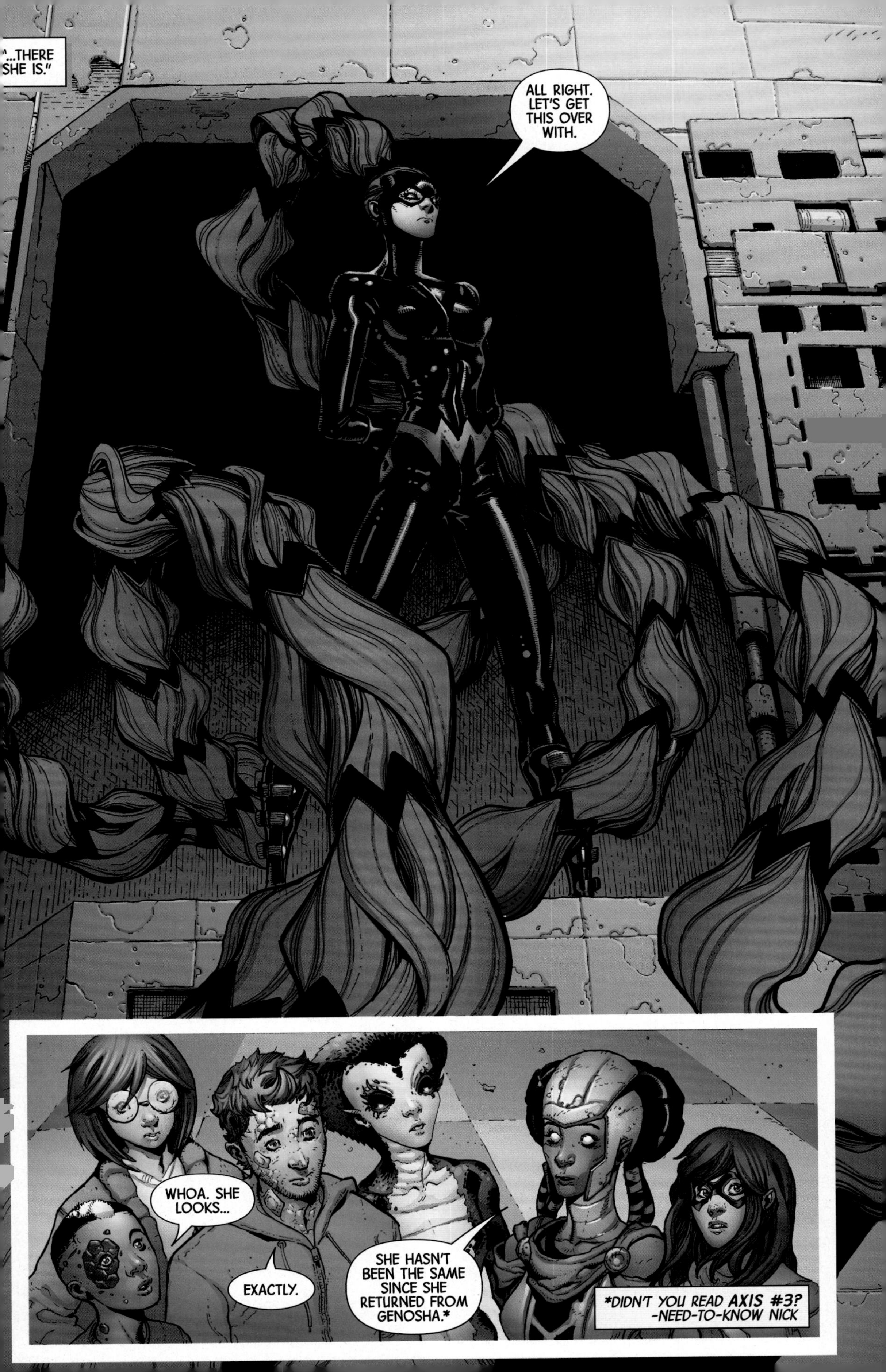
"...THERE SHE IS."
ALL RIGHT. LET'S GET THIS OVER WITH.
WHOA. SHE LOOKS...
EXACTLY.
SHE HASN'T BEEN THE SAME SINCE SHE RETURNED FROM GENOSHA.*
*DIDN'T YOU READ AXIS #3? -NEED-TO-KNOW NICK

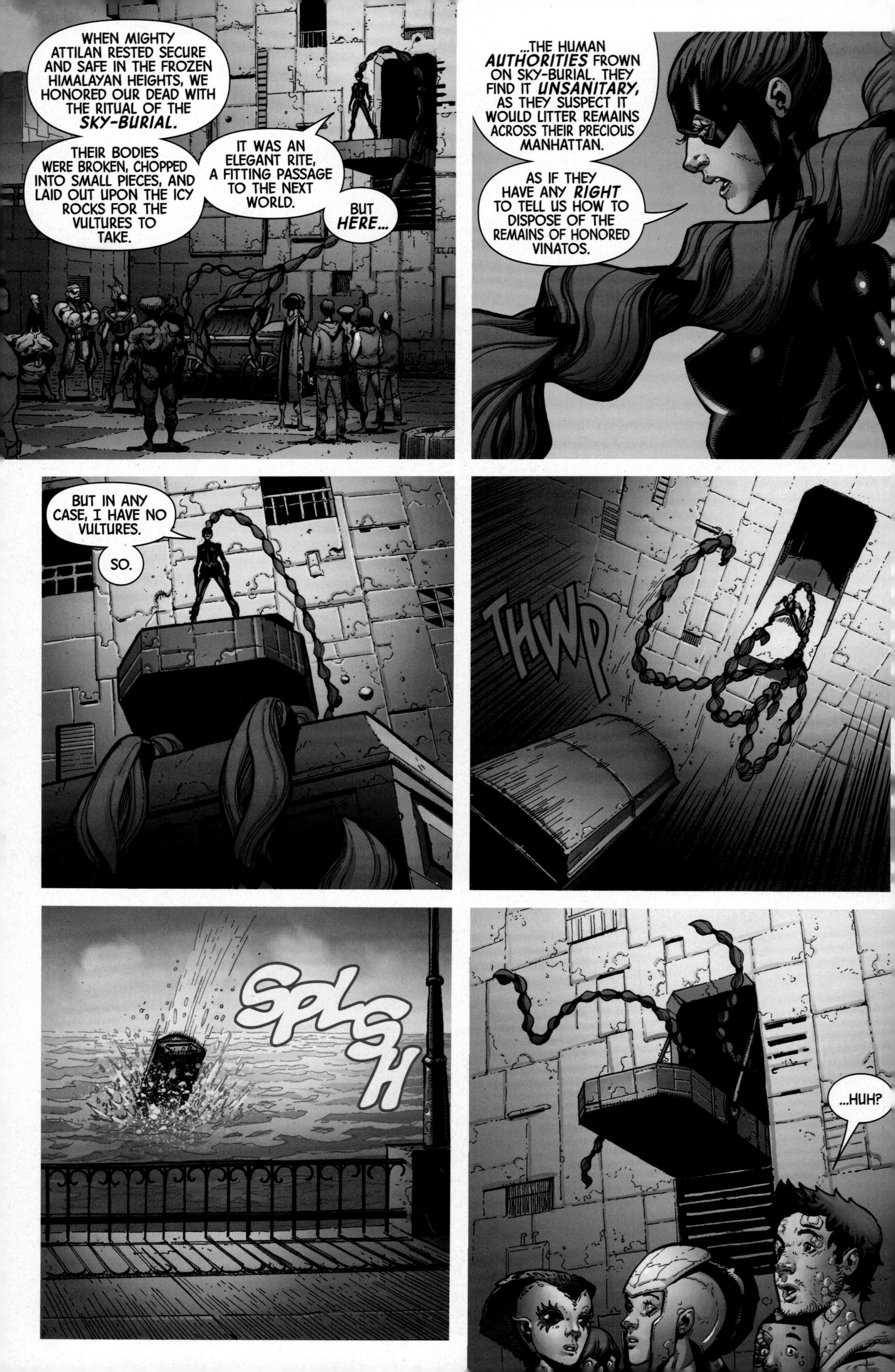
WHEN MIGHTY ATTILAN RESTED SECURE AND SAFE IN THE FROZEN HIMALAYAN HEIGHTS, WE HONORED OUR DEAD WITH THE RITUAL OF THE SKY-BURIAL.
THEIR BODIES WERE BROKEN, CHOPPED INTO SMALL PIECES, AND LAID OUT UPON THE ICY ROCKS FOR THE VULTURES TO TAKE.
IT WAS AN ELEGANT RITE, A FITTING PASSAGE TO THE NEXT WORLD.
BUT HERE...
...THE HUMAN AUTHORITIES FROWN ON SKY-BURIAL. THEY FIND IT UNSANITARY, AS THEY SUSPECT IT WOULD LITTER REMAINS ACROSS THEIR PRECIOUS MANHATTAN.
AS IF THEY HAVE ANY RIGHT TO TELL US HOW TO DISPOSE OF THE REMAINS OF HONORED VINATOS.
BUT IN ANY CASE, I HAVE NO VULTURES.
SO.
THWP
SPLASH
...HUH?

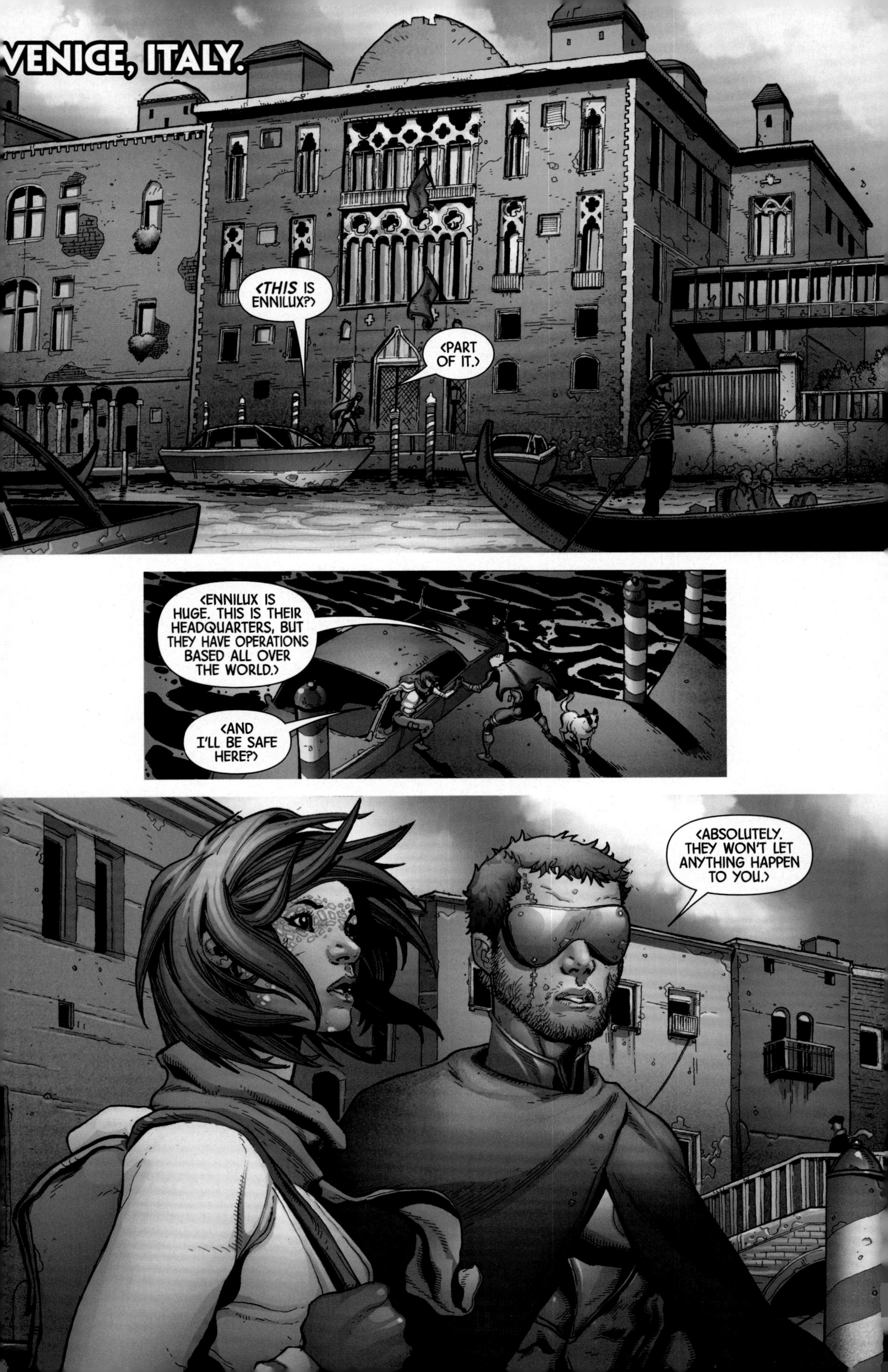
VENICE, ITALY.
<THIS IS ENNILUX?>
<PART OF IT.>
<ENNILUX IS HUGE. THIS IS THEIR HEADQUARTERS, BUT THEY HAVE OPERATIONS BASED ALL OVER THE WORLD.>
<AND I'LL BE SAFE HERE?>
<ABSOLUTELY. THEY WON'T LET ANYTHING HAPPEN TO YOU.>

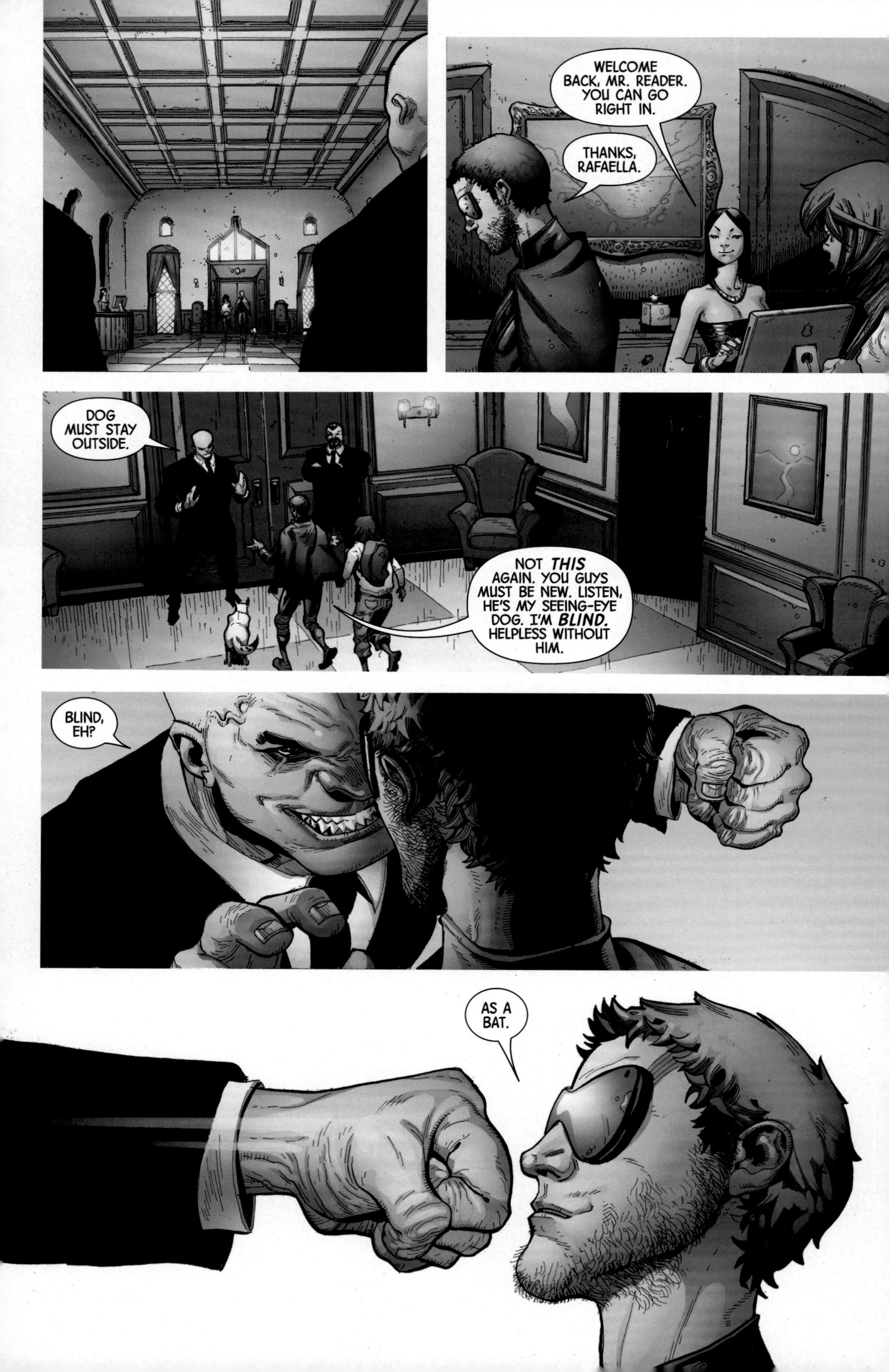
WELCOME BACK, MR. READER. YOU CAN GO RIGHT IN.
THANKS, RAFAELLA.
DOG MUST STAY OUTSIDE.
NOT THIS AGAIN. YOU GUYS MUST BE NEW. LISTEN, HE'S MY SEEING-EYE DOG. I'M BLIND. HELPLESS WITHOUT HIM.
BLIND, EH?
AS A BAT.

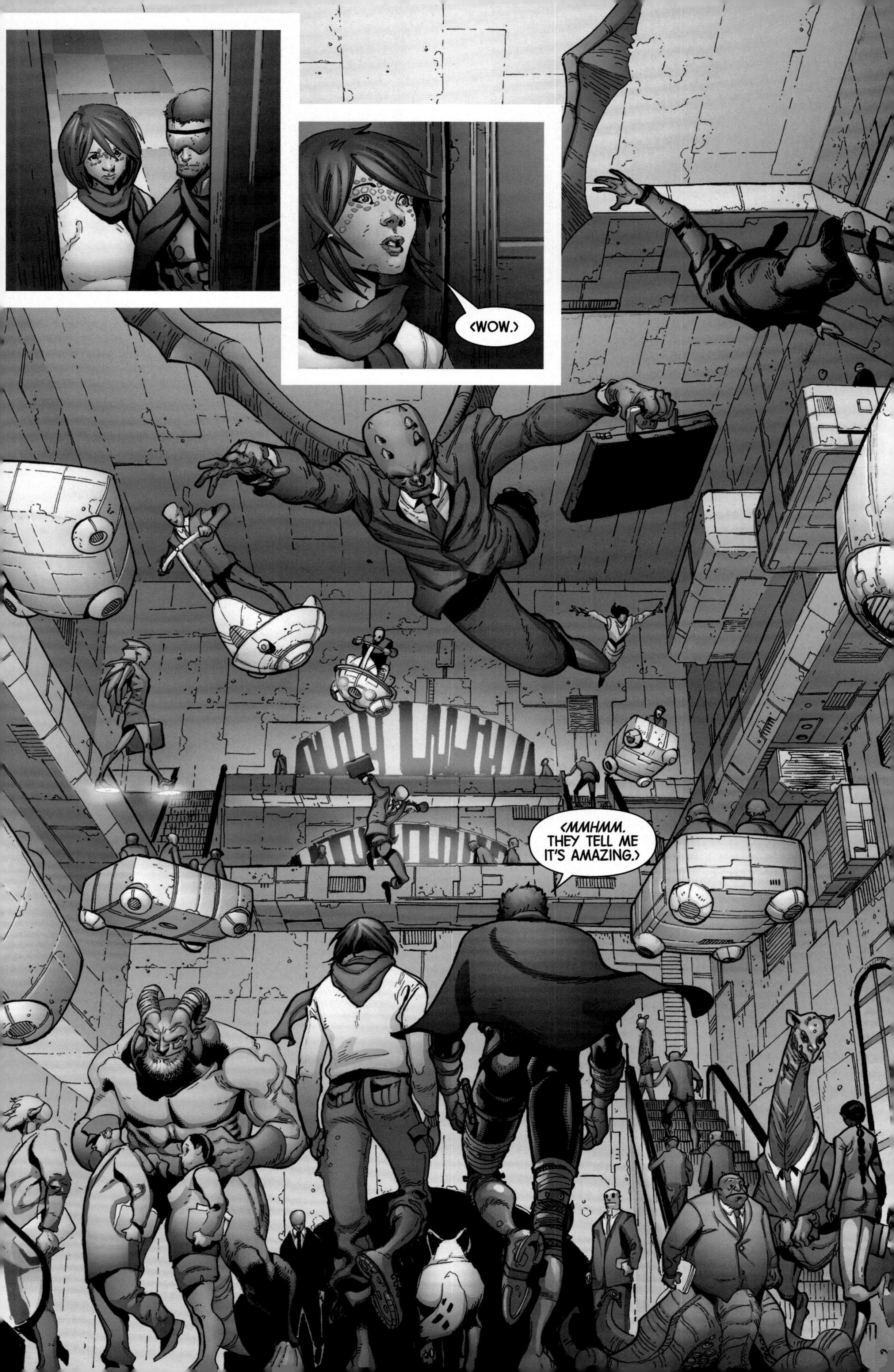
<WOW.>
<MMHMM. THEY TELL ME IT'S AMAZING.>

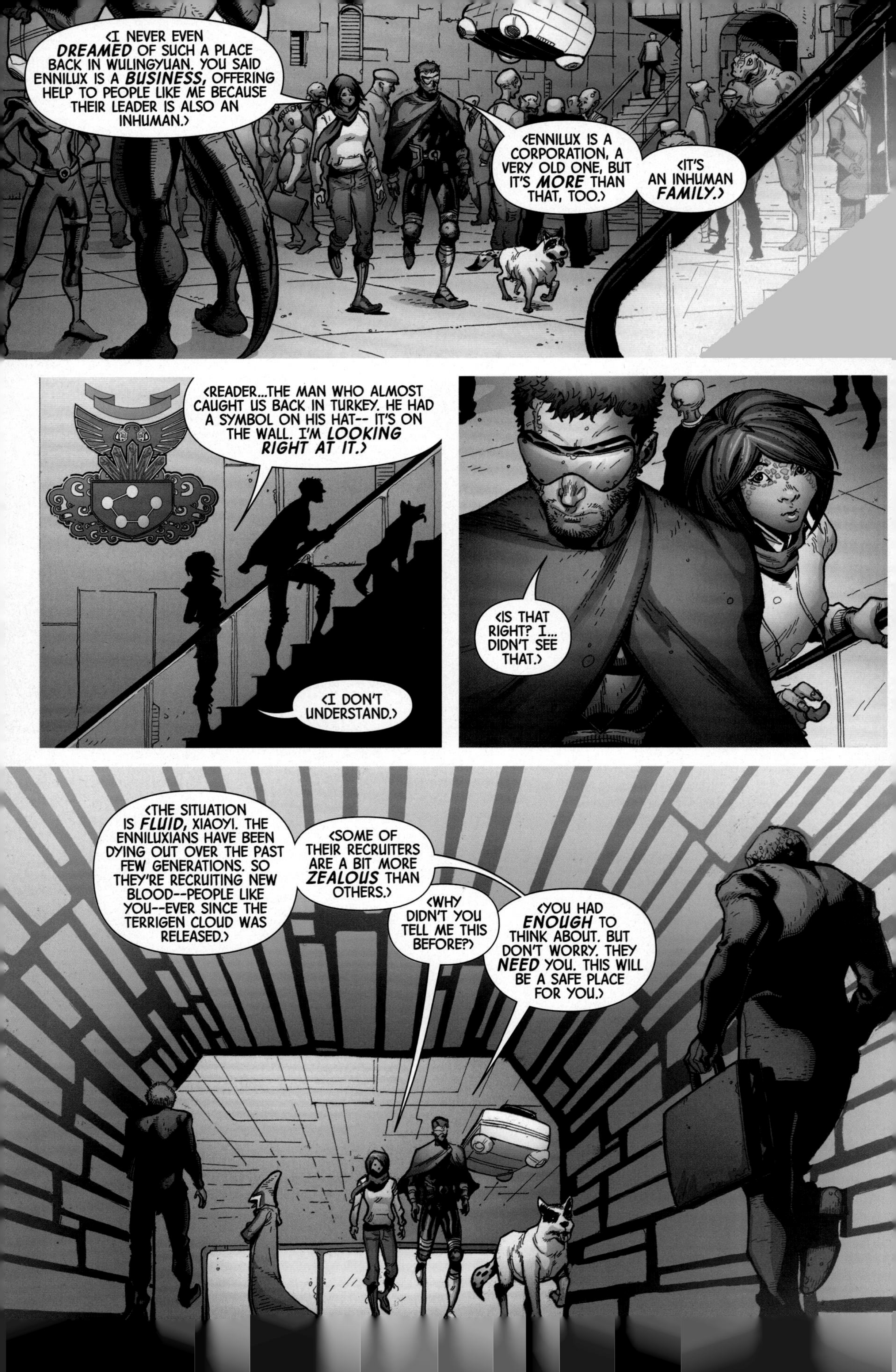
<I NEVER EVEN DREAMED OF SUCH A PLACE BACK IN WULINGYUAN. YOU SAID ENNILUX IS A BUSINESS, OFFERING HELP TO PEOPLE LIKE ME BECAUSE THEIR LEADER IS ALSO AN INHUMAN.>
<ENNILUX IS A CORPORATION, A VERY OLD ONE, BUT IT'S MORE THAN THAT, TOO.>
<IT'S AN INHUMAN FAMILY.>
<READER...THE MAN WHO ALMOST CAUGHT US BACK IN TURKEY. HE HAD A SYMBOL ON HIS HAT-- IT'S ON THE WALL. I'M LOOKING RIGHT AT IT.>
<I DON'T UNDERSTAND.>
<IS THAT RIGHT? I... DIDN'T SEE THAT.>
<THE SITUATION IS FLUID, XIAOYI. THE ENNILUXIANS HAVE BEEN DYING OUT OVER THE PAST FEW GENERATIONS. SO THEY'RE RECRUITING NEW BLOOD--PEOPLE LIKE YOU--EVER SINCE THE TERRIGEN CLOUD WAS RELEASED.>
<SOME OF THEIR RECRUITERS ARE A BIT MORE ZEALOUS THAN OTHERS.>
<WHY DIDN'T YOU TELL ME THIS BEFORE?>
<YOU HAD ENOUGH TO THINK ABOUT. BUT DON'T WORRY. THEY NEED YOU. THIS WILL BE A SAFE PLACE FOR YOU.>

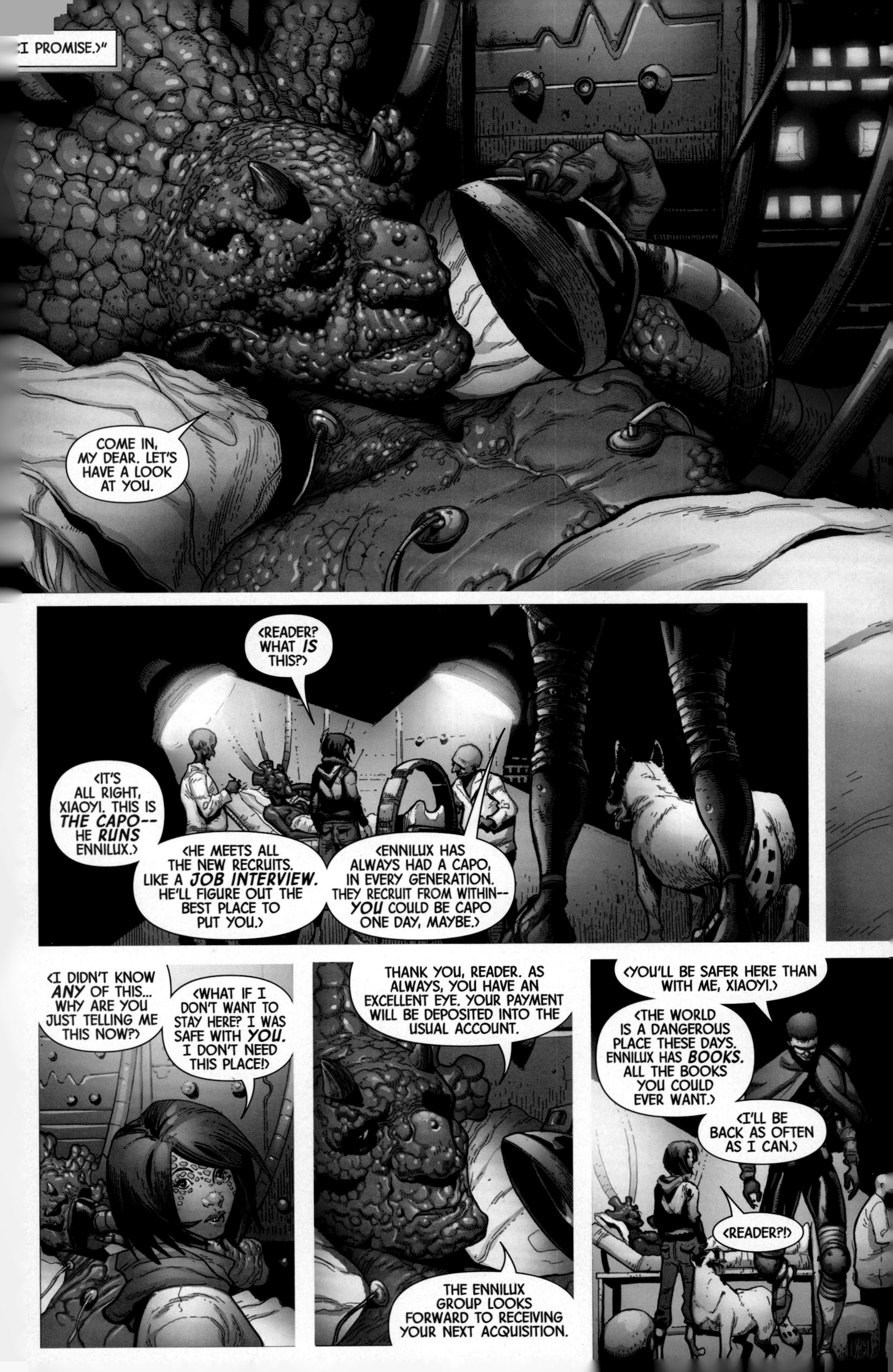

I PROMISE.>"
COME IN, MY DEAR. LET'S HAVE A LOOK AT YOU.
<READER? WHAT IS THIS?>
<IT'S ALL RIGHT, XIAOYI. THIS IS THE CAPO-- HE RUNS ENNILUX.>
<HE MEETS ALL THE NEW RECRUITS. LIKE A JOB INTERVIEW. HE'LL FIGURE OUT THE BEST PLACE TO PUT YOU.>
<ENNILUX HAS ALWAYS HAD A CAPO, IN EVERY GENERATION. THEY RECRUIT FROM WITHIN-- YOU COULD BE CAPO ONE DAY, MAYBE.>
<I DIDN'T KNOW ANY OF THIS... WHY ARE YOU JUST TELLING ME THIS NOW?>
<WHAT IF I DON'T WANT TO STAY HERE? I WAS SAFE WITH YOU. I DON'T NEED THIS PLACE!>
THANK YOU, READER. AS ALWAYS, YOU HAVE AN EXCELLENT EYE. YOUR PAYMENT WILL BE DEPOSITED INTO THE USUAL ACCOUNT.
THE ENNILUX GROUP LOOKS FORWARD TO RECEIVING YOUR NEXT ACQUISITION.
<YOU'LL BE SAFER HERE THAN WITH ME, XIAOYI.>
<THE WORLD IS A DANGEROUS PLACE THESE DAYS. ENNILUX HAS BOOKS. ALL THE BOOKS YOU COULD EVER WANT.>
<I'LL BE BACK AS OFTEN AS I CAN.>
<READER?!>

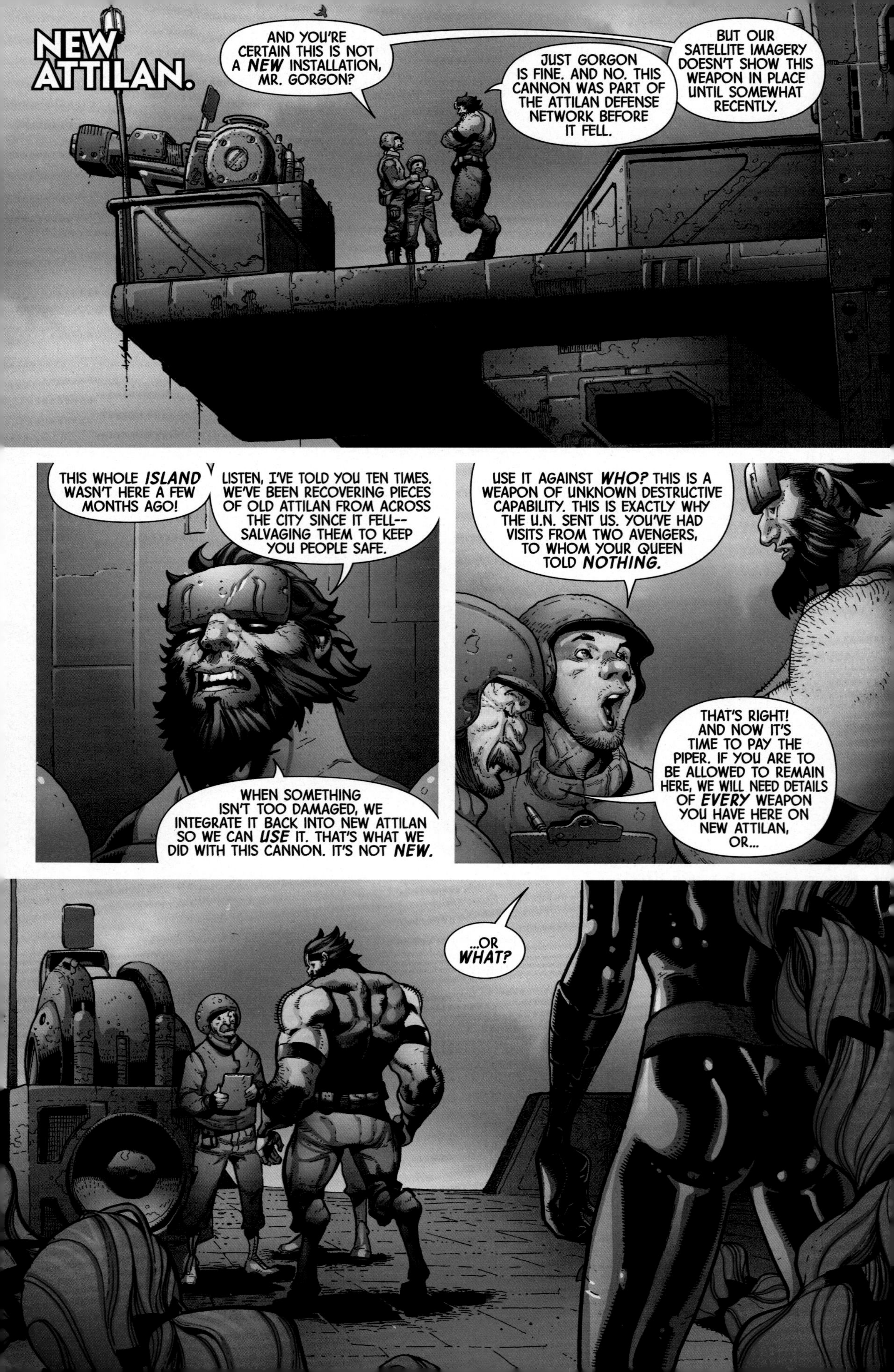
NEW ATTILAN.
AND YOU'RE CERTAIN THIS IS NOT A NEW INSTALLATION, MR. GORGON?
BUT OUR SATELLITE IMAGERY DOESN'T SHOW THIS WEAPON IN PLACE UNTIL SOMEWHAT RECENTLY.
JUST GORGON IS FINE. AND NO. THIS CANNON WAS PART OF THE ATTILAN DEFENSE NETWORK BEFORE IT FELL.
THIS WHOLE ISLAND WASN'T HERE A FEW MONTHS AGO!
LISTEN, I'VE TOLD YOU TEN TIMES. WE'VE BEEN RECOVERING PIECES OF OLD ATTILAN FROM ACROSS THE CITY SINCE IT FELL-- SALVAGING THEM TO KEEP YOU PEOPLE SAFE.
WHEN SOMETHING ISN'T TOO DAMAGED, WE INTEGRATE IT BACK INTO NEW ATTILAN SO WE CAN USE IT. THAT'S WHAT WE DID WITH THIS CANNON. IT'S NOT NEW.
USE IT AGAINST WHO? THIS IS A WEAPON OF UNKNOWN DESTRUCTIVE CAPABILITY. THIS IS EXACTLY WHY THE U.N. SENT US. YOU'VE HAD VISITS FROM TWO AVENGERS, TO WHOM YOUR QUEEN TOLD NOTHING.
THAT'S RIGHT! AND NOW IT'S TIME TO PAY THE PIPER. IF YOU ARE TO BE ALLOWED TO REMAIN HERE, WE WILL NEED DETAILS OF EVERY WEAPON YOU HAVE HERE ON NEW ATTILAN, OR...
...OR WHAT?

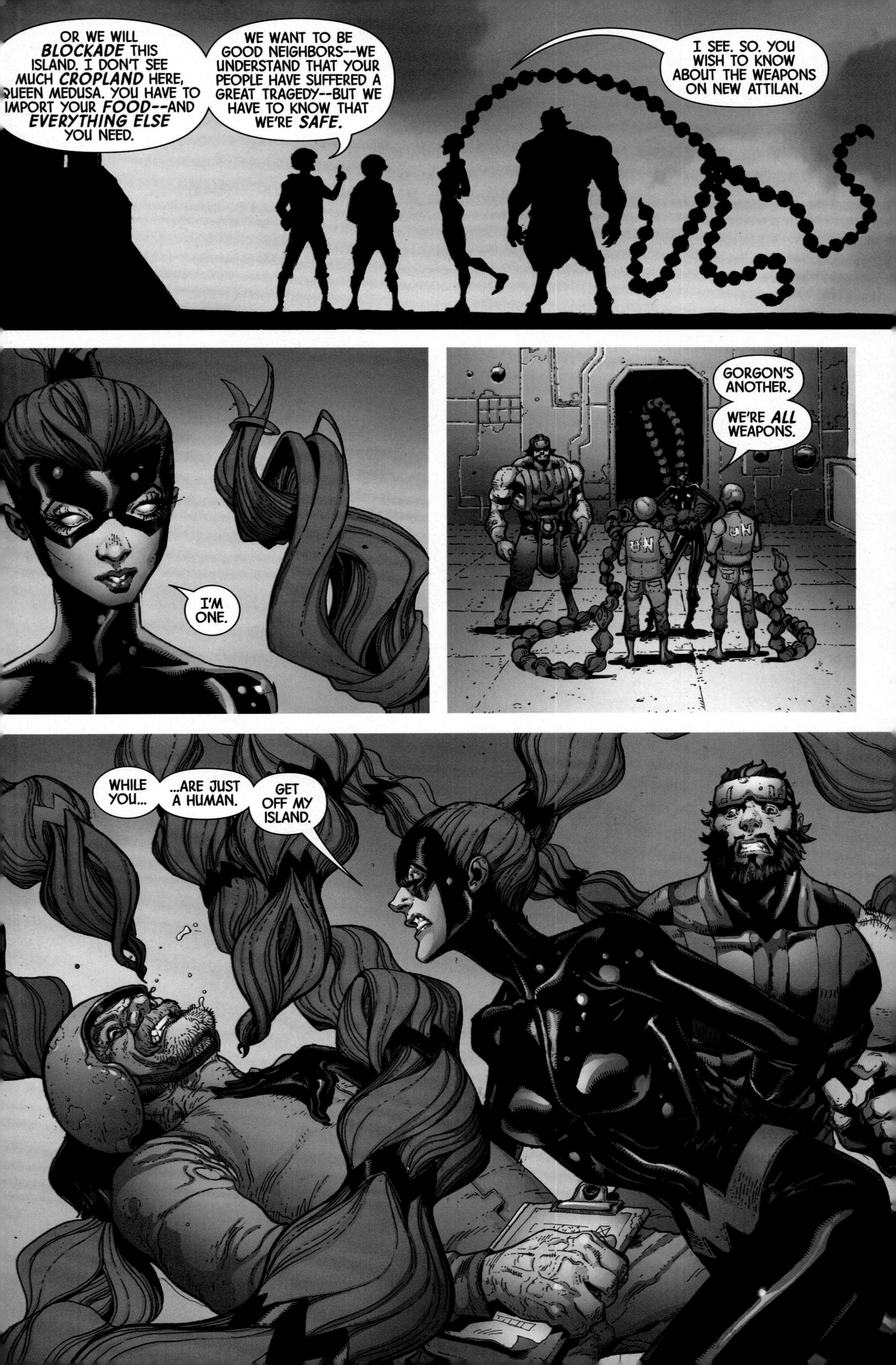
OR WE WILL BLOCKADE THIS ISLAND. I DON'T SEE MUCH CROPLAND HERE, QUEEN MEDUSA. YOU HAVE TO IMPORT YOUR FOOD--AND EVERYTHING ELSE YOU NEED.
WE WANT TO BE GOOD NEIGHBORS--WE UNDERSTAND THAT YOUR PEOPLE HAVE SUFFERED A GREAT TRAGEDY--BUT WE HAVE TO KNOW THAT WE'RE SAFE.
I SEE. SO. YOU WISH TO KNOW ABOUT THE WEAPONS ON NEW ATTILAN.
I'M ONE.
GORGON'S ANOTHER.
WE'RE ALL WEAPONS.
WHILE YOU...
...ARE JUST A HUMAN.
GET OFF MY ISLAND.

ENNILUX.

‹WHAT DO YOU *WANT* FROM ME? PLEASE...JUST *TALK* TO ME.›

SHE'S EXACTLY WHAT WE'VE BEEN SEARCHING FOR, SIR.

VERY GOOD. I WAS CONCERNED THAT WE WOULD *NEVER* FIND A SUITABLE CANDIDATE.

THE RELEASE OF THE TERRIGEN CLOUD HELPED. OUR SAMPLE SET WAS INCREASED A THOUSANDFOLD.

IT IS UNSETTLING THAT SHE WAS NOT PRODUCED FROM OUR IN-COMPANY BREEDING PROGRAMS, BUT AT THIS POINT, I WILL TAKE WHAT I CAN GET.

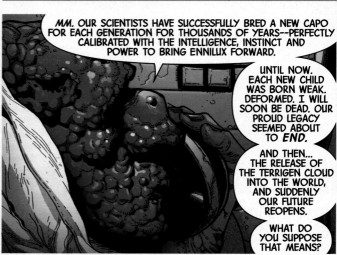

MM. OUR SCIENTISTS HAVE SUCCESSFULLY BRED A NEW CAPO FOR EACH GENERATION FOR THOUSANDS OF YEARS--PERFECTLY CALIBRATED WITH THE INTELLIGENCE, INSTINCT AND POWER TO BRING ENNILUX FORWARD.

UNTIL NOW. EACH NEW CHILD WAS BORN WEAK. DEFORMED. I WILL SOON BE DEAD. OUR PROUD LEGACY SEEMED ABOUT TO *END.*

AND THEN... THE RELEASE OF THE TERRIGEN CLOUD INTO THE WORLD, AND SUDDENLY OUR FUTURE REOPENS.

WHAT DO YOU SUPPOSE THAT MEANS?

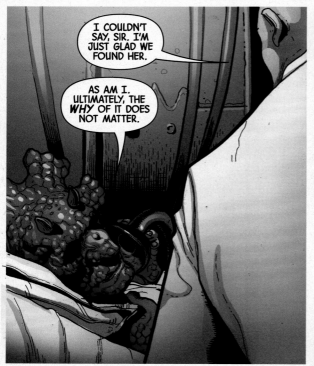

I COULDN'T SAY, SIR. I'M JUST GLAD WE FOUND HER.

AS AM I. ULTIMATELY, THE *WHY* OF IT DOES NOT MATTER.

PREPARE HER FOR THE TRANSFER.

TRANSFER? WHAT DO YOU...

WE'RE READY, SIR. WE'LL COMMENCE BY WIPING THE VESSEL'S MIND, AND THEN THE IMPLANTATION PROCEDURE WILL BEGIN.

AS YOU KNOW, WE CAN PRESERVE HER MENTAL TEMPLATE AND PUT IT IN YOUR *CURRENT* BODY, IF YOU CHOOSE.

SHE WOULD NOT LIVE LONG, BUT IT WOULD BE *SOMETHING.*

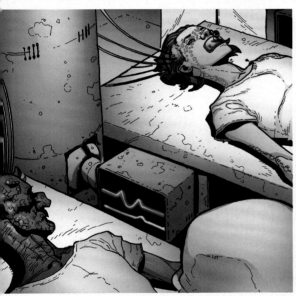

NO--THAT ALWAYS CAUSES DIFFICULTIES. BEST TO END HER TIME HERE AND NOW. I AM INHUMAN...

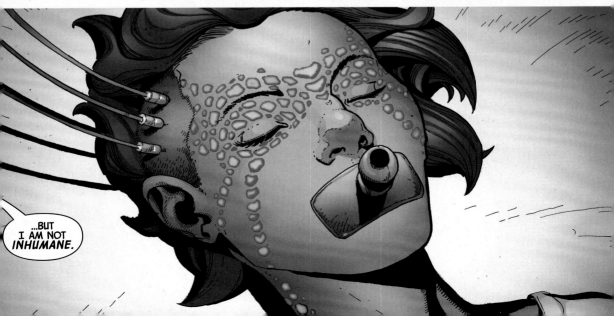

...BUT I AM NOT *INHUMANE.*

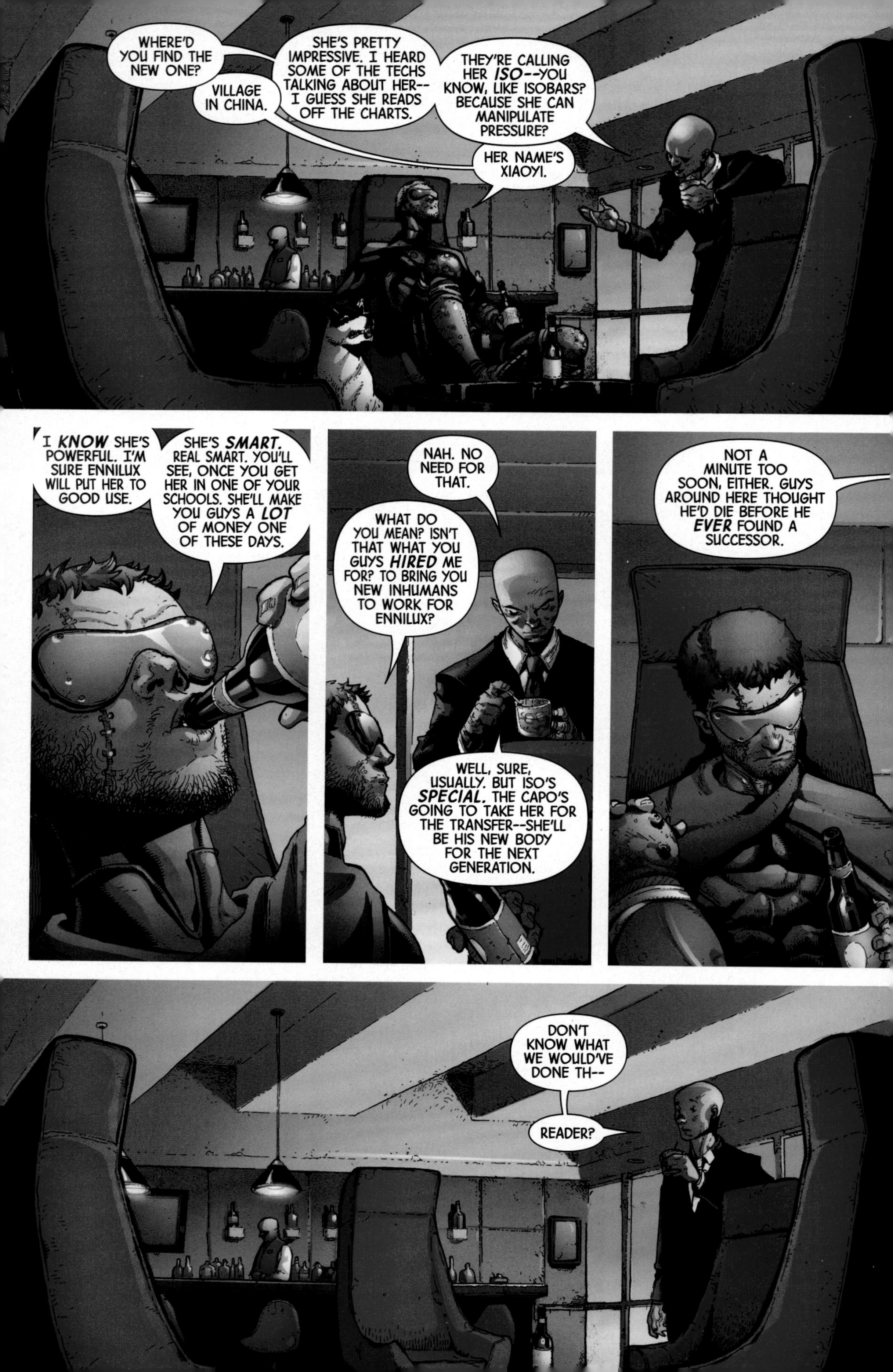

WHERE'D YOU FIND THE NEW ONE?
VILLAGE IN CHINA.
SHE'S PRETTY IMPRESSIVE. I HEARD SOME OF THE TECHS TALKING ABOUT HER-- I GUESS SHE READS OFF THE CHARTS.
THEY'RE CALLING HER ISO--YOU KNOW, LIKE ISOBARS? BECAUSE SHE CAN MANIPULATE PRESSURE?
HER NAME'S XIAOYI.
I KNOW SHE'S POWERFUL. I'M SURE ENNILUX WILL PUT HER TO GOOD USE.
SHE'S SMART. REAL SMART. YOU'LL SEE, ONCE YOU GET HER IN ONE OF YOUR SCHOOLS. SHE'LL MAKE YOU GUYS A LOT OF MONEY ONE OF THESE DAYS.
NAH. NO NEED FOR THAT.
WHAT DO YOU MEAN? ISN'T THAT WHAT YOU GUYS HIRED ME FOR? TO BRING YOU NEW INHUMANS TO WORK FOR ENNILUX?
WELL, SURE, USUALLY. BUT ISO'S SPECIAL. THE CAPO'S GOING TO TAKE HER FOR THE TRANSFER--SHE'LL BE HIS NEW BODY FOR THE NEXT GENERATION.
NOT A MINUTE TOO SOON, EITHER. GUYS AROUND HERE THOUGHT HE'D DIE BEFORE HE EVER FOUND A SUCCESSOR.
DON'T KNOW WHAT WE WOULD'VE DONE TH--
READER?

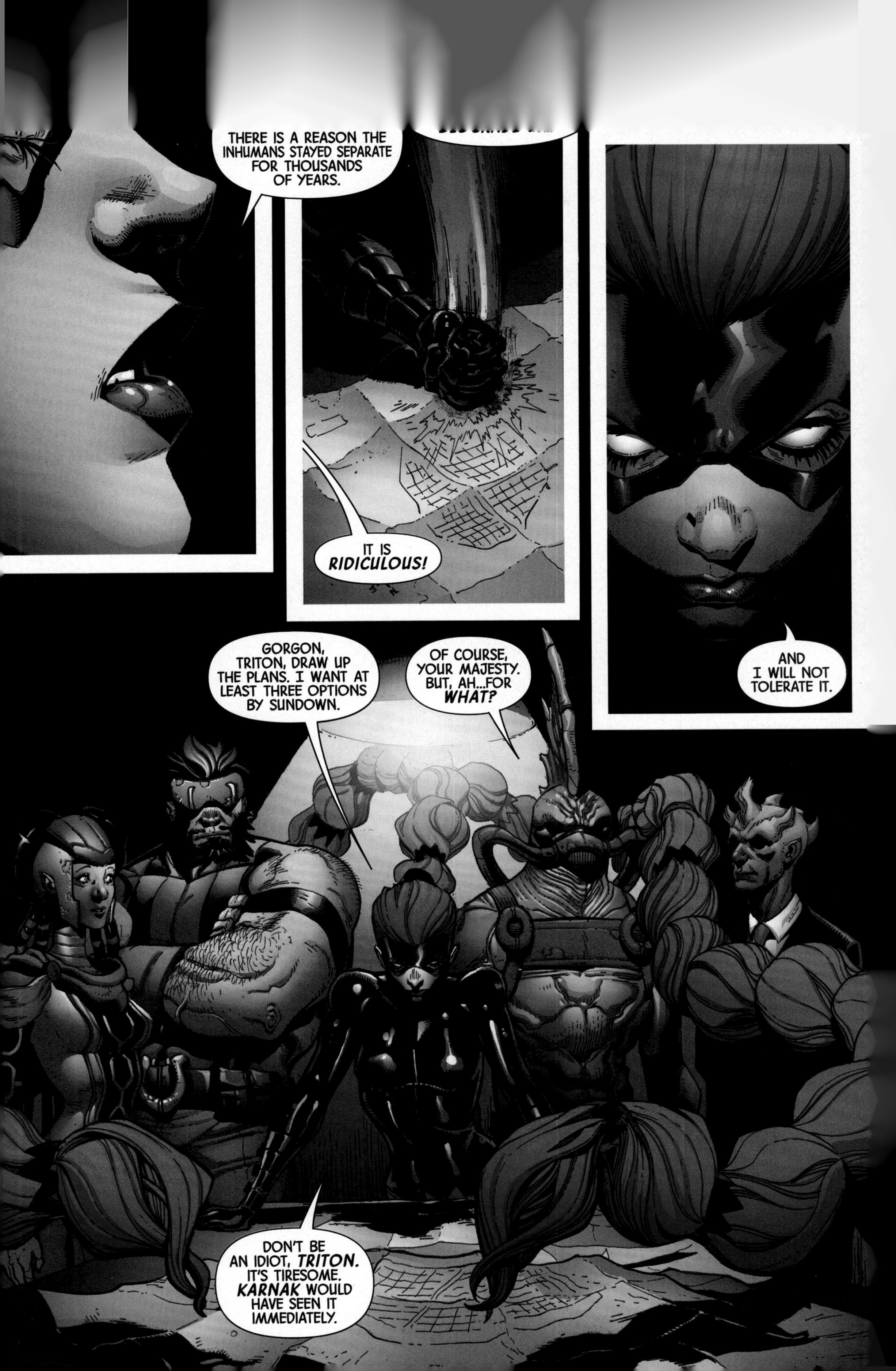
THERE IS A REASON THE INHUMANS STAYED SEPARATE FOR THOUSANDS OF YEARS.
IT IS *RIDICULOUS!*
AND I WILL NOT TOLERATE IT.
GORGON, TRITON, DRAW UP THE PLANS. I WANT AT LEAST THREE OPTIONS BY SUNDOWN.
OF COURSE, YOUR MAJESTY. BUT, AH...FOR *WHAT?*
DON'T BE AN IDIOT, *TRITON.* IT'S TIRESOME. *KARNAK* WOULD HAVE SEEN IT IMMEDIATELY.

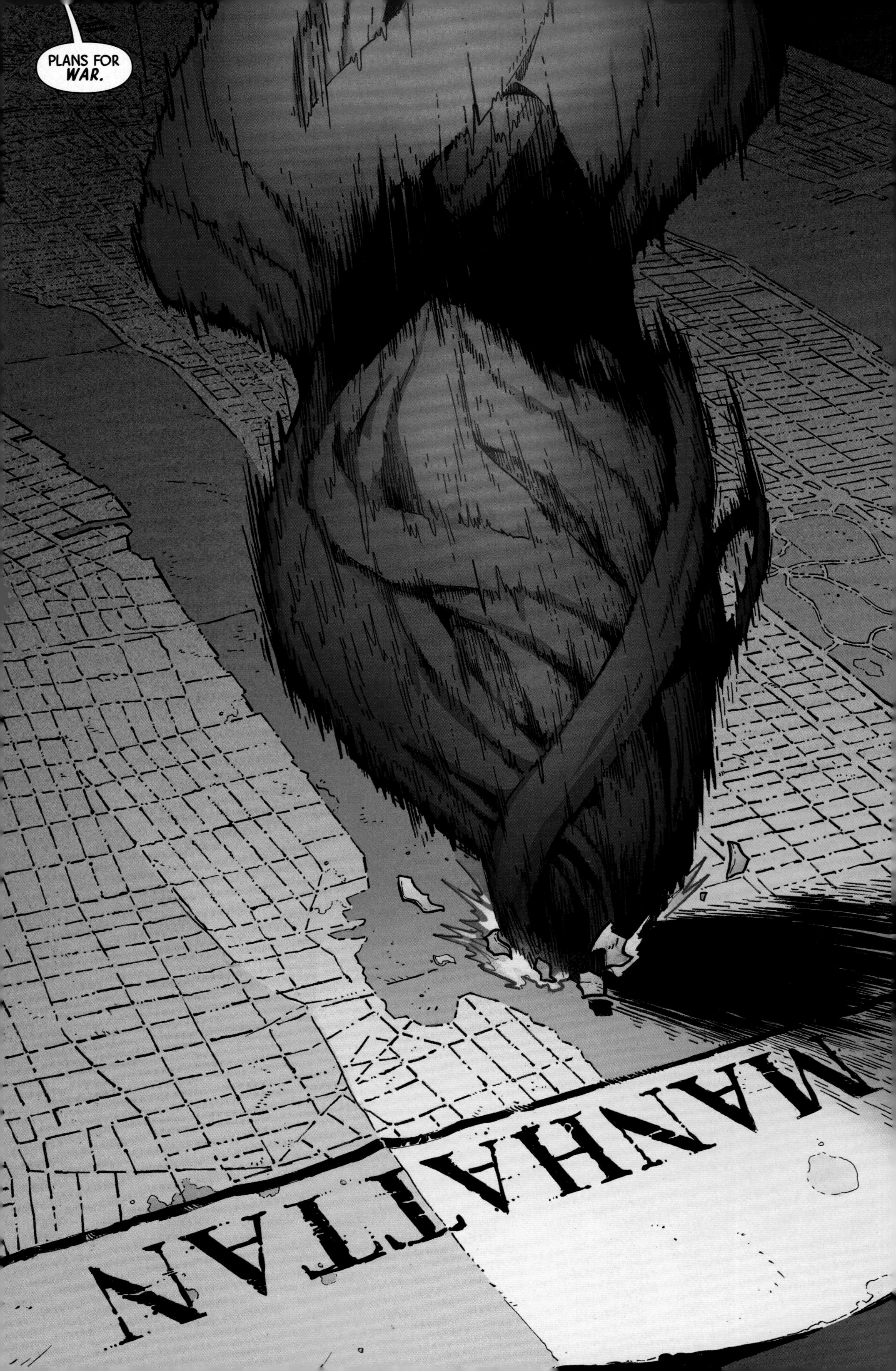
PLANS FOR WAR.
MANHATTAN

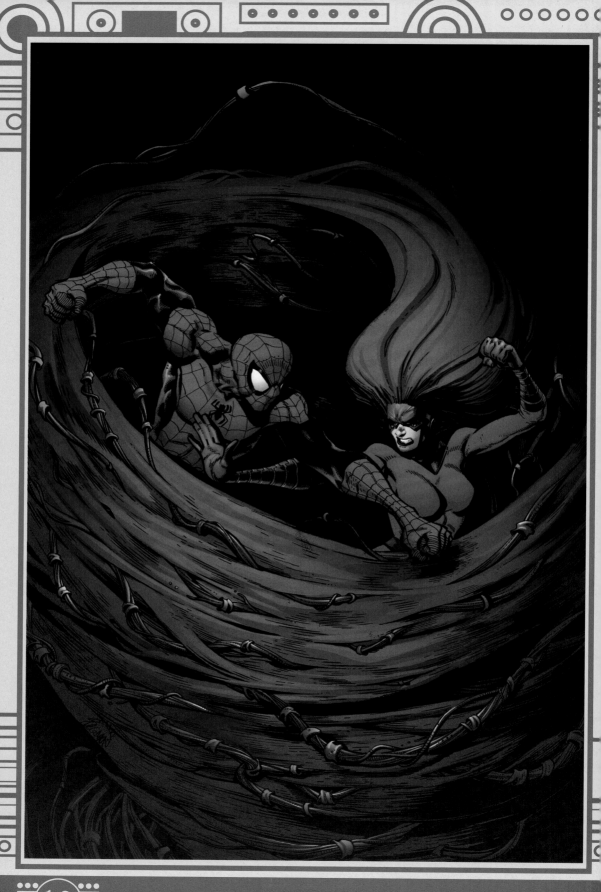

PART TEN: THE DARK QUEEN

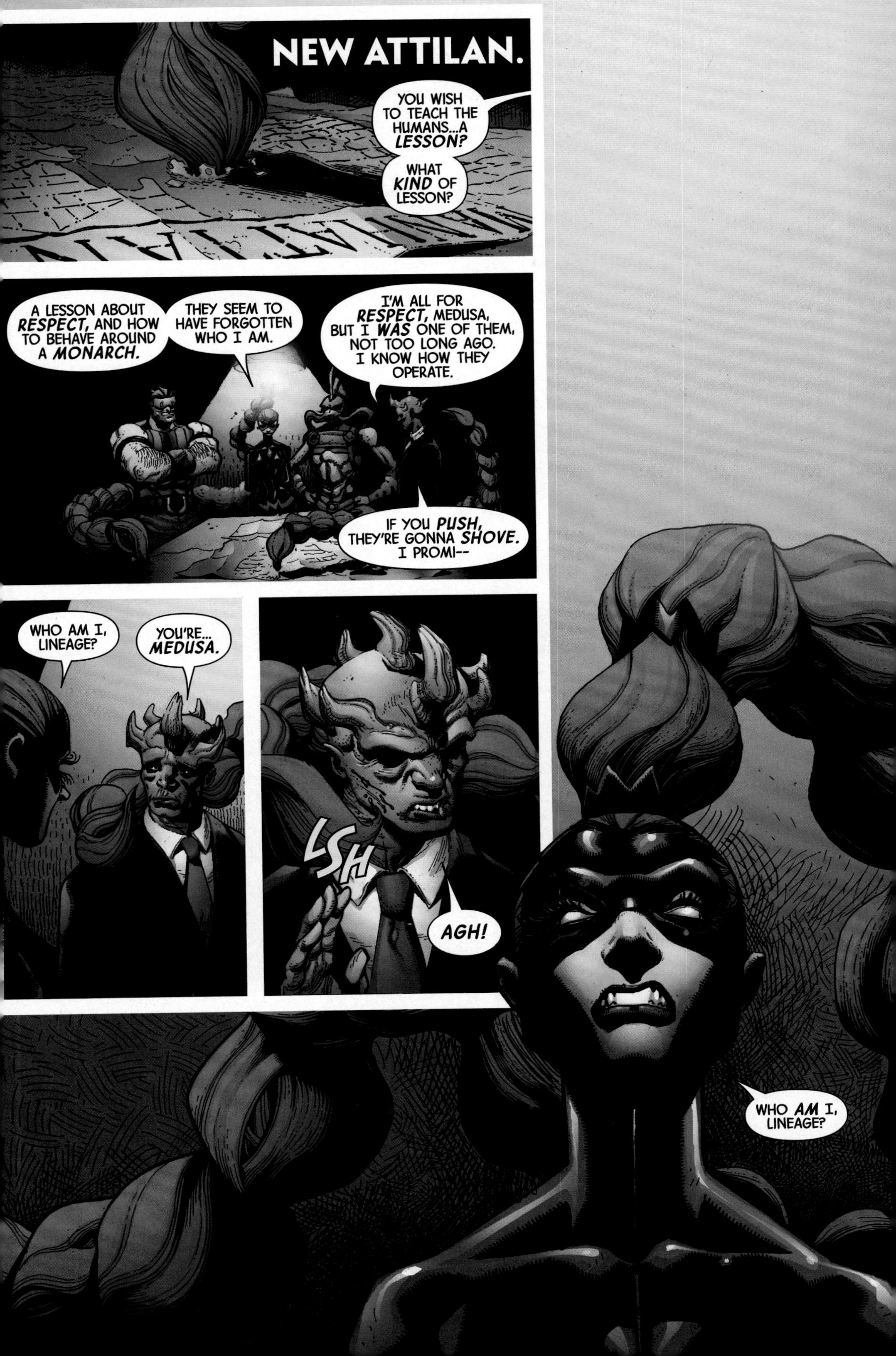
NEW ATTILAN.
YOU WISH TO TEACH THE HUMANS...A LESSON?
WHAT KIND OF LESSON?
A LESSON ABOUT RESPECT, AND HOW TO BEHAVE AROUND A MONARCH.
THEY SEEM TO HAVE FORGOTTEN WHO I AM.
I'M ALL FOR RESPECT, MEDUSA, BUT I WAS ONE OF THEM, NOT TOO LONG AGO. I KNOW HOW THEY OPERATE.
IF YOU PUSH, THEY'RE GONNA SHOVE. I PROMI--
WHO AM I, LINEAGE?
YOU'RE... MEDUSA.
LSH
AGH!
WHO AM I, LINEAGE?

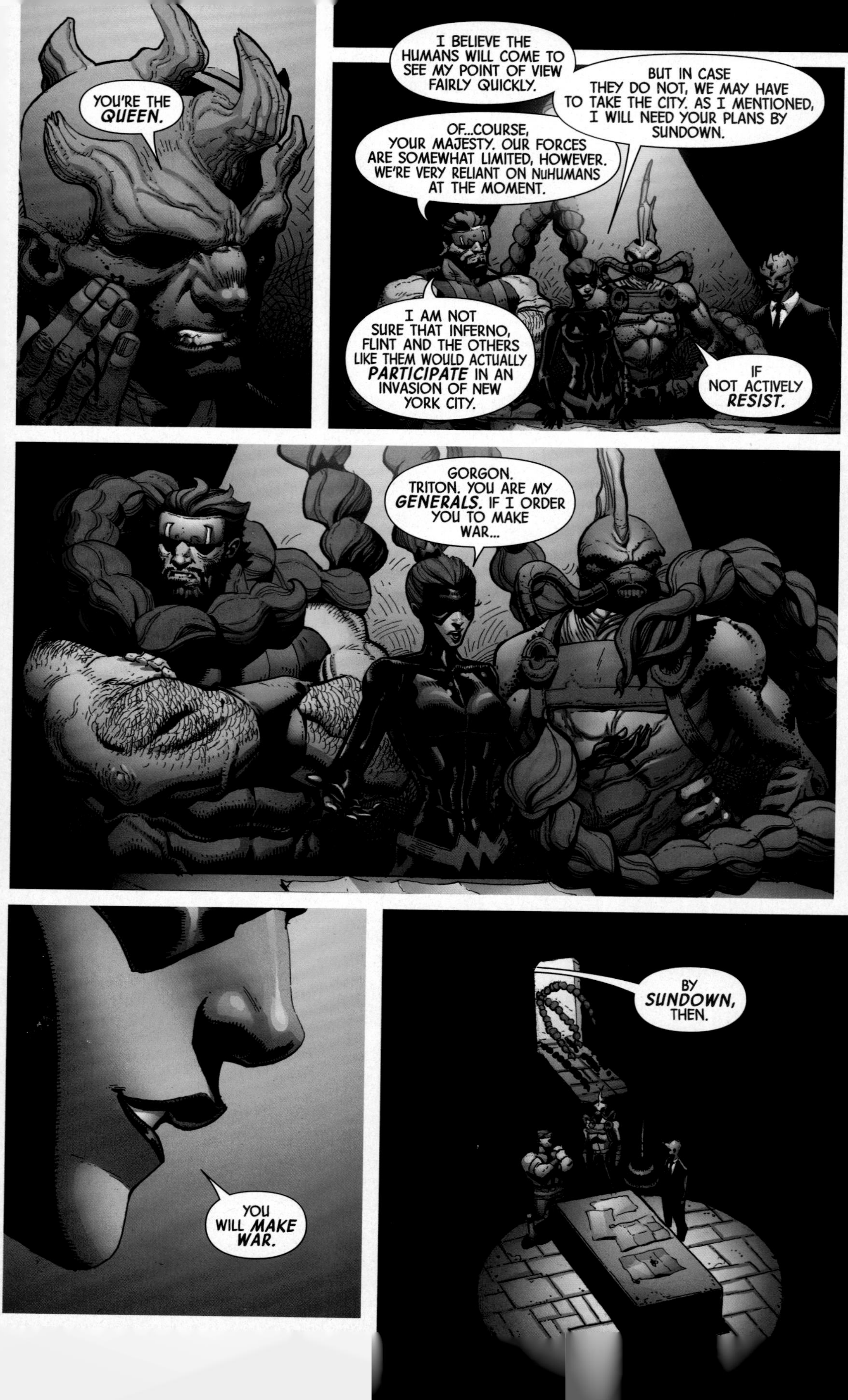
YOU'RE THE QUEEN.
I BELIEVE THE HUMANS WILL COME TO SEE MY POINT OF VIEW FAIRLY QUICKLY.
BUT IN CASE THEY DO NOT, WE MAY HAVE TO TAKE THE CITY. AS I MENTIONED, I WILL NEED YOUR PLANS BY SUNDOWN.
OF...COURSE, YOUR MAJESTY. OUR FORCES ARE SOMEWHAT LIMITED, HOWEVER. WE'RE VERY RELIANT ON NuHUMANS AT THE MOMENT.
I AM NOT SURE THAT INFERNO, FLINT AND THE OTHERS LIKE THEM WOULD ACTUALLY PARTICIPATE IN AN INVASION OF NEW YORK CITY.
IF NOT ACTIVELY RESIST.
GORGON. TRITON. YOU ARE MY GENERALS. IF I ORDER YOU TO MAKE WAR...
YOU WILL MAKE WAR.
BY SUNDOWN, THEN.

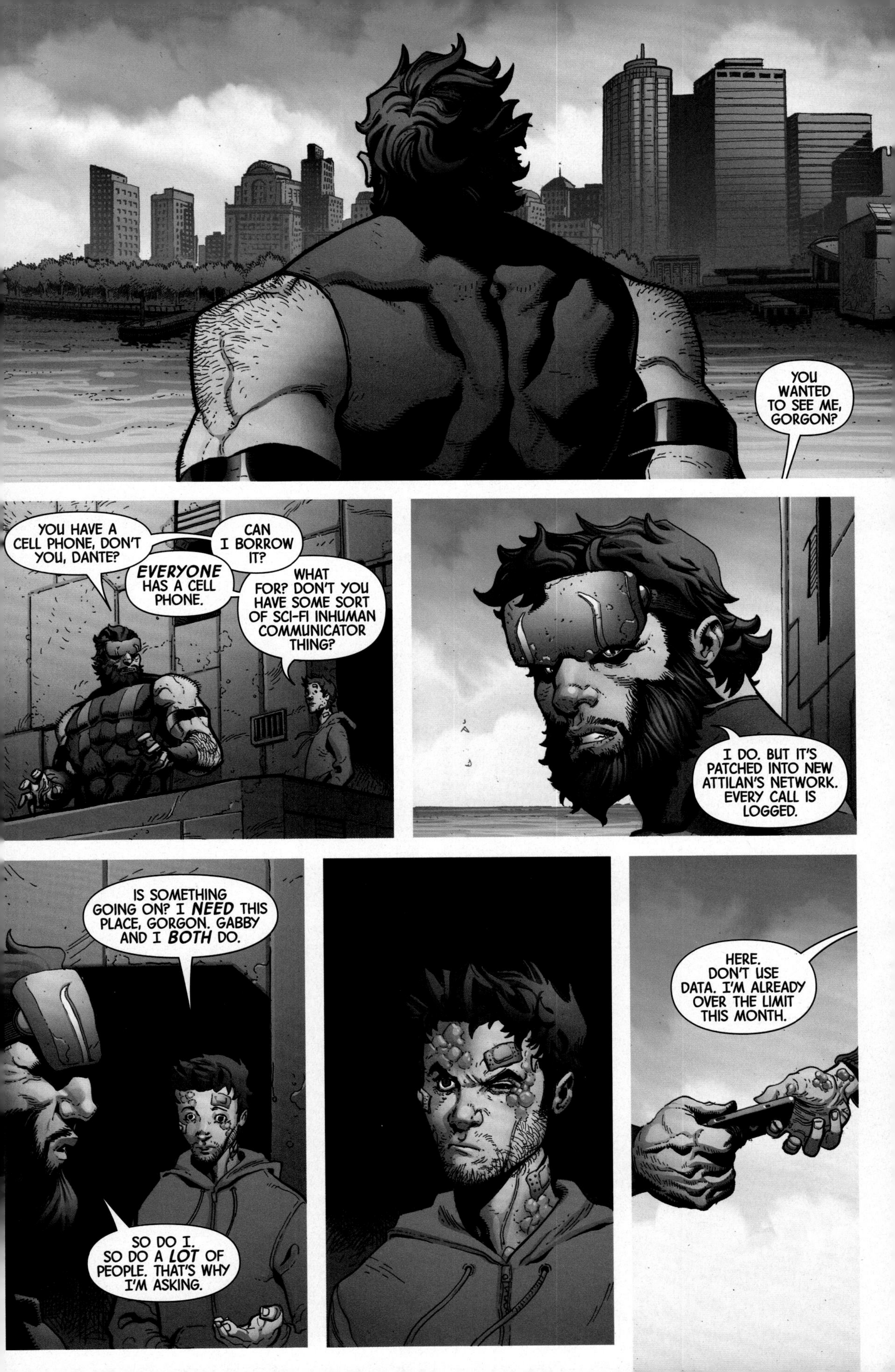
YOU WANTED TO SEE ME, GORGON?
YOU HAVE A CELL PHONE, DON'T YOU, DANTE?
CAN I BORROW IT?
EVERYONE HAS A CELL PHONE.
WHAT FOR? DON'T YOU HAVE SOME SORT OF SCI-FI INHUMAN COMMUNICATOR THING?
I DO. BUT IT'S PATCHED INTO NEW ATTILAN'S NETWORK. EVERY CALL IS LOGGED.
IS SOMETHING GOING ON? I NEED THIS PLACE, GORGON. GABBY AND I BOTH DO.
SO DO I. SO DO A LOT OF PEOPLE. THAT'S WHY I'M ASKING.
HERE. DON'T USE DATA. I'M ALREADY OVER THE LIMIT THIS MONTH.

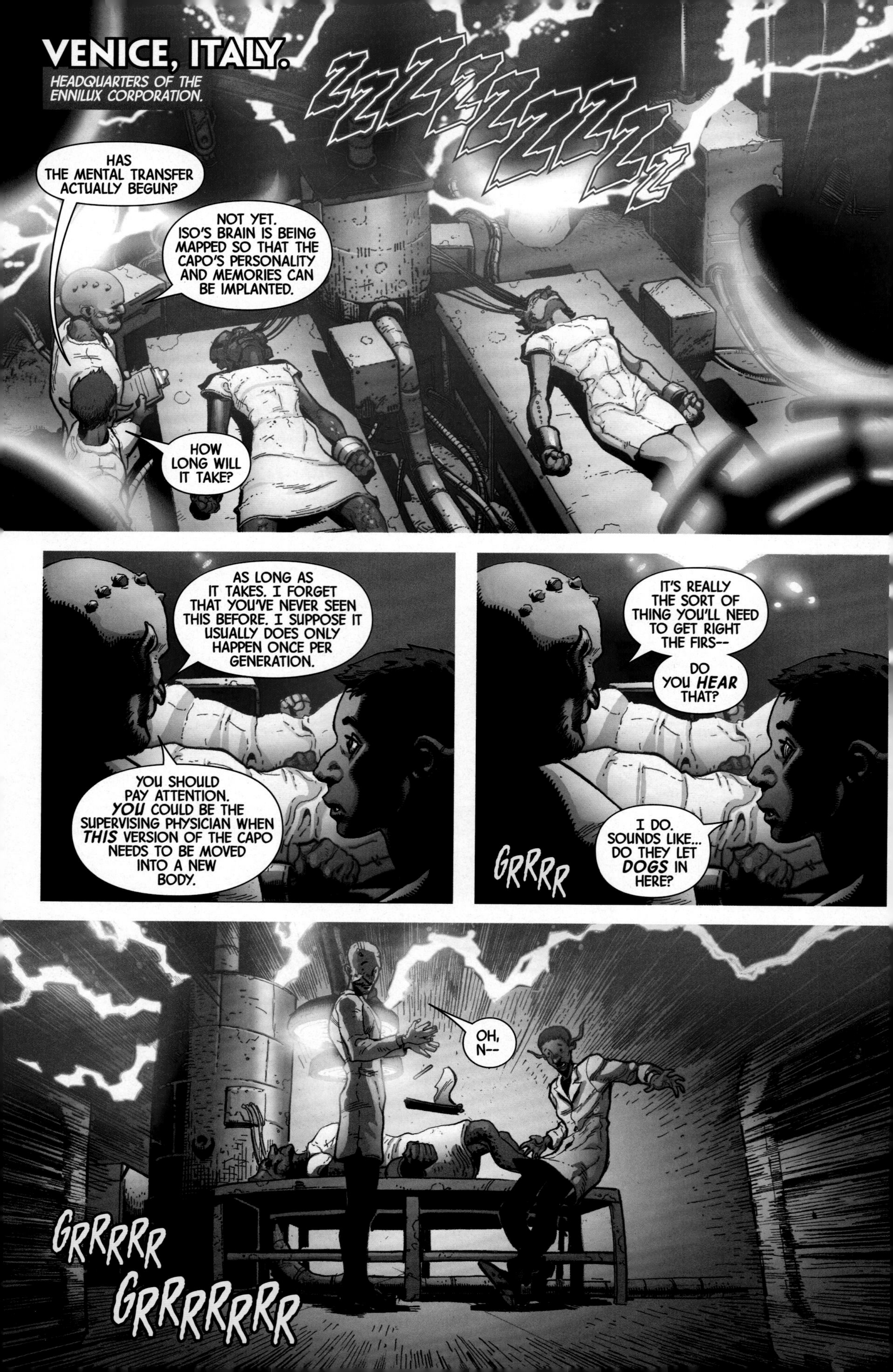
VENICE, ITALY.
HEADQUARTERS OF THE ENNILUX CORPORATION.
ZZZZZZZZZZZ
HAS THE MENTAL TRANSFER ACTUALLY BEGUN?
NOT YET. ISO'S BRAIN IS BEING MAPPED SO THAT THE CAPO'S PERSONALITY AND MEMORIES CAN BE IMPLANTED.
HOW LONG WILL IT TAKE?
AS LONG AS IT TAKES. I FORGET THAT YOU'VE NEVER SEEN THIS BEFORE. I SUPPOSE IT USUALLY DOES ONLY HAPPEN ONCE PER GENERATION.
YOU SHOULD PAY ATTENTION. YOU COULD BE THE SUPERVISING PHYSICIAN WHEN THIS VERSION OF THE CAPO NEEDS TO BE MOVED INTO A NEW BODY.
IT'S REALLY THE SORT OF THING YOU'LL NEED TO GET RIGHT THE FIRS--
DO YOU HEAR THAT?
I DO. SOUNDS LIKE... DO THEY LET DOGS IN HERE?
GRRRR
OH, N--
GRRRRR
GRRRRRRR

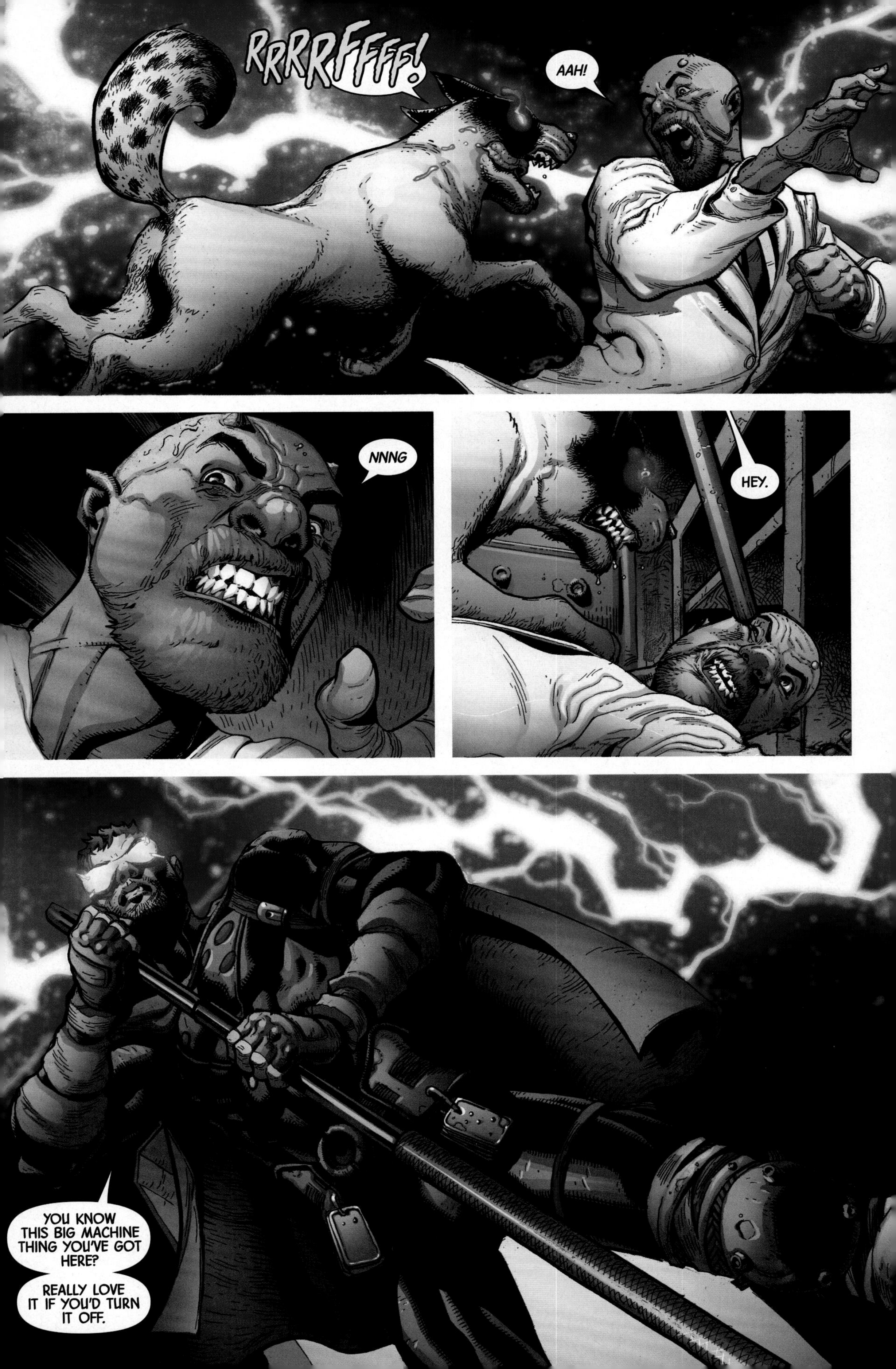
RRRRFFFFF!
AAH!
NNNG
HEY.
YOU KNOW THIS BIG MACHINE THING YOU'VE GOT HERE?
REALLY LOVE IT IF YOU'D TURN IT OFF.

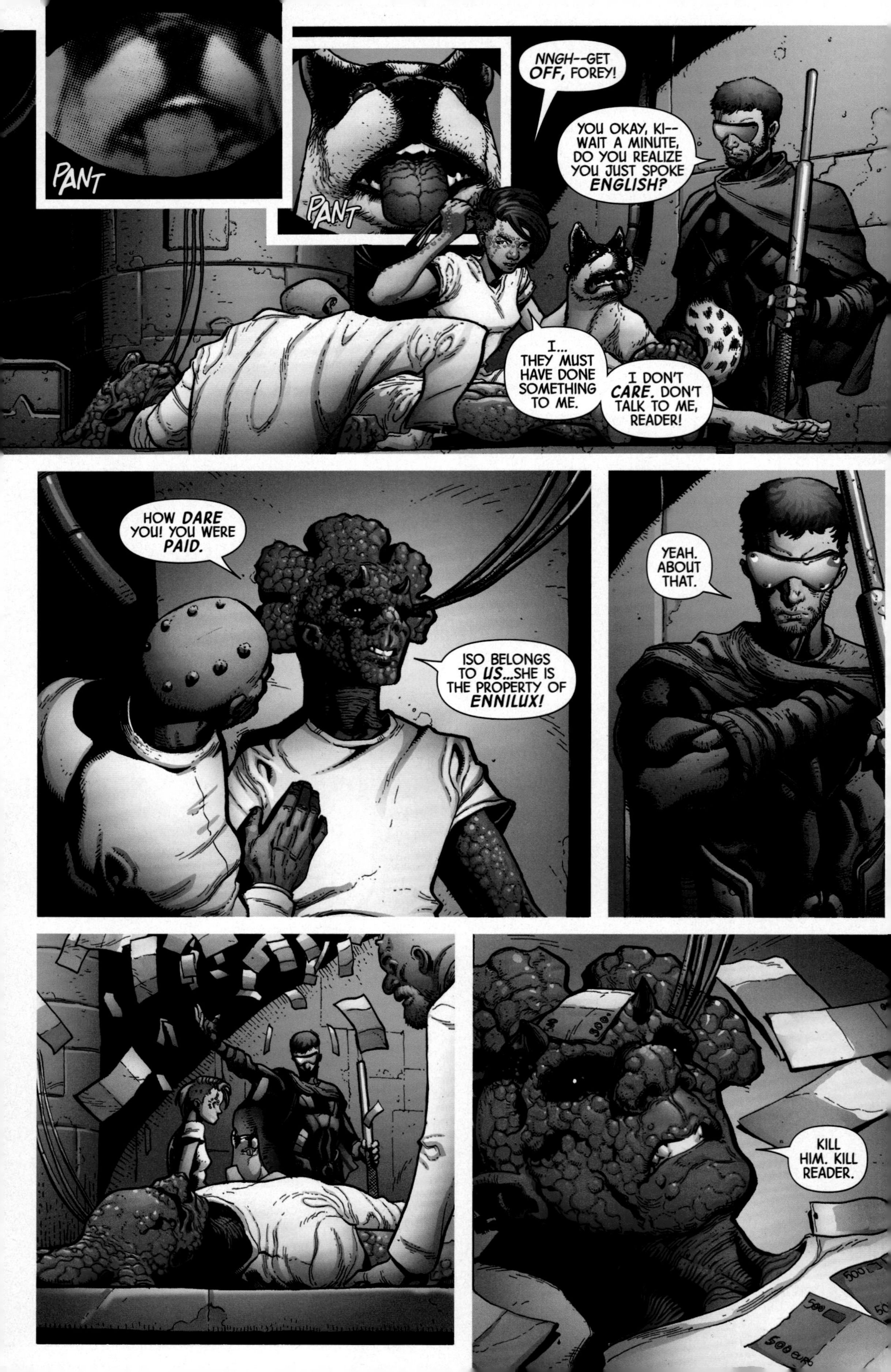
PANT
PANT
NNGH--GET OFF, FOREY!
YOU OKAY, KI-- WAIT A MINUTE, DO YOU REALIZE YOU JUST SPOKE ENGLISH?
I... THEY MUST HAVE DONE SOMETHING TO ME.
I DON'T CARE. DON'T TALK TO ME, READER!
HOW DARE YOU! YOU WERE PAID.
ISO BELONGS TO US...SHE IS THE PROPERTY OF ENNILUX!
YEAH. ABOUT THAT.
KILL HIM. KILL READER.

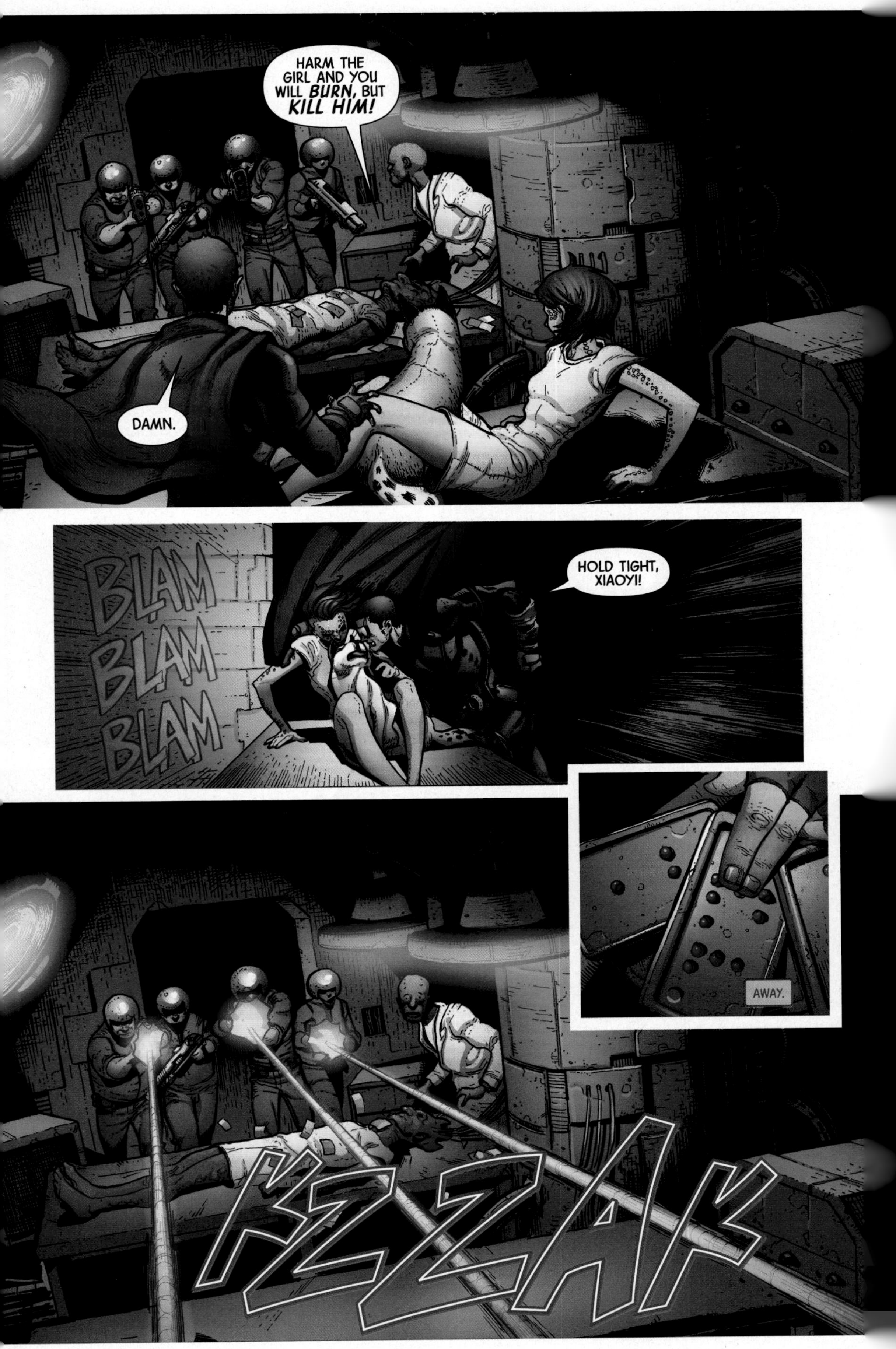
HARM THE GIRL AND YOU WILL BURN, BUT KILL HIM!
DAMN.
BLAM BLAM BLAM
HOLD TIGHT, XIAOYI!
AWAY.
KZZAK

THE UNITED NATIONS.

GENERAL ASSEMBLY.

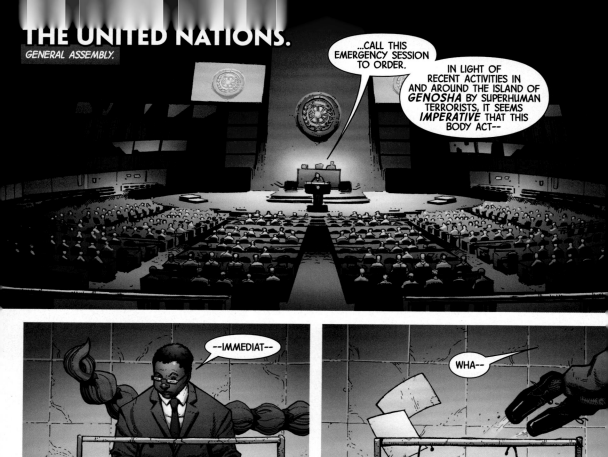

...CALL THIS EMERGENCY SESSION TO ORDER.

IN LIGHT OF RECENT ACTIVITIES IN AND AROUND THE ISLAND OF *GENOSHA* BY SUPERHUMAN TERRORISTS, IT SEEMS *IMPERATIVE* THAT THIS BODY ACT--

--IMMEDIAT--

WHA--

HUMAN NATIONS OF THE WORLD.

I THOUGHT IT WAS TIME WE *TALKED.*

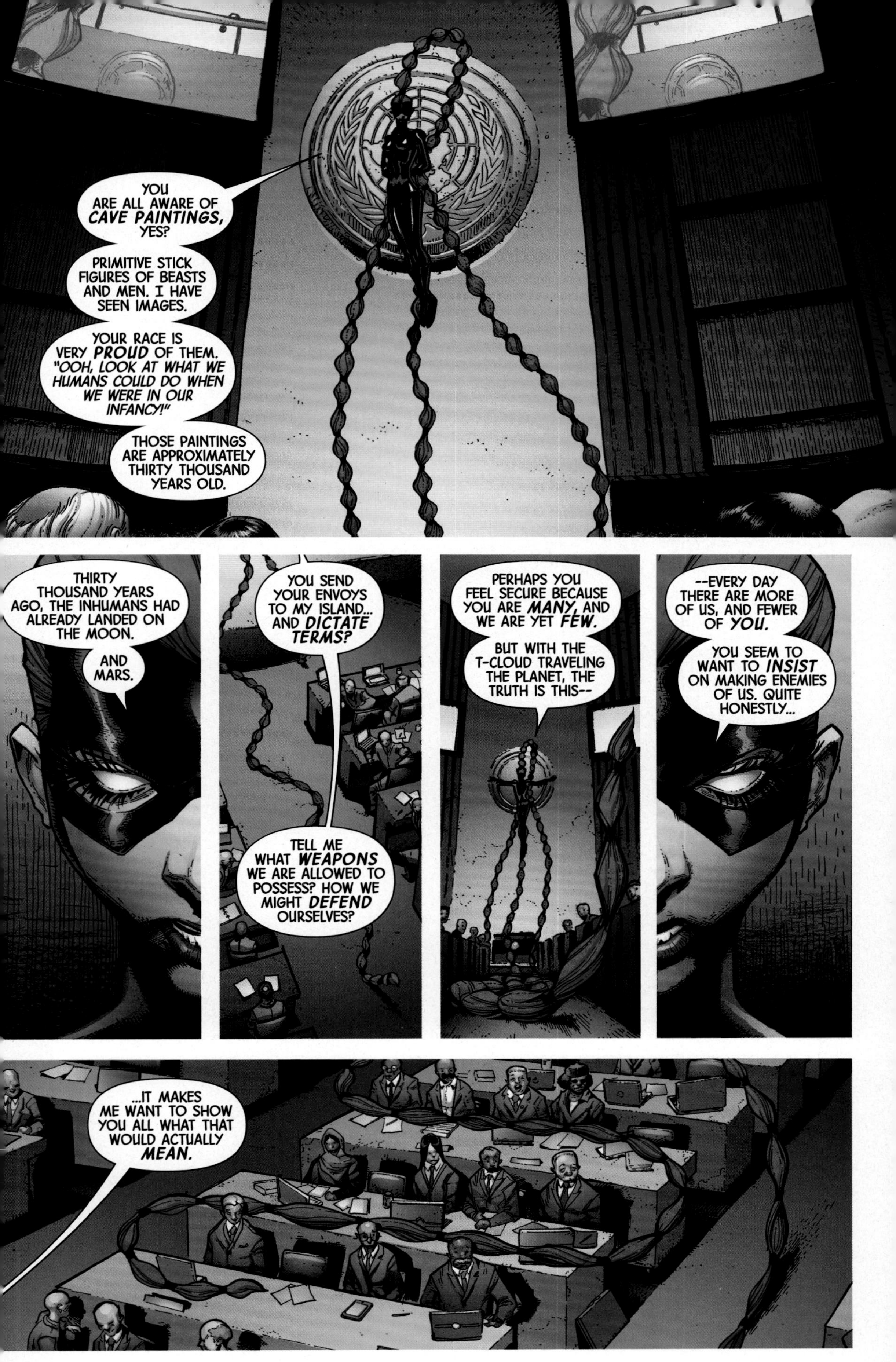

YOU ARE ALL AWARE OF CAVE PAINTINGS, YES?
PRIMITIVE STICK FIGURES OF BEASTS AND MEN. I HAVE SEEN IMAGES.
YOUR RACE IS VERY PROUD OF THEM. "OOH, LOOK AT WHAT WE HUMANS COULD DO WHEN WE WERE IN OUR INFANCY!"
THOSE PAINTINGS ARE APPROXIMATELY THIRTY THOUSAND YEARS OLD.
THIRTY THOUSAND YEARS AGO, THE INHUMANS HAD ALREADY LANDED ON THE MOON.
AND MARS.
YOU SEND YOUR ENVOYS TO MY ISLAND... AND DICTATE TERMS?
TELL ME WHAT WEAPONS WE ARE ALLOWED TO POSSESS? HOW WE MIGHT DEFEND OURSELVES?
PERHAPS YOU FEEL SECURE BECAUSE YOU ARE MANY, AND WE ARE YET FEW.
BUT WITH THE T-CLOUD TRAVELING THE PLANET, THE TRUTH IS THIS--
--EVERY DAY THERE ARE MORE OF US, AND FEWER OF YOU.
YOU SEEM TO WANT TO INSIST ON MAKING ENEMIES OF US. QUITE HONESTLY...
...IT MAKES ME WANT TO SHOW YOU ALL WHAT THAT WOULD ACTUALLY MEAN.

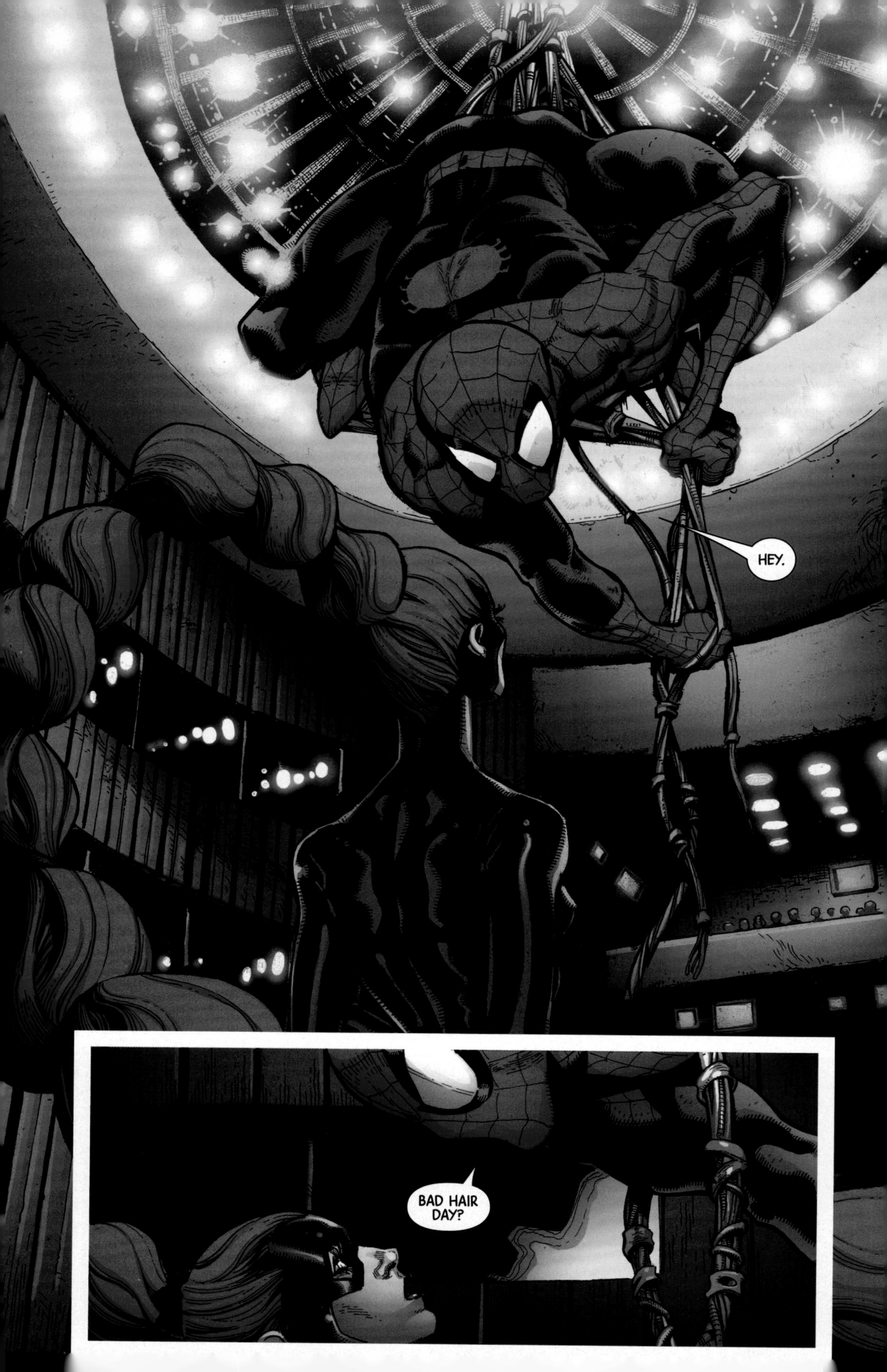
HEY.
BAD HAIR DAY?

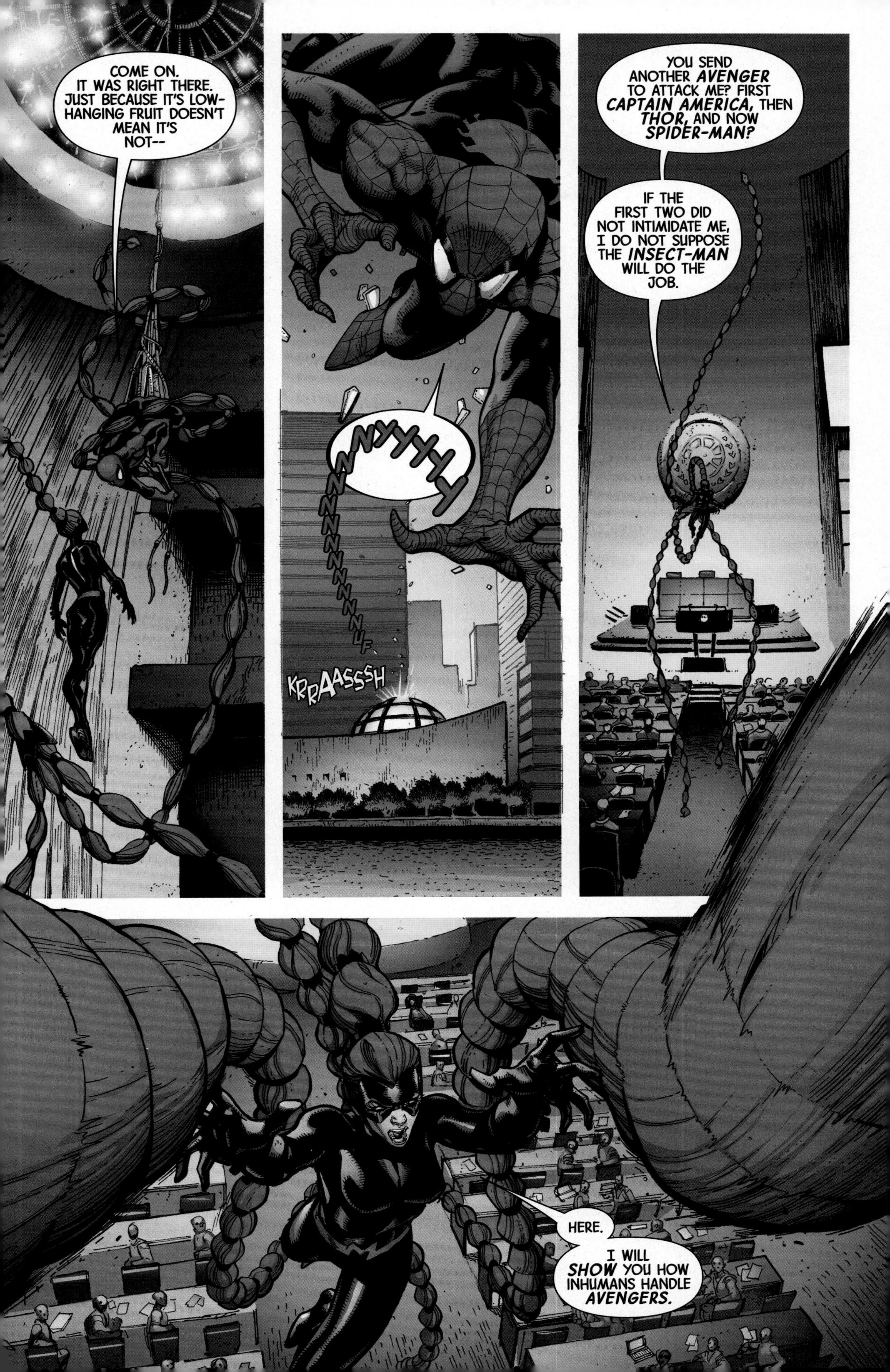
COME ON. IT WAS RIGHT THERE. JUST BECAUSE IT'S LOW-HANGING FRUIT DOESN'T MEAN IT'S NOT--
NNNNNNNNNNNNYYYYYYY
NNNNNNNNNNNNNUF
KRRAASSSH
YOU SEND ANOTHER AVENGER TO ATTACK ME? FIRST CAPTAIN AMERICA, THEN THOR, AND NOW SPIDER-MAN?
IF THE FIRST TWO DID NOT INTIMIDATE ME, I DO NOT SUPPOSE THE INSECT-MAN WILL DO THE JOB.
HERE.
I WILL SHOW YOU HOW INHUMANS HANDLE AVENGERS.

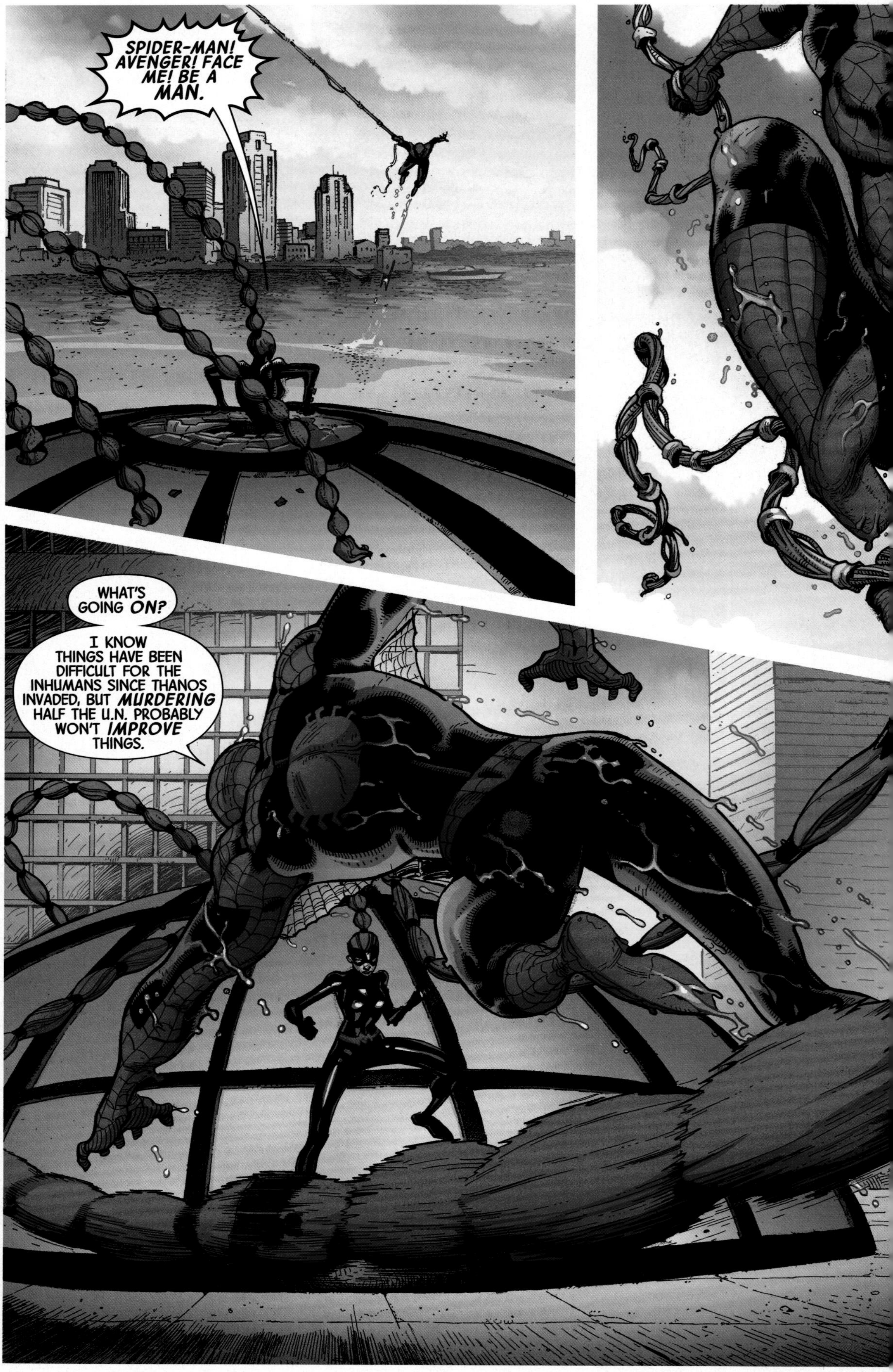
SPIDER-MAN! AVENGER! FACE ME! BE A MAN.
WHAT'S GOING ON?
I KNOW THINGS HAVE BEEN DIFFICULT FOR THE INHUMANS SINCE THANOS INVADED, BUT MURDERING HALF THE U.N. PROBABLY WON'T IMPROVE THINGS.

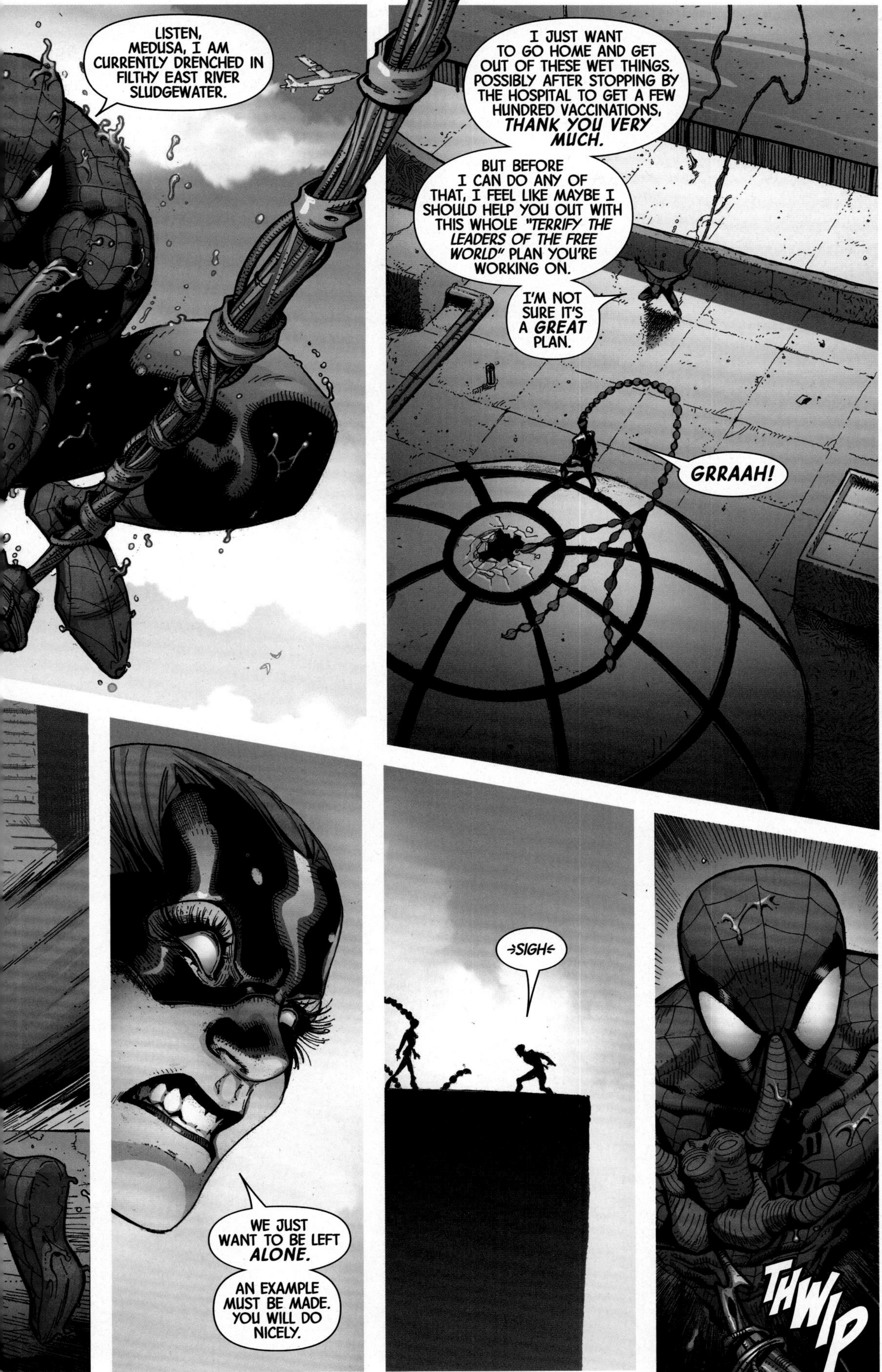

LISTEN, MEDUSA, I AM CURRENTLY DRENCHED IN FILTHY EAST RIVER SLUDGEWATER.
I JUST WANT TO GO HOME AND GET OUT OF THESE WET THINGS. POSSIBLY AFTER STOPPING BY THE HOSPITAL TO GET A FEW HUNDRED VACCINATIONS, THANK YOU VERY MUCH.
BUT BEFORE I CAN DO ANY OF THAT, I FEEL LIKE MAYBE I SHOULD HELP YOU OUT WITH THIS WHOLE "TERRIFY THE LEADERS OF THE FREE WORLD" PLAN YOU'RE WORKING ON.
I'M NOT SURE IT'S A GREAT PLAN.
GRRAAH!
WE JUST WANT TO BE LEFT ALONE.
AN EXAMPLE MUST BE MADE. YOU WILL DO NICELY.
SIGH
THWIP

VENICE.

SPLSH

YOU *LOST* HER!

WE DIDN'T... THEY JUST *VANISHED*, SIR. THIS IS NOT AN EXCUSE, BUT YOU KNOW WHAT *READER'S* CAPABLE OF.

THAT CERTAINLY *SOUNDS* LIKE AN EXCUSE, CAPTAIN.

YOU *SOLD* ME!

DID YOU GET *PAID?*

YES, BUT NOT FOR YOU.

NO, THAT'S NOT WHAT I--

ENNILUX HIRED ME TO BRING THEM NEWLY BORN INHUMANS-- THEY NEED PEOPLE, THAT'S ALL. I GET PAID TO BRING THEM NEW RECRUITS SAFELY.

IT WAS JUST A *JOB.*

I HAD *NO IDEA* THEY WOULD TRY TO...STEAL YOUR *MIND.*

ALL RIGHT. LET'S GO GET HER BACK.

CAPO, YOU AREN'T THINKING ABOUT GOING *YOURSELF?* IN YOUR STATE, THAT WOULD MEAN--

I *KNOW* WHAT IT WOULD MEAN. IF I DON'T GET HER BACK, I'LL DIE ANYWAY.

DESPERATE TIMES.

WAS I FREE TO LEAVE? WERE *ANY* OF THE PEOPLE YOU BROUGHT TO ENNILUX FREE TO LEAVE?

I DON'T *KNOW*--I NEVER *THOUGHT* ABOUT IT, XIAOYI.

ENNILUX SEEMED SAFER THAN THE REST OF THE WORLD. I MEAN, YOU KNOW WHAT WE SAW OUT THERE--IT'S *DANGEROUS* FOR INHUMANS, OLD *OR* NEW.

SO YOU *SOLD* US. SIMPLE AS THAT.

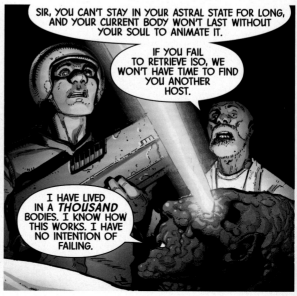

SIR, YOU CAN'T STAY IN YOUR ASTRAL STATE FOR LONG, AND YOUR CURRENT BODY WON'T LAST WITHOUT YOUR SOUL TO ANIMATE IT.

IF YOU FAIL TO RETRIEVE ISO, WE WON'T HAVE TIME TO FIND YOU ANOTHER HOST.

I HAVE LIVED IN A *THOUSAND* BODIES. I KNOW HOW THIS WORKS. I HAVE NO INTENTION OF FAILING.

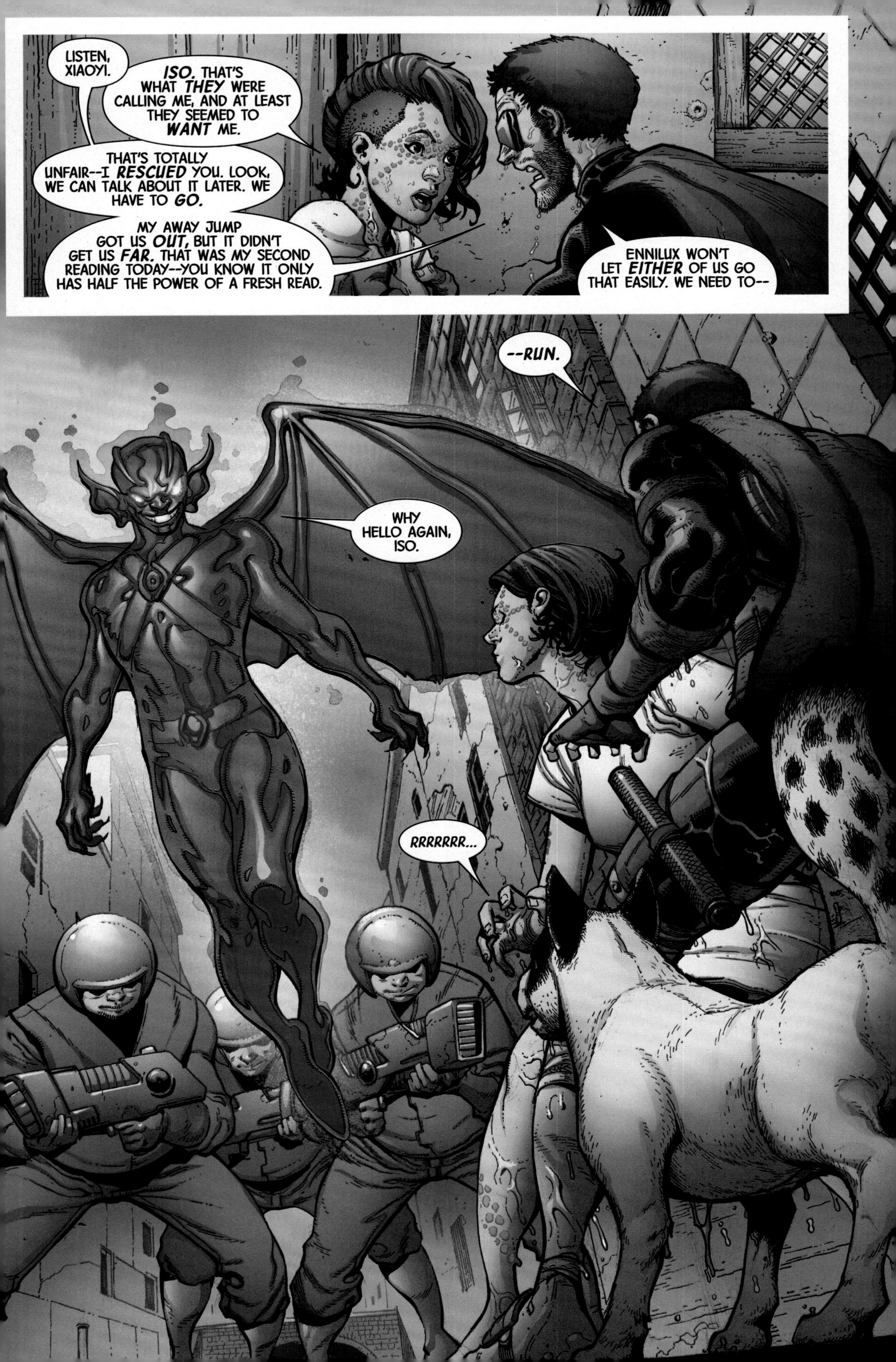
LISTEN, XIAOYI.
ISO. THAT'S WHAT THEY WERE CALLING ME, AND AT LEAST THEY SEEMED TO WANT ME.
THAT'S TOTALLY UNFAIR--I RESCUED YOU. LOOK, WE CAN TALK ABOUT IT LATER. WE HAVE TO GO.
MY AWAY JUMP GOT US OUT, BUT IT DIDN'T GET US FAR. THAT WAS MY SECOND READING TODAY--YOU KNOW IT ONLY HAS HALF THE POWER OF A FRESH READ.
ENNILUX WON'T LET EITHER OF US GO THAT EASILY. WE NEED TO--
--RUN.
WHY HELLO AGAIN, ISO.
RRRRRRR...

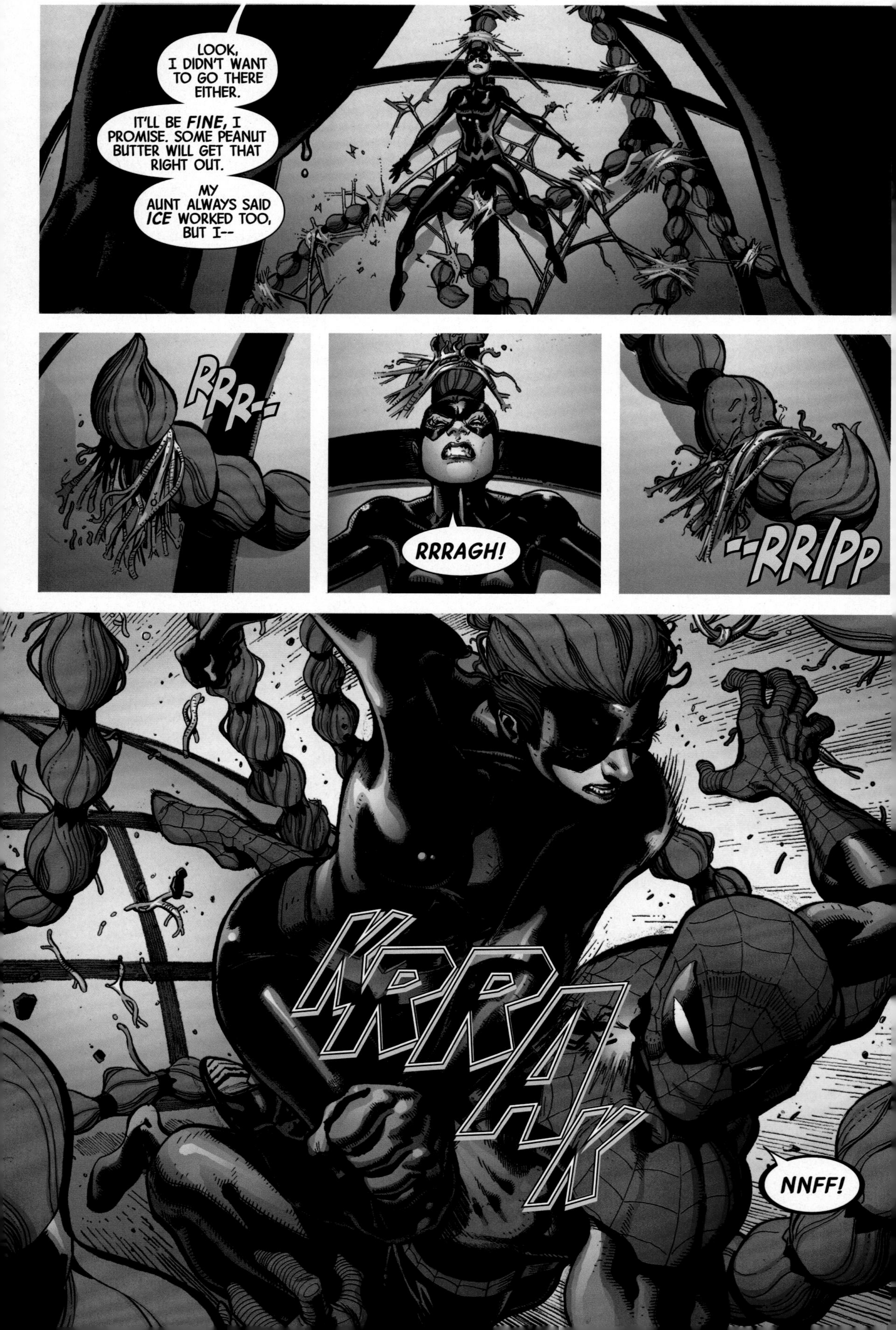
LOOK, I DIDN'T WANT TO GO THERE EITHER.
IT'LL BE *FINE*, I PROMISE. SOME PEANUT BUTTER WILL GET THAT RIGHT OUT.
MY AUNT ALWAYS SAID *ICE* WORKED TOO, BUT I--
RRR--
RRRAGH!
--RRIPP
KRRAK
NNFF!

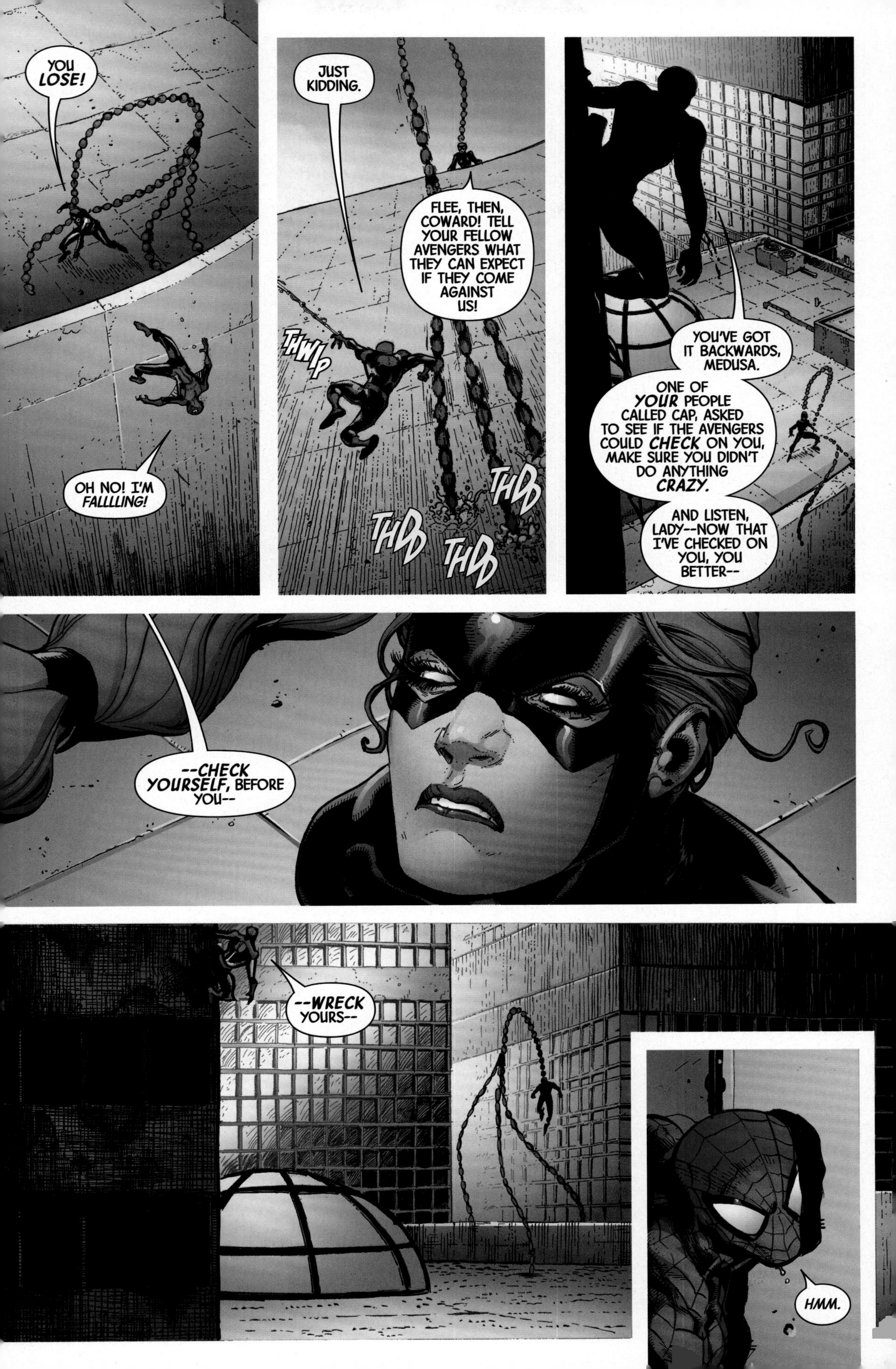
YOU LOSE!
OH NO! I'M FALLLLING!
JUST KIDDING.
FLEE, THEN, COWARD! TELL YOUR FELLOW AVENGERS WHAT THEY CAN EXPECT IF THEY COME AGAINST US!
THWIP
THDD
THDD
THDD
YOU'VE GOT IT BACKWARDS, MEDUSA.
ONE OF YOUR PEOPLE CALLED CAP, ASKED TO SEE IF THE AVENGERS COULD CHECK ON YOU, MAKE SURE YOU DIDN'T DO ANYTHING CRAZY.
AND LISTEN, LADY--NOW THAT I'VE CHECKED ON YOU, YOU BETTER--
--CHECK YOURSELF, BEFORE YOU--
--WRECK YOURS--
HMM.

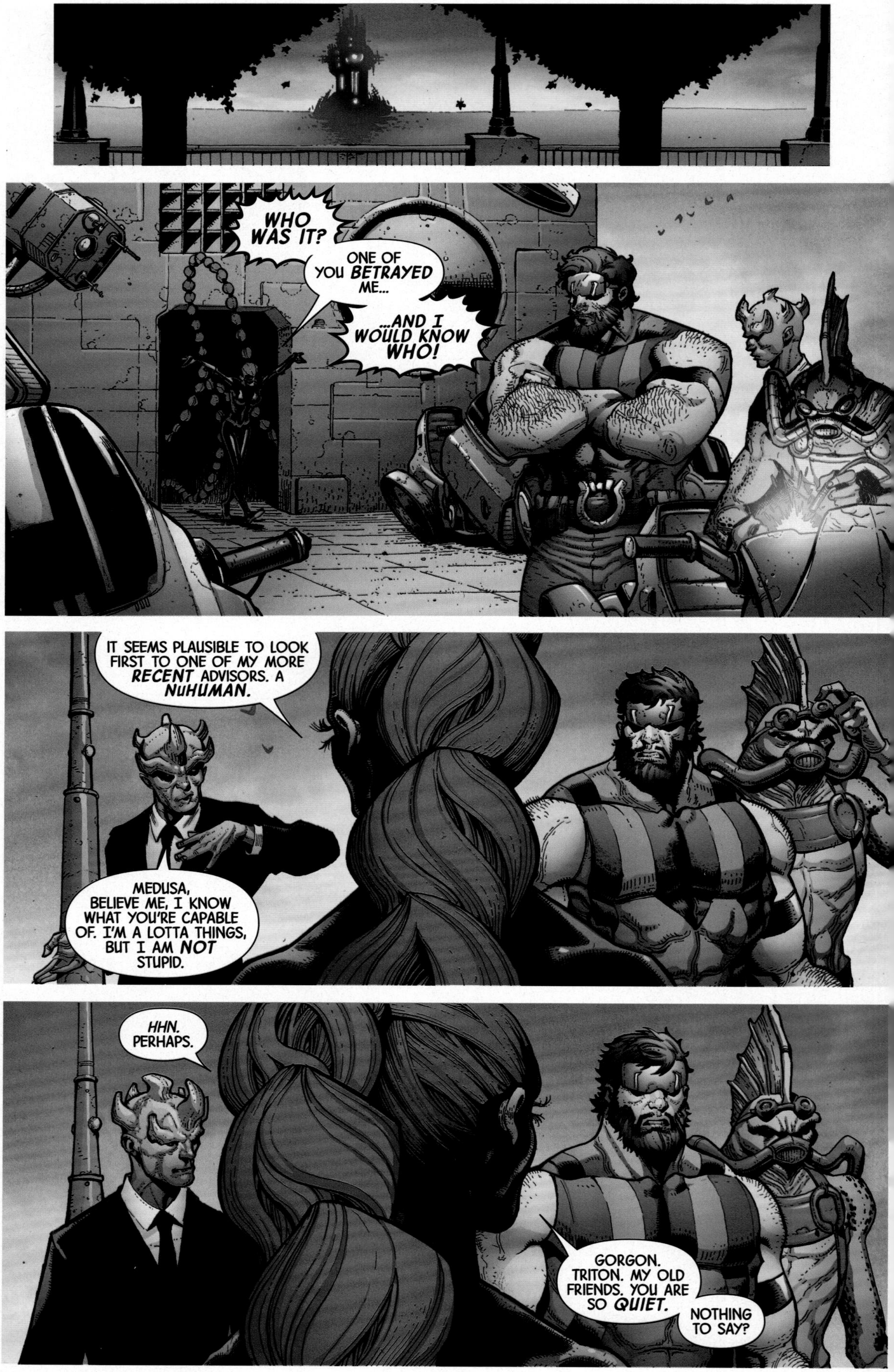
WHO WAS IT?
ONE OF YOU BETRAYED ME...
...AND I WOULD KNOW WHO!
IT SEEMS PLAUSIBLE TO LOOK FIRST TO ONE OF MY MORE RECENT ADVISORS. A NuHUMAN.
MEDUSA, BELIEVE ME, I KNOW WHAT YOU'RE CAPABLE OF. I'M A LOTTA THINGS, BUT I AM NOT STUPID.
HHN. PERHAPS.
GORGON. TRITON. MY OLD FRIENDS. YOU ARE SO QUIET.
NOTHING TO SAY?

MEDUSA, YOU ARE MY QUEEN, AND YOU ARE MY FAMILY.

I DID NOT, AND WOULD NEVER BETRAY YOU. EVERYTHING I DO, I DO TO PROTECT YOU--AND WHAT YOU ARE TRYING TO BUILD.

BUT SOMETHING HAS HAPPENED TO YOU. WE MUST BE VIGILANT--TRITON AND I WERE CONCERNED THAT PERHAPS MAXIMUS, OR SOME OTHER ENEMY, HAS TAKEN CONTROL OF YOUR MIND. WE--

YOU DID IT. YOU CALLED THE AVENGERS.

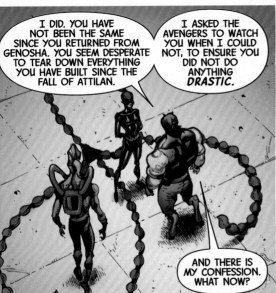

I DID. YOU HAVE NOT BEEN THE SAME SINCE YOU RETURNED FROM GENOSHA. YOU SEEM DESPERATE TO TEAR DOWN EVERYTHING YOU HAVE BUILT SINCE THE FALL OF ATTILAN.

I ASKED THE AVENGERS TO WATCH YOU WHEN I COULD NOT, TO ENSURE YOU DID NOT DO ANYTHING DRASTIC.

AND THERE IS MY CONFESSION. WHAT NOW?

HAVE YOU TURNED ON ME AS WELL, TRITON?

NEVER. I AM TRYING TO SAVE YOU, AND OUR PEOPLE. GORGON AND I WILL DO WHAT WE HAVE TO DO.

NO. YOU WON'T.

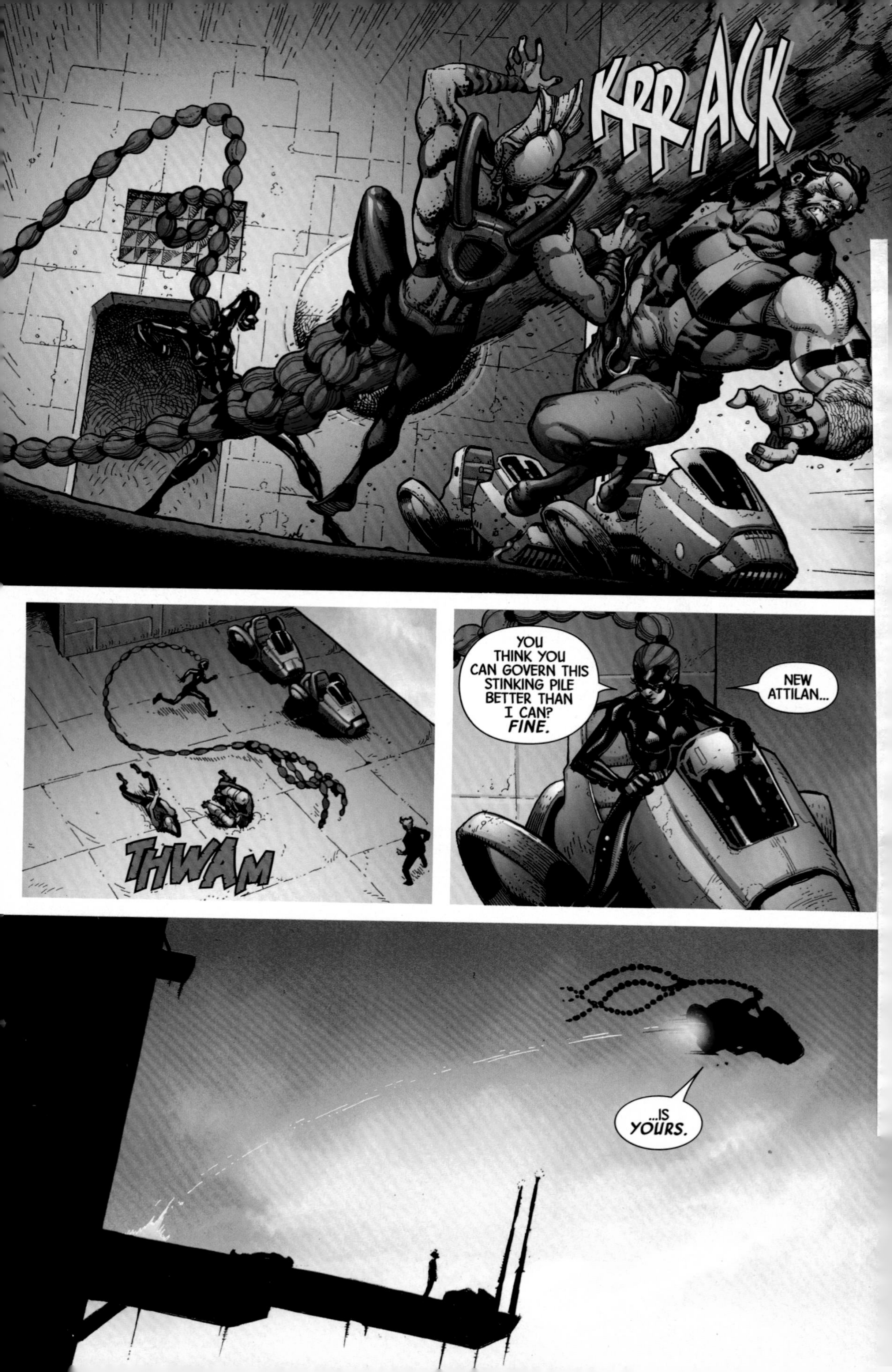
KRRACK
THWAM
YOU THINK YOU CAN GOVERN THIS STINKING PILE BETTER THAN I CAN? FINE.
NEW ATTILAN...
...IS YOURS.

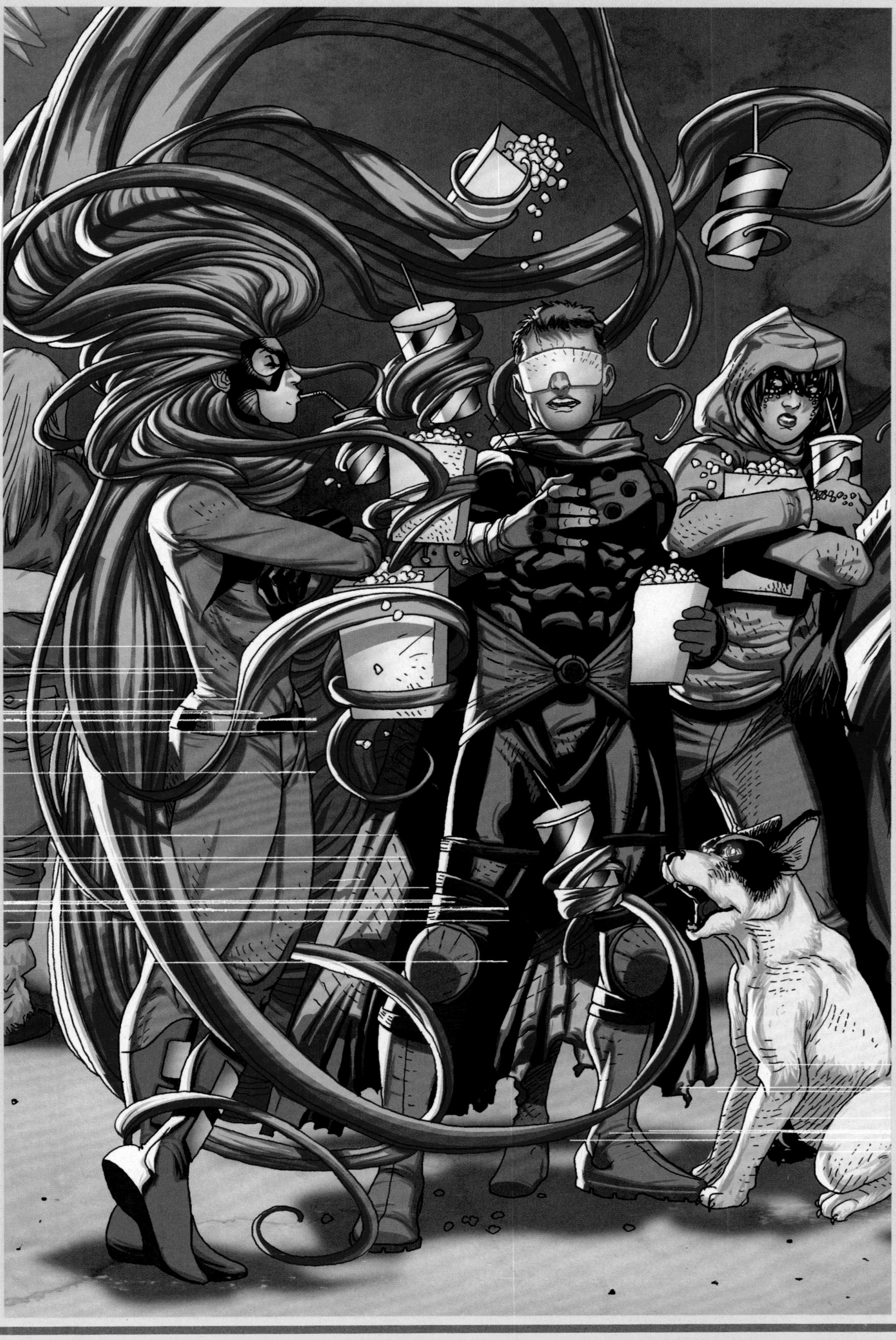

WELCOME HOME VARIANT
BY SALVADOR LARROCA & ISRAEL SILVA

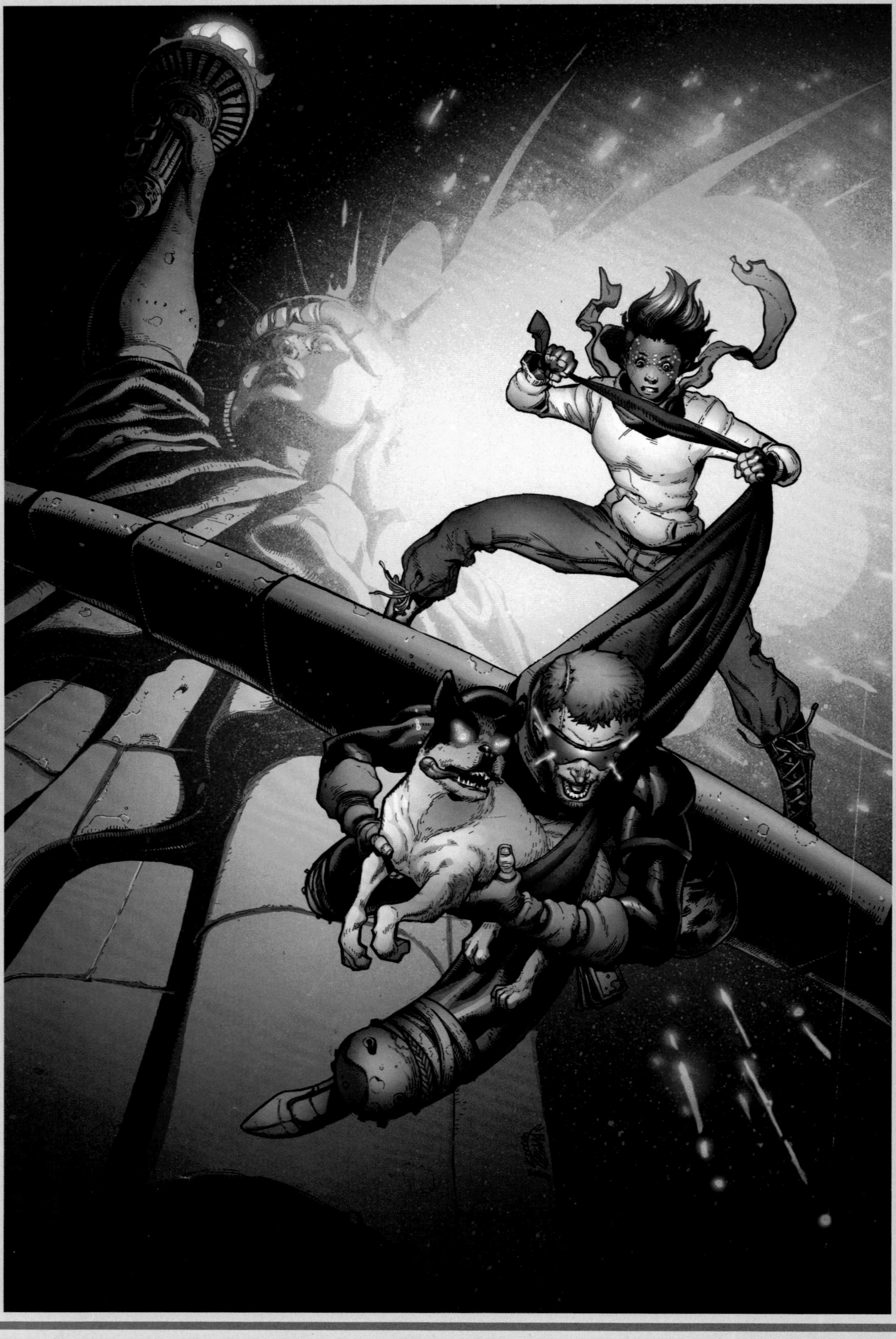

11 PART ELEVEN: ESCAPES

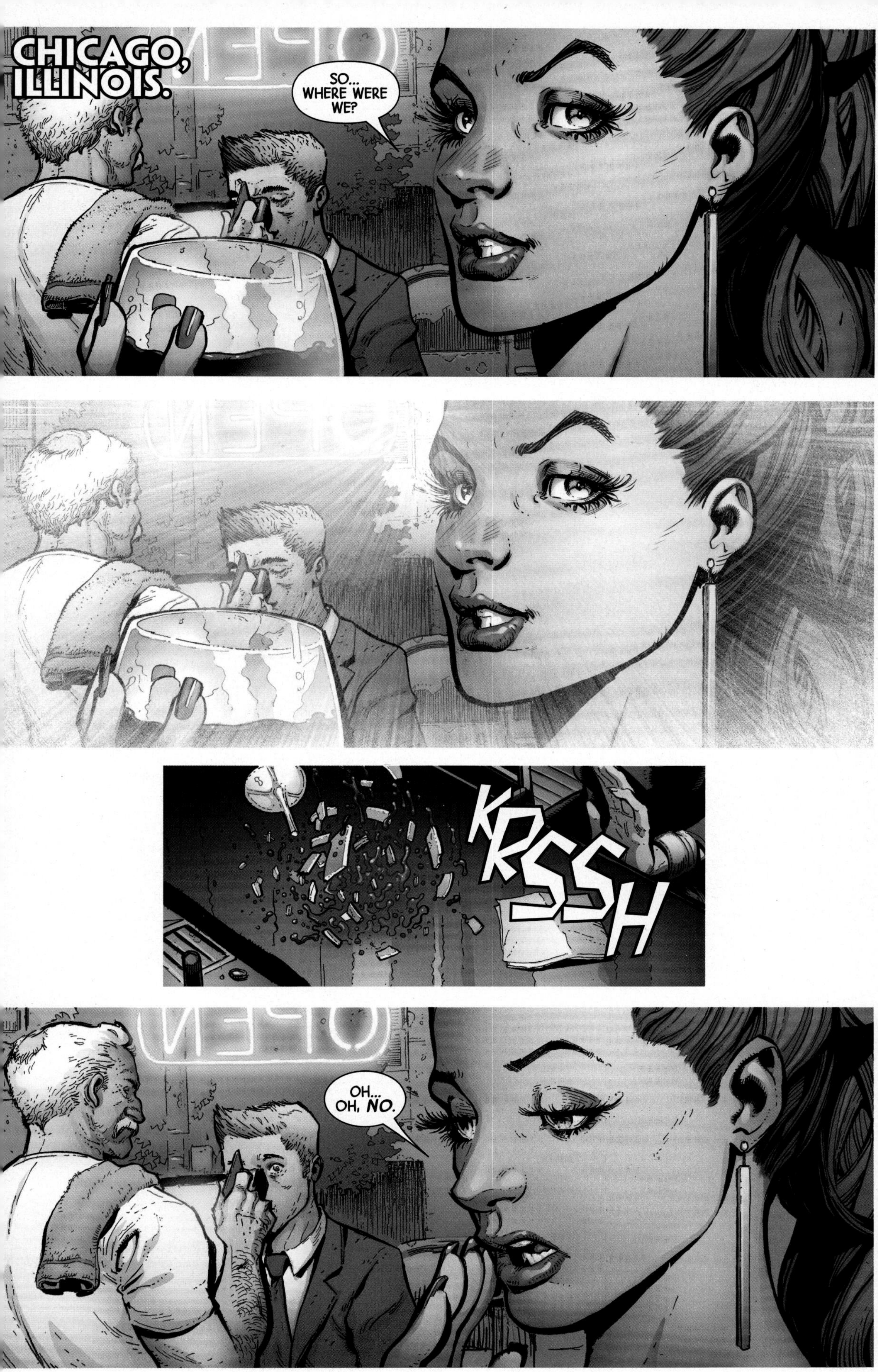
CHICAGO, ILLINOIS.
SO... WHERE WERE WE?
KRSSH
OH... OH, NO.

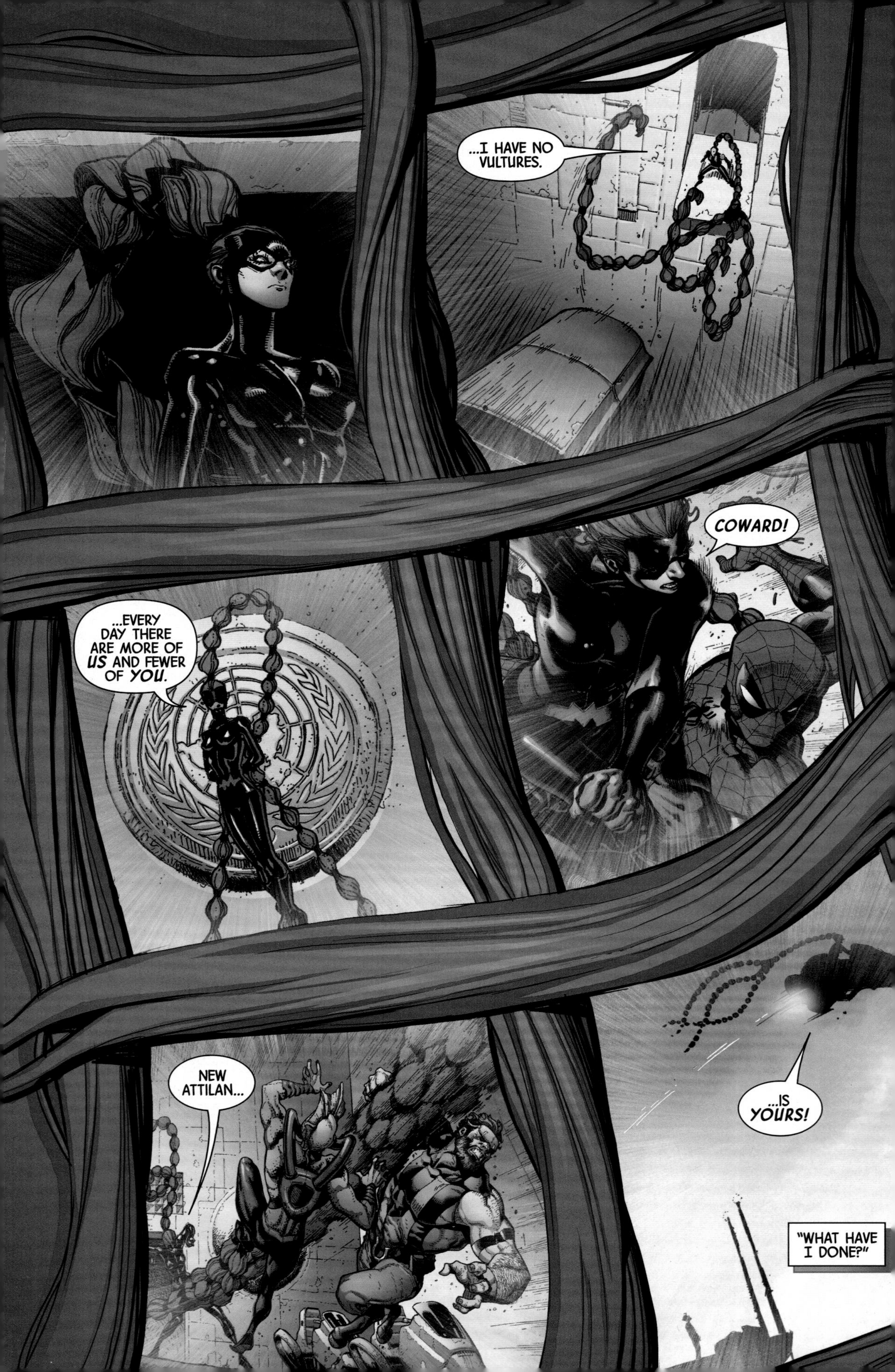
...I HAVE NO VULTURES.
...EVERY DAY THERE ARE MORE OF US AND FEWER OF YOU.
COWARD!
NEW ATTILAN...
...IS YOURS!
"WHAT HAVE I DONE?"

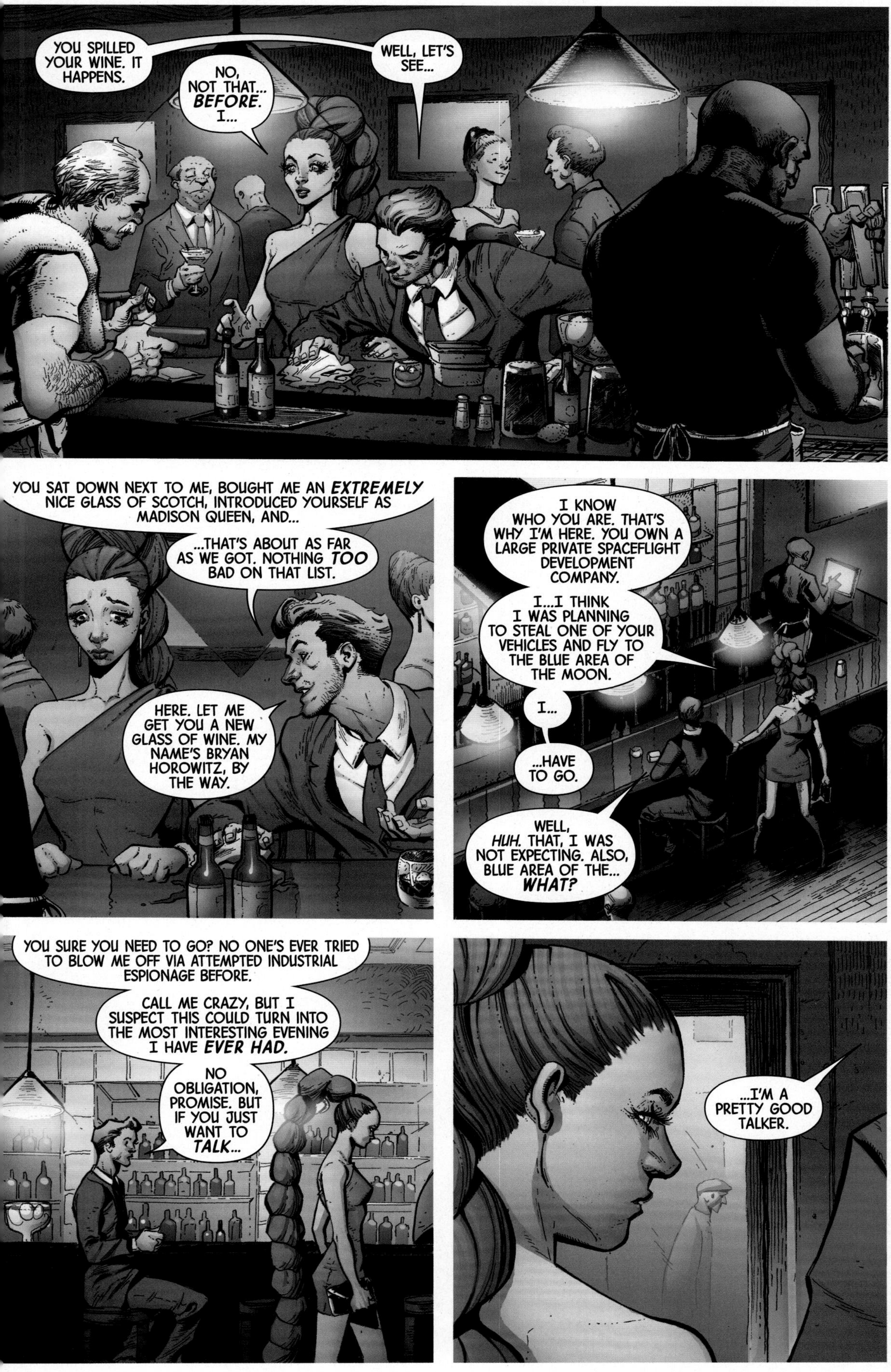
YOU SPILLED YOUR WINE. IT HAPPENS.
NO, NOT THAT... BEFORE. I...
WELL, LET'S SEE...
YOU SAT DOWN NEXT TO ME, BOUGHT ME AN EXTREMELY NICE GLASS OF SCOTCH, INTRODUCED YOURSELF AS MADISON QUEEN, AND...
...THAT'S ABOUT AS FAR AS WE GOT. NOTHING TOO BAD ON THAT LIST.
HERE. LET ME GET YOU A NEW GLASS OF WINE. MY NAME'S BRYAN HOROWITZ, BY THE WAY.
I KNOW WHO YOU ARE. THAT'S WHY I'M HERE. YOU OWN A LARGE PRIVATE SPACEFLIGHT DEVELOPMENT COMPANY.
I...I THINK I WAS PLANNING TO STEAL ONE OF YOUR VEHICLES AND FLY TO THE BLUE AREA OF THE MOON.
I...
...HAVE TO GO.
WELL, HUH. THAT, I WAS NOT EXPECTING. ALSO, BLUE AREA OF THE... WHAT?
YOU SURE YOU NEED TO GO? NO ONE'S EVER TRIED TO BLOW ME OFF VIA ATTEMPTED INDUSTRIAL ESPIONAGE BEFORE.
CALL ME CRAZY, BUT I SUSPECT THIS COULD TURN INTO THE MOST INTERESTING EVENING I HAVE EVER HAD.
NO OBLIGATION, PROMISE. BUT IF YOU JUST WANT TO TALK...
...I'M A PRETTY GOOD TALKER.

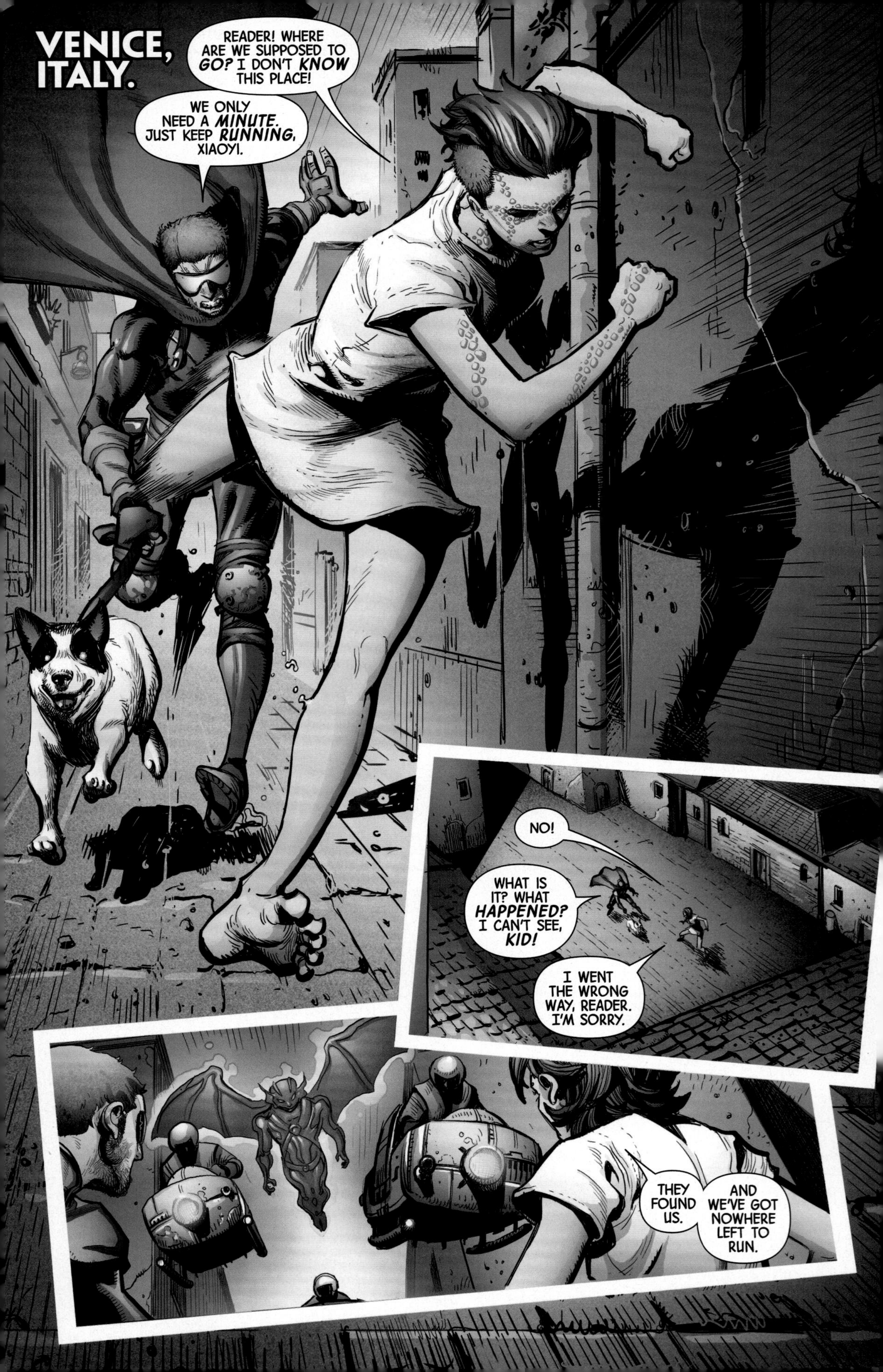
VENICE, ITALY.
READER! WHERE ARE WE SUPPOSED TO GO? I DON'T KNOW THIS PLACE!
WE ONLY NEED A MINUTE. JUST KEEP RUNNING, XIAOYI.
NO!
WHAT IS IT? WHAT HAPPENED? I CAN'T SEE, KID!
I WENT THE WRONG WAY, READER. I'M SORRY.
THEY FOUND US.
AND WE'VE GOT NOWHERE LEFT TO RUN.

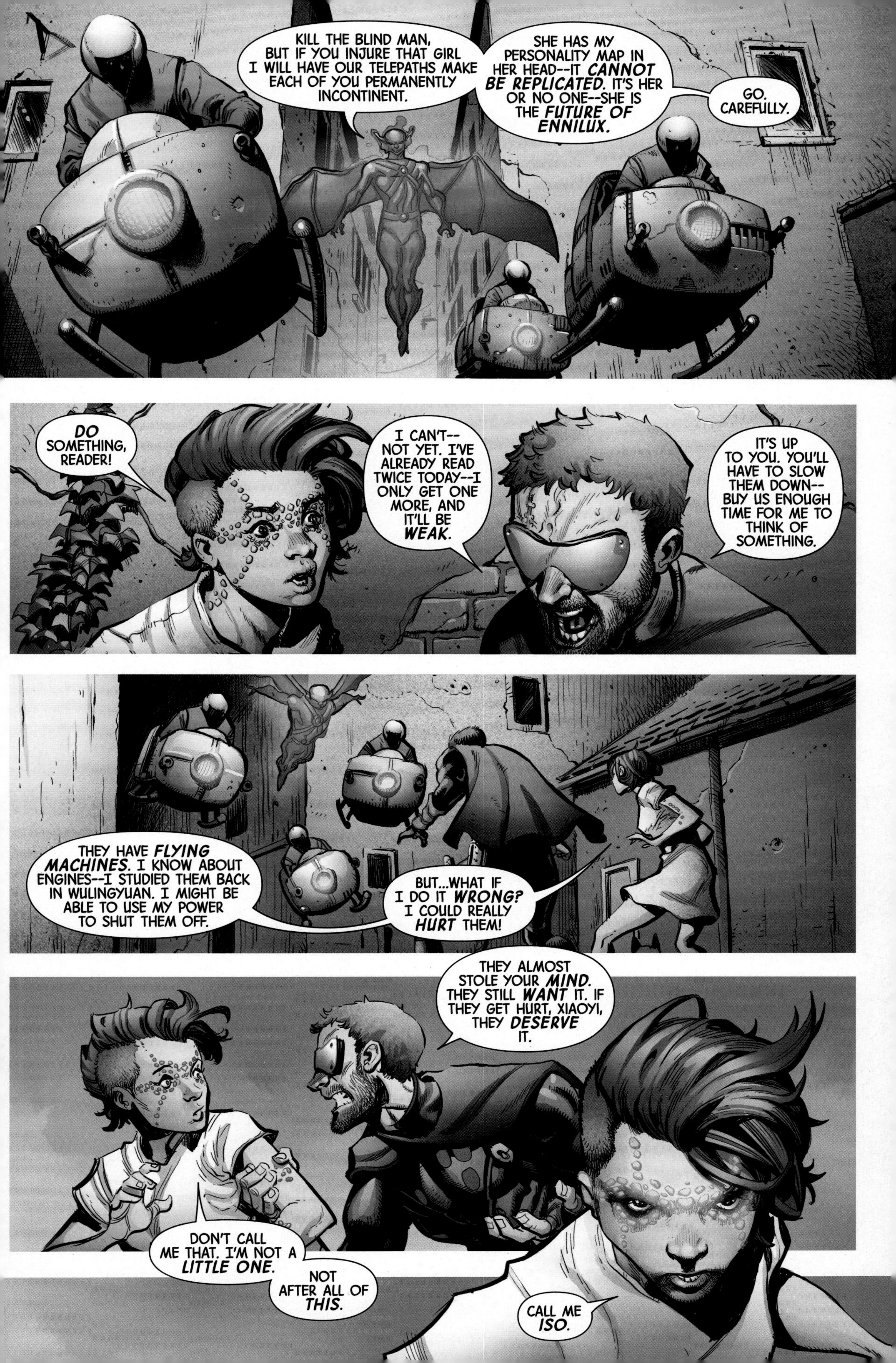
KILL THE BLIND MAN, BUT IF YOU INJURE THAT GIRL I WILL HAVE OUR TELEPATHS MAKE EACH OF YOU PERMANENTLY INCONTINENT.
SHE HAS MY PERSONALITY MAP IN HER HEAD--IT *CANNOT BE REPLICATED*. IT'S HER OR NO ONE--SHE IS THE *FUTURE OF ENNILUX.*
GO. CAREFULLY.
DO SOMETHING, READER!
I CAN'T--NOT YET. I'VE ALREADY READ TWICE TODAY--I ONLY GET ONE MORE, AND IT'LL BE *WEAK*.
IT'S UP TO YOU. YOU'LL HAVE TO SLOW THEM DOWN--BUY US ENOUGH TIME FOR ME TO THINK OF SOMETHING.
THEY HAVE *FLYING MACHINES*. I KNOW ABOUT ENGINES--I STUDIED THEM BACK IN WULINGYUAN. I MIGHT BE ABLE TO USE MY POWER TO SHUT THEM OFF.
BUT...WHAT IF I DO IT *WRONG?* I COULD REALLY *HURT* THEM!
THEY ALMOST STOLE YOUR *MIND*. THEY STILL *WANT* IT. IF THEY GET HURT, XIAOYI, THEY *DESERVE* IT.
DON'T CALL ME THAT. I'M NOT A *LITTLE ONE*.
NOT AFTER ALL OF *THIS*.
CALL ME *ISO*.

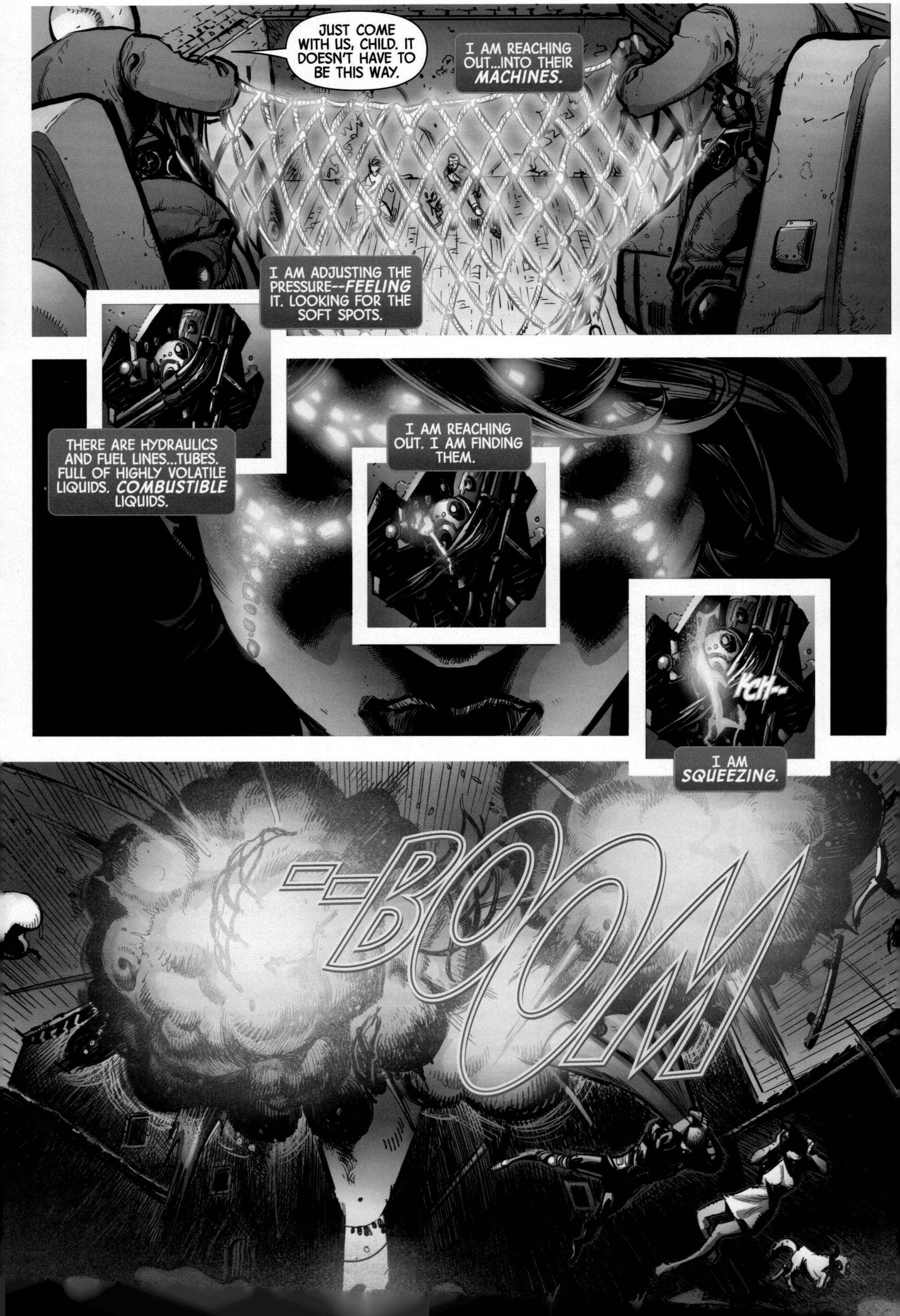
JUST COME WITH US, CHILD. IT DOESN'T HAVE TO BE THIS WAY.
I AM REACHING OUT...INTO THEIR MACHINES.
I AM ADJUSTING THE PRESSURE--FEELING IT. LOOKING FOR THE SOFT SPOTS.
THERE ARE HYDRAULICS AND FUEL LINES...TUBES. FULL OF HIGHLY VOLATILE LIQUIDS. COMBUSTIBLE LIQUIDS.
I AM REACHING OUT. I AM FINDING THEM.
KCH--
I AM SQUEEZING.
--BOOOM

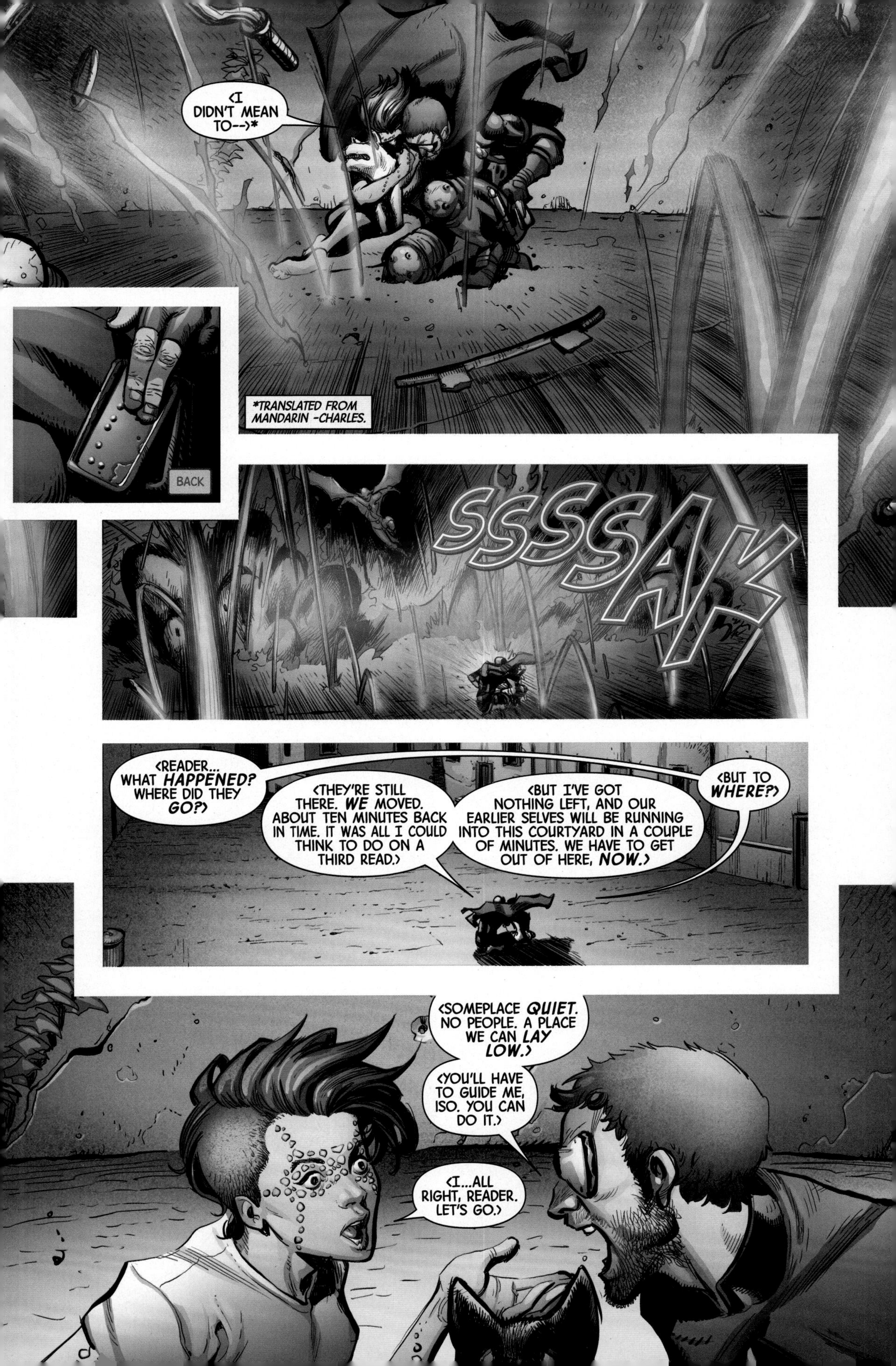

<I DIDN'T MEAN TO-->*
*TRANSLATED FROM MANDARIN -CHARLES.
BACK
SSSSAK
<READER... WHAT HAPPENED? WHERE DID THEY GO?>
<THEY'RE STILL THERE. WE MOVED. ABOUT TEN MINUTES BACK IN TIME. IT WAS ALL I COULD THINK TO DO ON A THIRD READ.>
<BUT I'VE GOT NOTHING LEFT, AND OUR EARLIER SELVES WILL BE RUNNING INTO THIS COURTYARD IN A COUPLE OF MINUTES. WE HAVE TO GET OUT OF HERE, NOW.>
<BUT TO WHERE?>
<SOMEPLACE QUIET. NO PEOPLE. A PLACE WE CAN LAY LOW.>
<YOU'LL HAVE TO GUIDE ME, ISO. YOU CAN DO IT.>
<I...ALL RIGHT, READER. LET'S GO.>

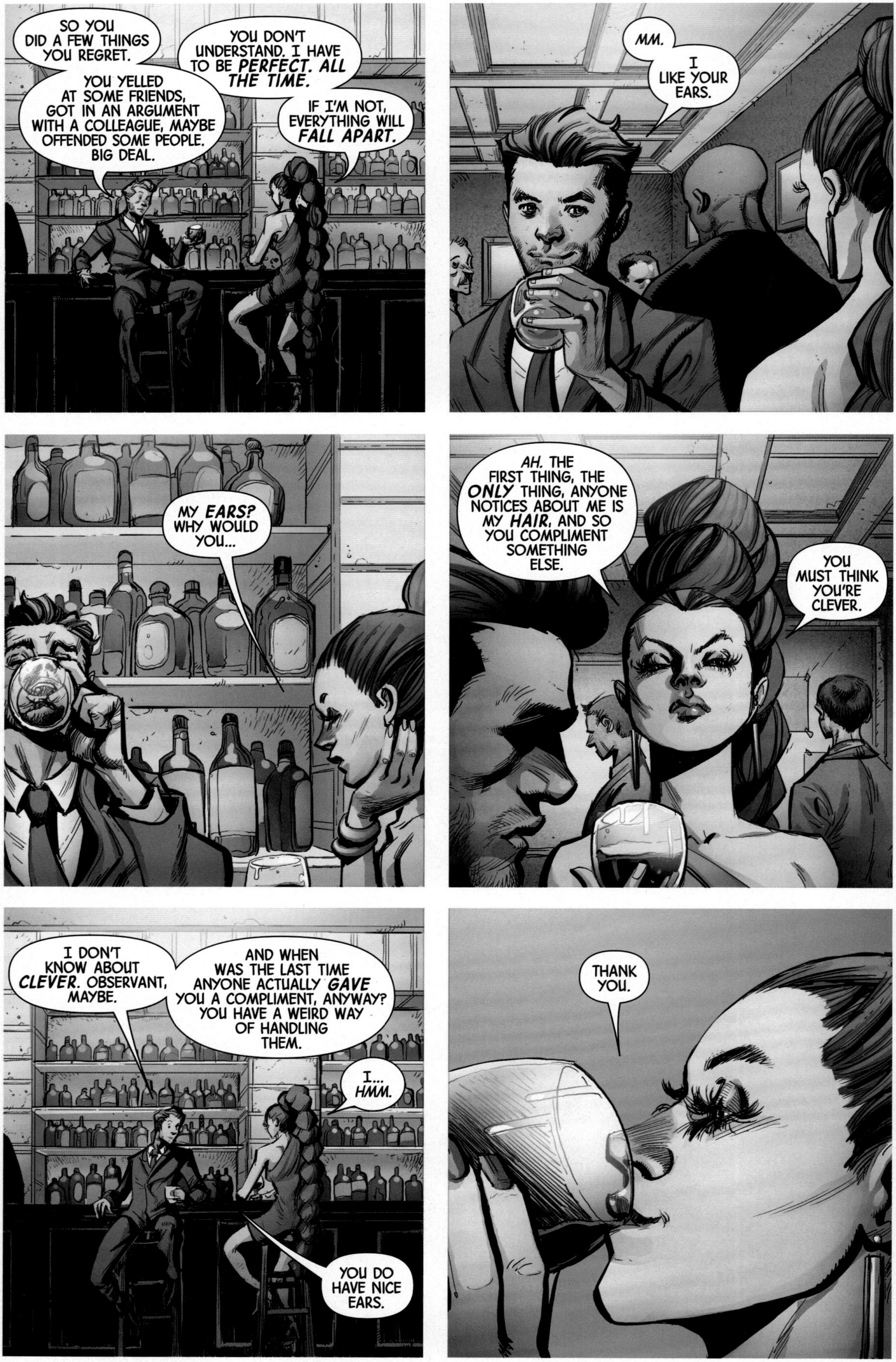
SO YOU DID A FEW THINGS YOU REGRET.
YOU YELLED AT SOME FRIENDS, GOT IN AN ARGUMENT WITH A COLLEAGUE, MAYBE OFFENDED SOME PEOPLE. BIG DEAL.
YOU DON'T UNDERSTAND. I HAVE TO BE *PERFECT. ALL THE TIME.*
IF I'M NOT, EVERYTHING WILL *FALL APART.*
MM.
I LIKE YOUR EARS.
MY *EARS?* WHY WOULD YOU...
AH. THE FIRST THING, THE *ONLY* THING, ANYONE NOTICES ABOUT ME IS MY *HAIR*, AND SO YOU COMPLIMENT SOMETHING ELSE.
YOU MUST THINK YOU'RE CLEVER.
I DON'T KNOW ABOUT *CLEVER*. OBSERVANT, MAYBE.
AND WHEN WAS THE LAST TIME ANYONE ACTUALLY *GAVE* YOU A COMPLIMENT, ANYWAY? YOU HAVE A WEIRD WAY OF HANDLING THEM.
I... *HMM.*
YOU DO HAVE NICE EARS.
THANK YOU.

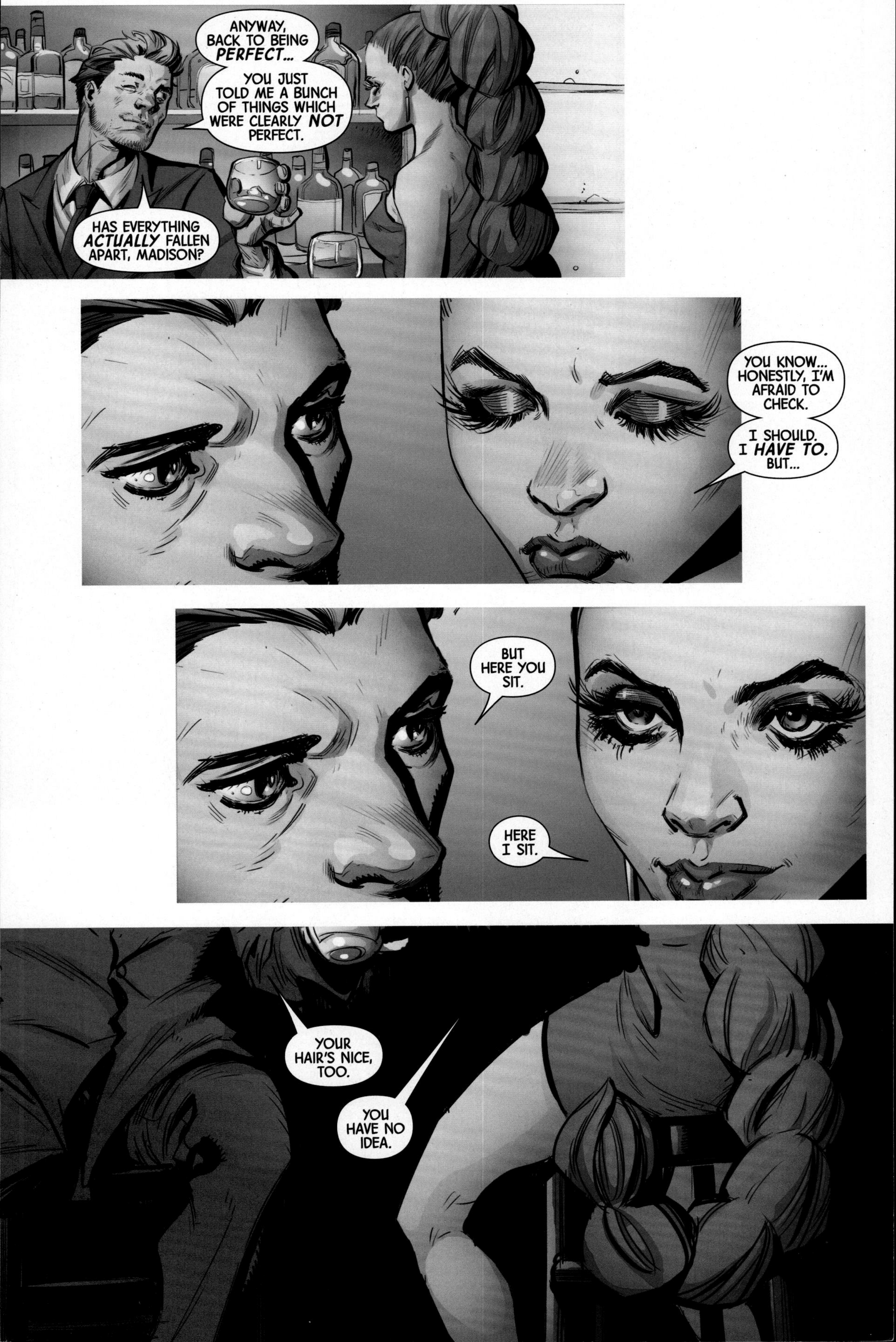
ANYWAY, BACK TO BEING PERFECT...
YOU JUST TOLD ME A BUNCH OF THINGS WHICH WERE CLEARLY NOT PERFECT.
HAS EVERYTHING ACTUALLY FALLEN APART, MADISON?
YOU KNOW... HONESTLY, I'M AFRAID TO CHECK.
I SHOULD. I HAVE TO. BUT...
BUT HERE YOU SIT.
HERE I SIT.
YOUR HAIR'S NICE, TOO.
YOU HAVE NO IDEA.

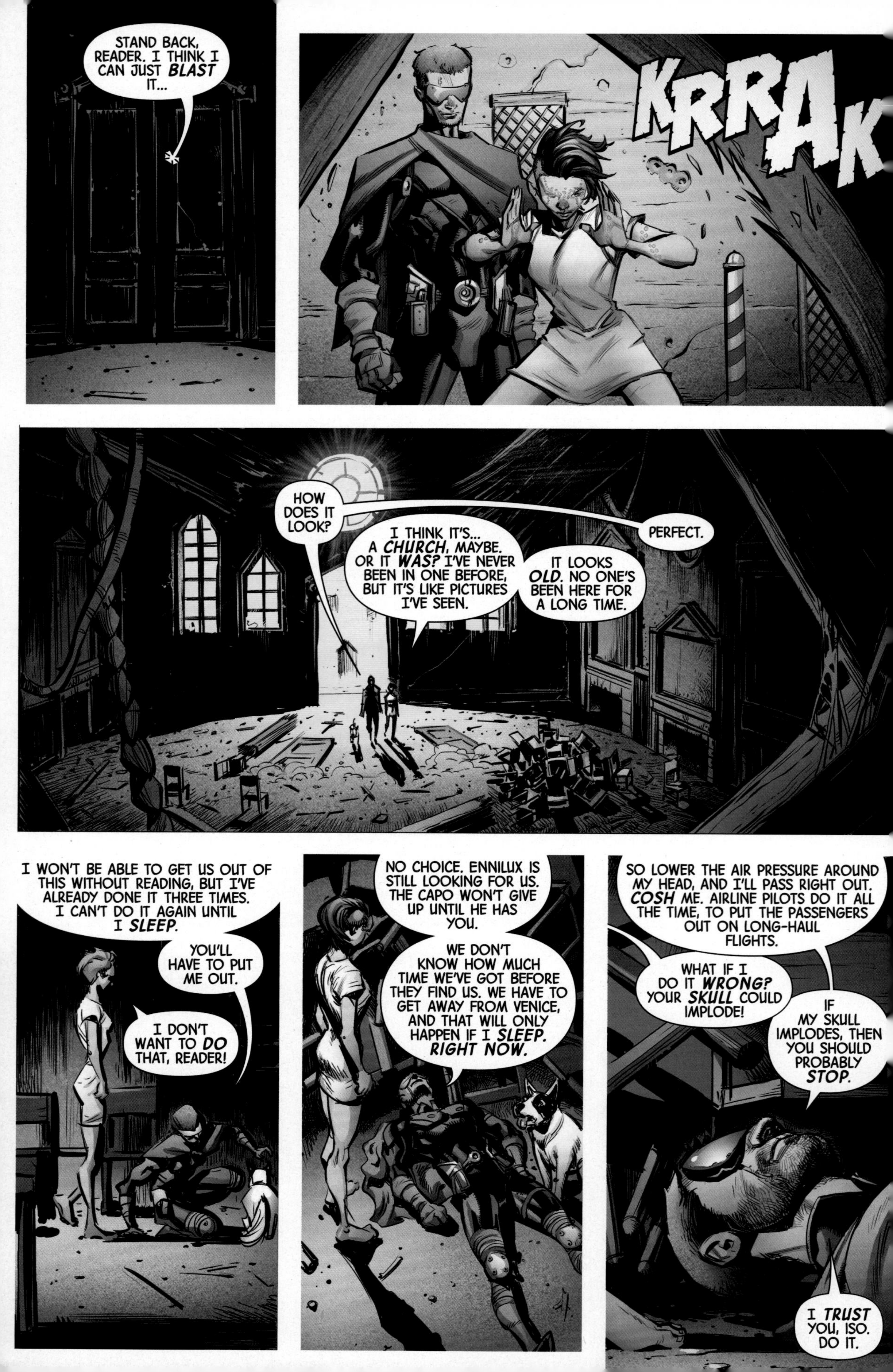
STAND BACK, READER. I THINK I CAN JUST BLAST IT...
KRRAK
HOW DOES IT LOOK?
I THINK IT'S... A CHURCH, MAYBE. OR IT WAS? I'VE NEVER BEEN IN ONE BEFORE, BUT IT'S LIKE PICTURES I'VE SEEN.
IT LOOKS OLD. NO ONE'S BEEN HERE FOR A LONG TIME.
PERFECT.
I WON'T BE ABLE TO GET US OUT OF THIS WITHOUT READING, BUT I'VE ALREADY DONE IT THREE TIMES. I CAN'T DO IT AGAIN UNTIL I SLEEP.
YOU'LL HAVE TO PUT ME OUT.
I DON'T WANT TO DO THAT, READER!
NO CHOICE. ENNILUX IS STILL LOOKING FOR US. THE CAPO WON'T GIVE UP UNTIL HE HAS YOU.
WE DON'T KNOW HOW MUCH TIME WE'VE GOT BEFORE THEY FIND US. WE HAVE TO GET AWAY FROM VENICE, AND THAT WILL ONLY HAPPEN IF I SLEEP. RIGHT NOW.
SO LOWER THE AIR PRESSURE AROUND MY HEAD, AND I'LL PASS RIGHT OUT. COSH ME. AIRLINE PILOTS DO IT ALL THE TIME, TO PUT THE PASSENGERS OUT ON LONG-HAUL FLIGHTS.
WHAT IF I DO IT WRONG? YOUR SKULL COULD IMPLODE!
IF MY SKULL IMPLODES, THEN YOU SHOULD PROBABLY STOP.
I TRUST YOU, ISO. DO IT.

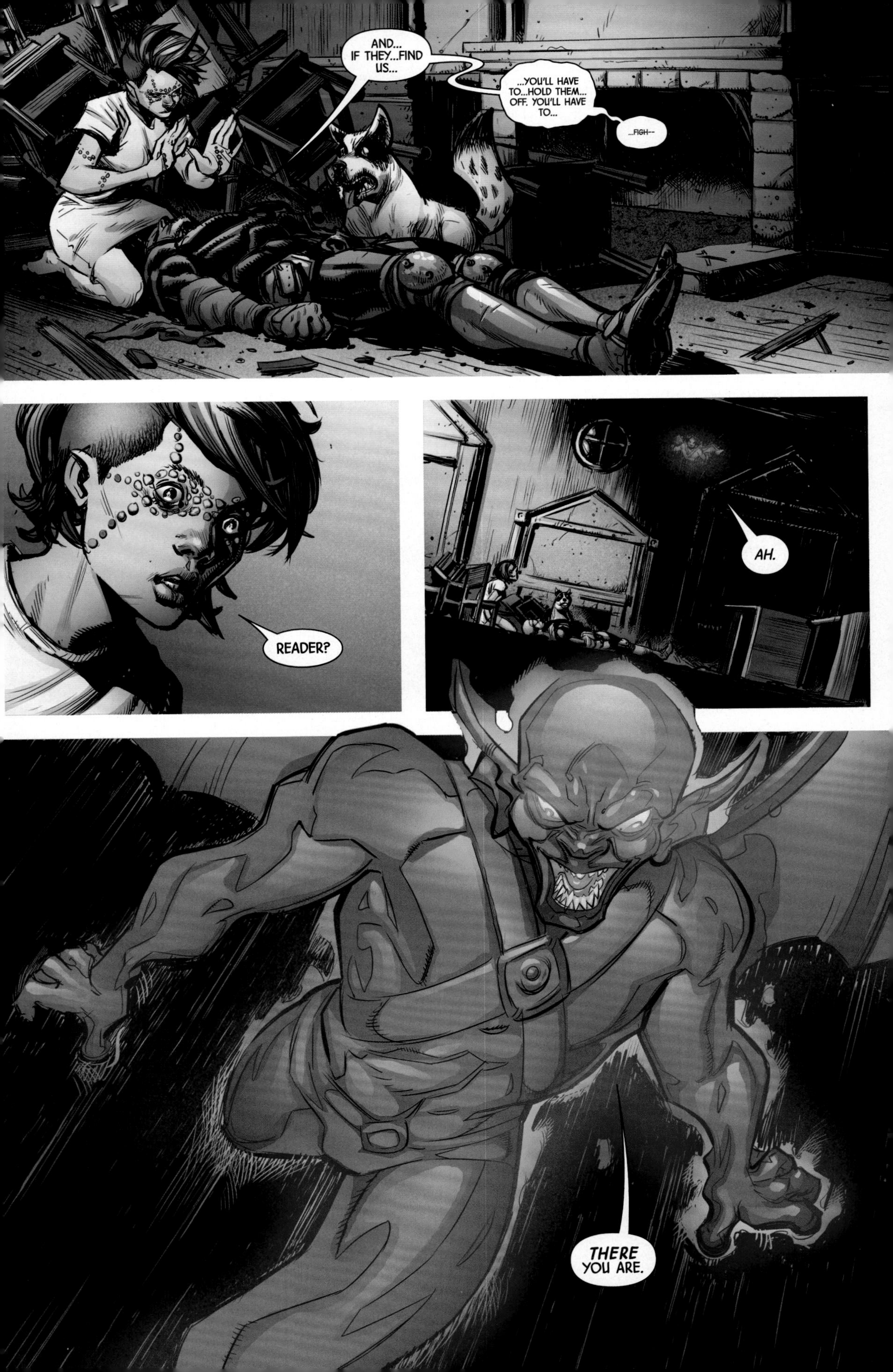
AND... IF THEY...FIND US...
...YOU'LL HAVE TO...HOLD THEM... OFF. YOU'LL HAVE TO...
...FIGH--
READER?
AH.
THERE YOU ARE.

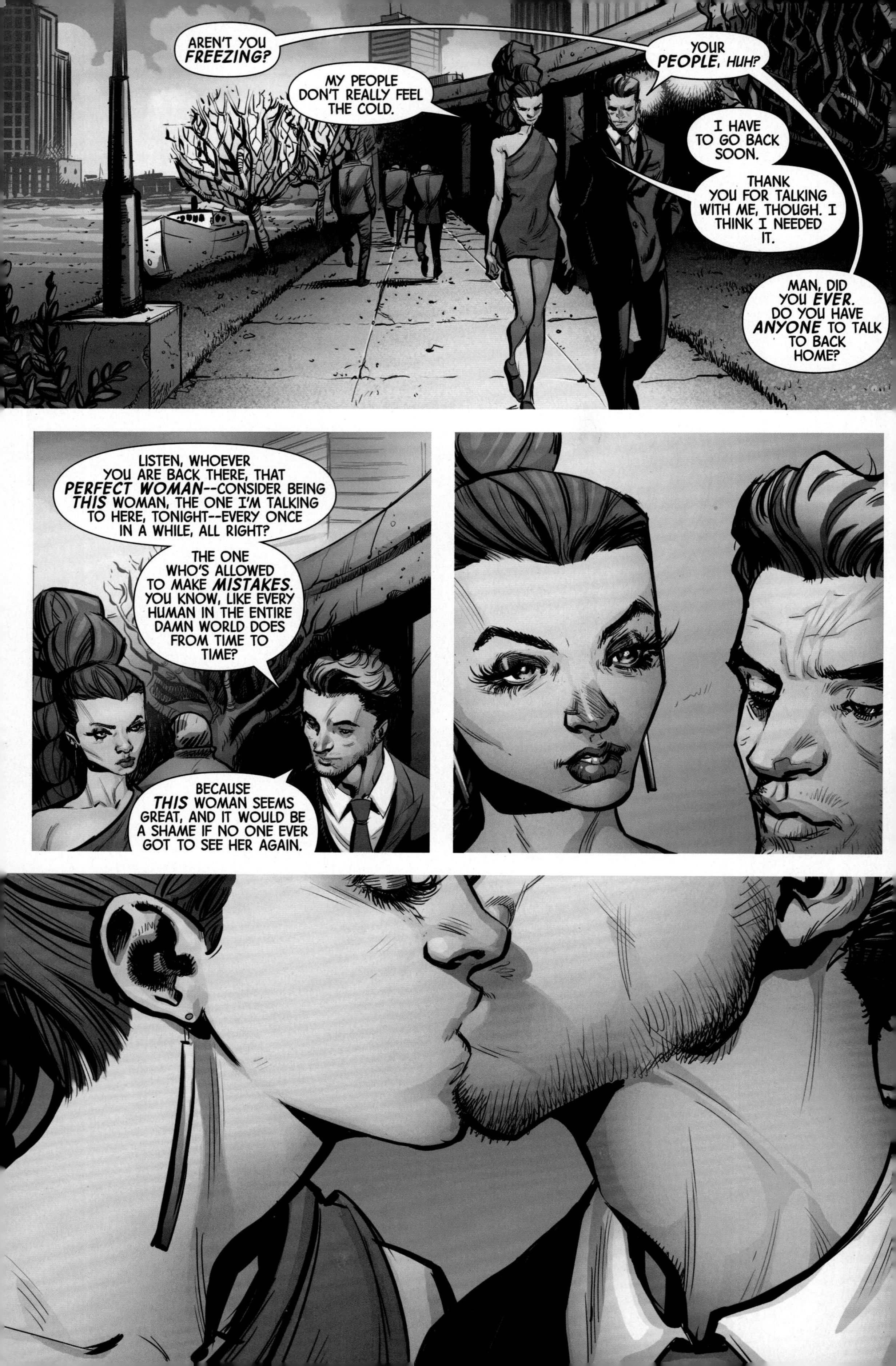
AREN'T YOU FREEZING?
MY PEOPLE DON'T REALLY FEEL THE COLD.
YOUR PEOPLE, HUH?
I HAVE TO GO BACK SOON.
THANK YOU FOR TALKING WITH ME, THOUGH. I THINK I NEEDED IT.
MAN, DID YOU EVER. DO YOU HAVE ANYONE TO TALK TO BACK HOME?
LISTEN, WHOEVER YOU ARE BACK THERE, THAT PERFECT WOMAN--CONSIDER BEING THIS WOMAN, THE ONE I'M TALKING TO HERE, TONIGHT--EVERY ONCE IN A WHILE, ALL RIGHT?
THE ONE WHO'S ALLOWED TO MAKE MISTAKES. YOU KNOW, LIKE EVERY HUMAN IN THE ENTIRE DAMN WORLD DOES FROM TIME TO TIME?
BECAUSE THIS WOMAN SEEMS GREAT, AND IT WOULD BE A SHAME IF NO ONE EVER GOT TO SEE HER AGAIN.

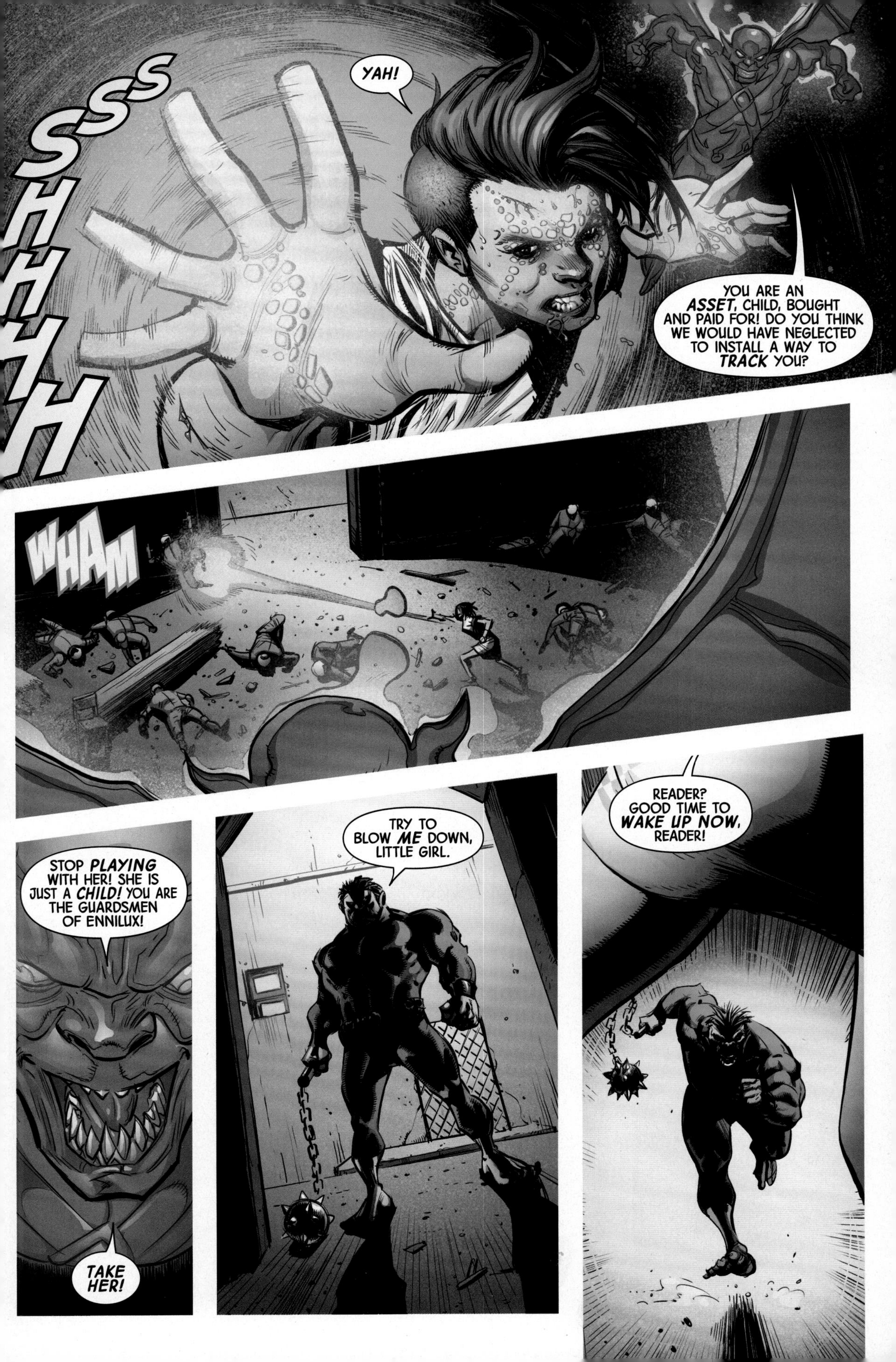
SSSSHHHHHH
YAH!
YOU ARE AN ASSET, CHILD, BOUGHT AND PAID FOR! DO YOU THINK WE WOULD HAVE NEGLECTED TO INSTALL A WAY TO TRACK YOU?
WHAM
STOP PLAYING WITH HER! SHE IS JUST A CHILD! YOU ARE THE GUARDSMEN OF ENNILUX!
TAKE HER!
TRY TO BLOW ME DOWN, LITTLE GIRL.
READER? GOOD TIME TO WAKE UP NOW, READER!

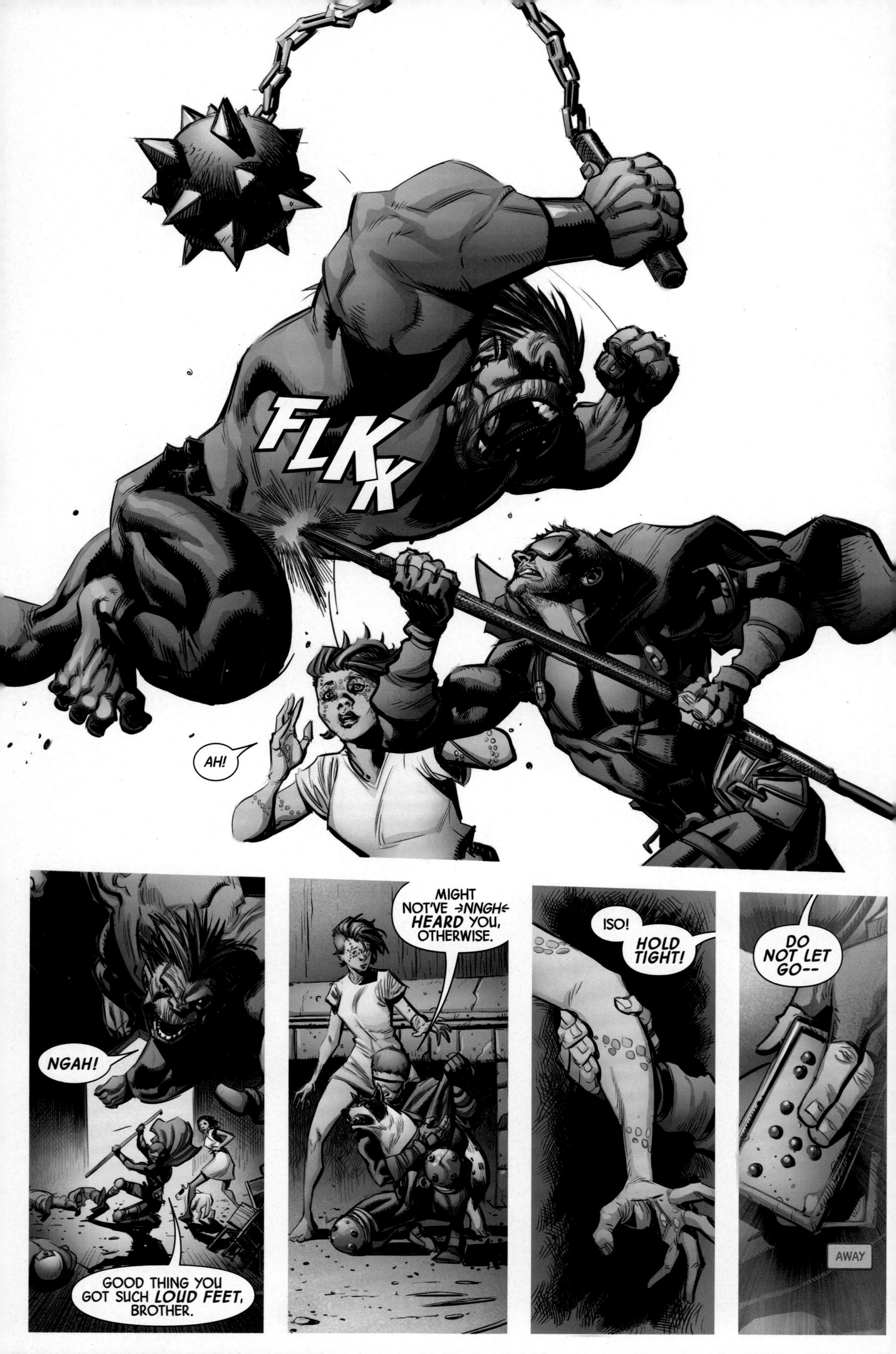
FLKK
AH!
NGAH!
GOOD THING YOU GOT SUCH LOUD FEET, BROTHER.
MIGHT NOT'VE →NNGH← HEARD YOU, OTHERWISE.
ISO! HOLD TIGHT!
DO NOT LET GO--
AWAY

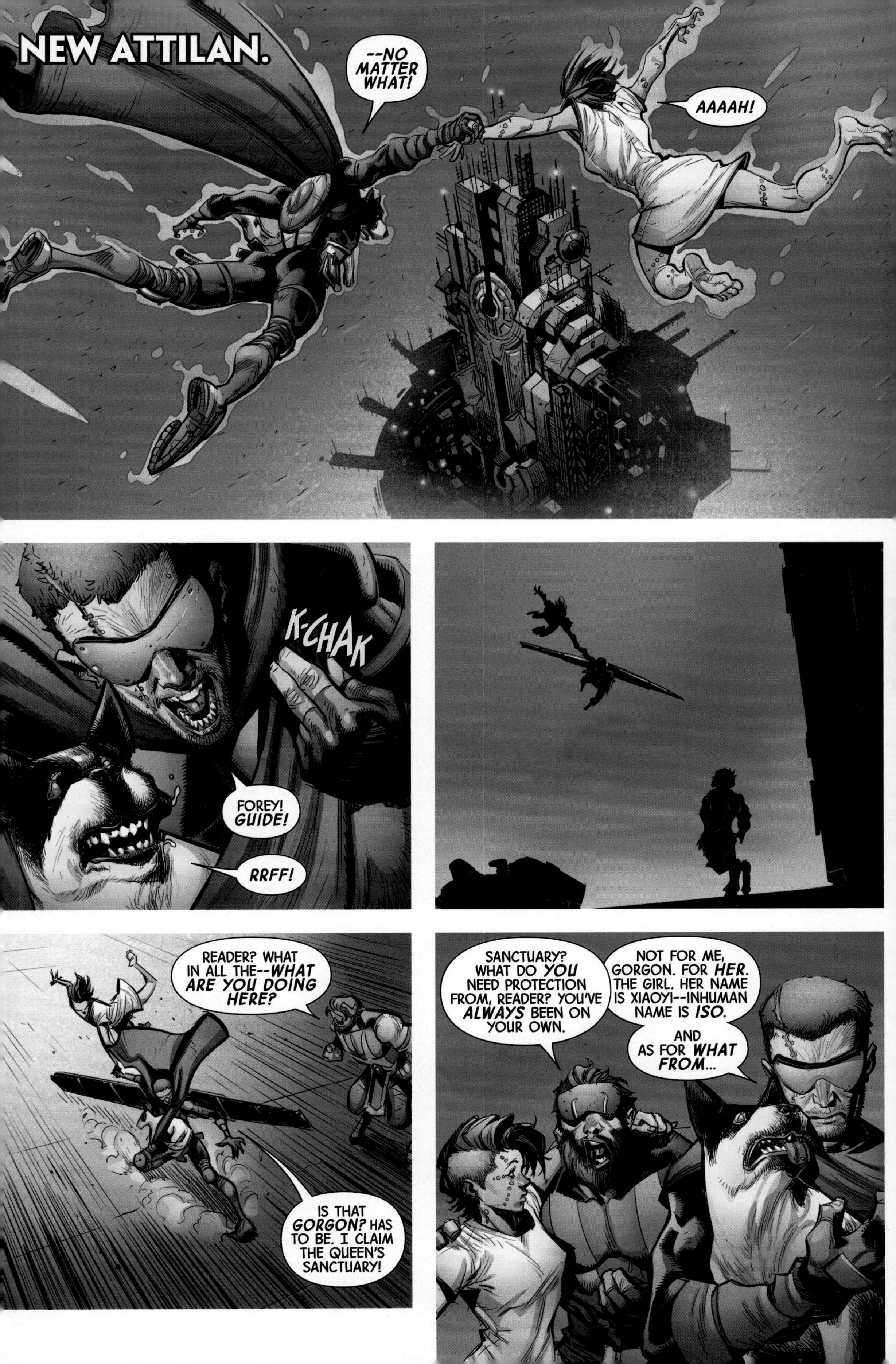
NEW ATTILAN.
--NO MATTER WHAT!
AAAAH!
K-CHAK
FOREY! GUIDE!
RRFF!
READER? WHAT IN ALL THE--WHAT ARE YOU DOING HERE?
IS THAT GORGON? HAS TO BE. I CLAIM THE QUEEN'S SANCTUARY!
SANCTUARY? WHAT DO YOU NEED PROTECTION FROM, READER? YOU'VE ALWAYS BEEN ON YOUR OWN.
NOT FOR ME, GORGON. FOR HER. THE GIRL. HER NAME IS XIAOYI--INHUMAN NAME IS ISO.
AND AS FOR WHAT FROM...

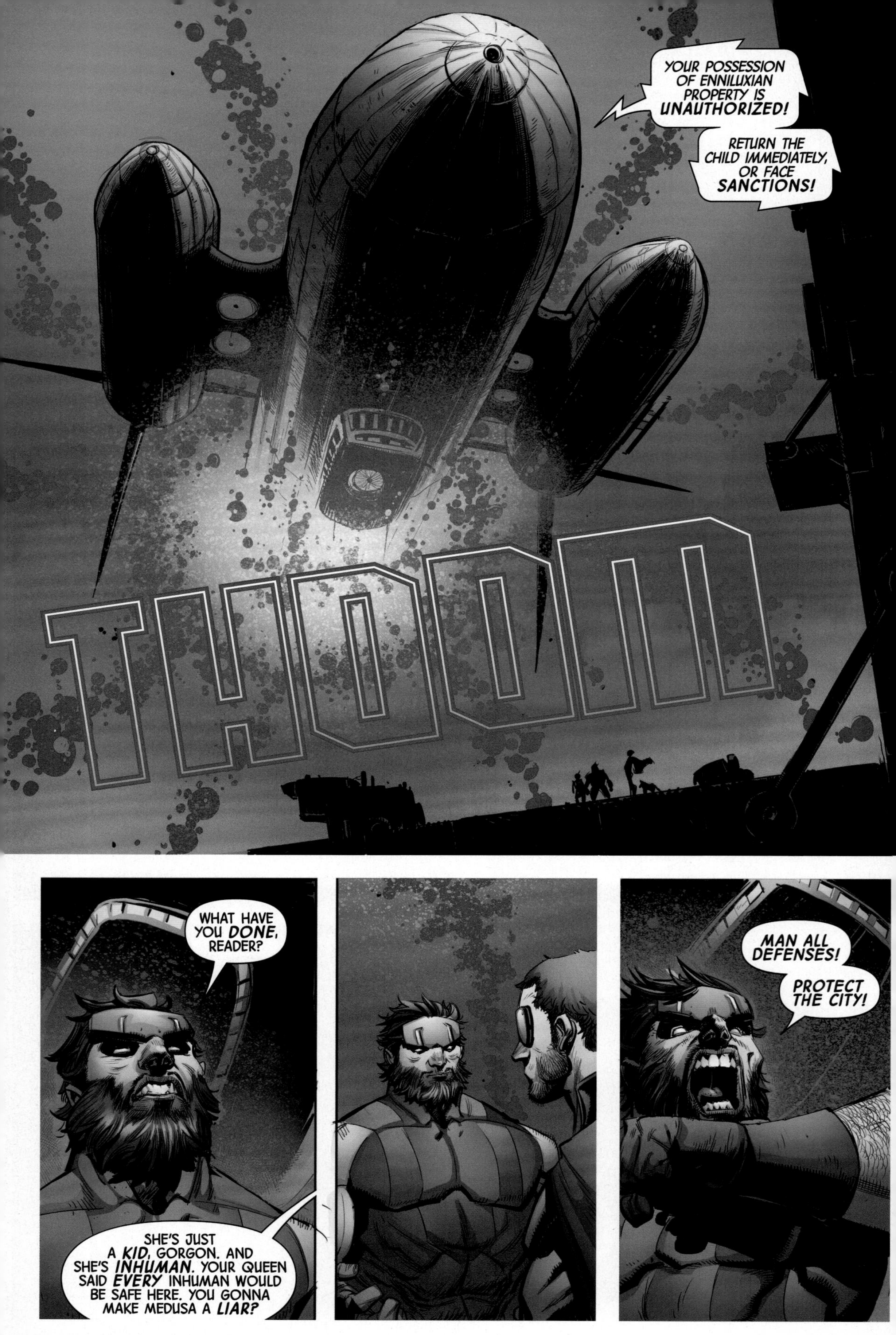
YOUR POSSESSION OF ENNILUXIAN PROPERTY IS UNAUTHORIZED!
RETURN THE CHILD IMMEDIATELY, OR FACE SANCTIONS!
THOOM
WHAT HAVE YOU DONE, READER?
SHE'S JUST A KID, GORGON. AND SHE'S INHUMAN. YOUR QUEEN SAID EVERY INHUMAN WOULD BE SAFE HERE. YOU GONNA MAKE MEDUSA A LIAR?
MAN ALL DEFENSES!
PROTECT THE CITY!

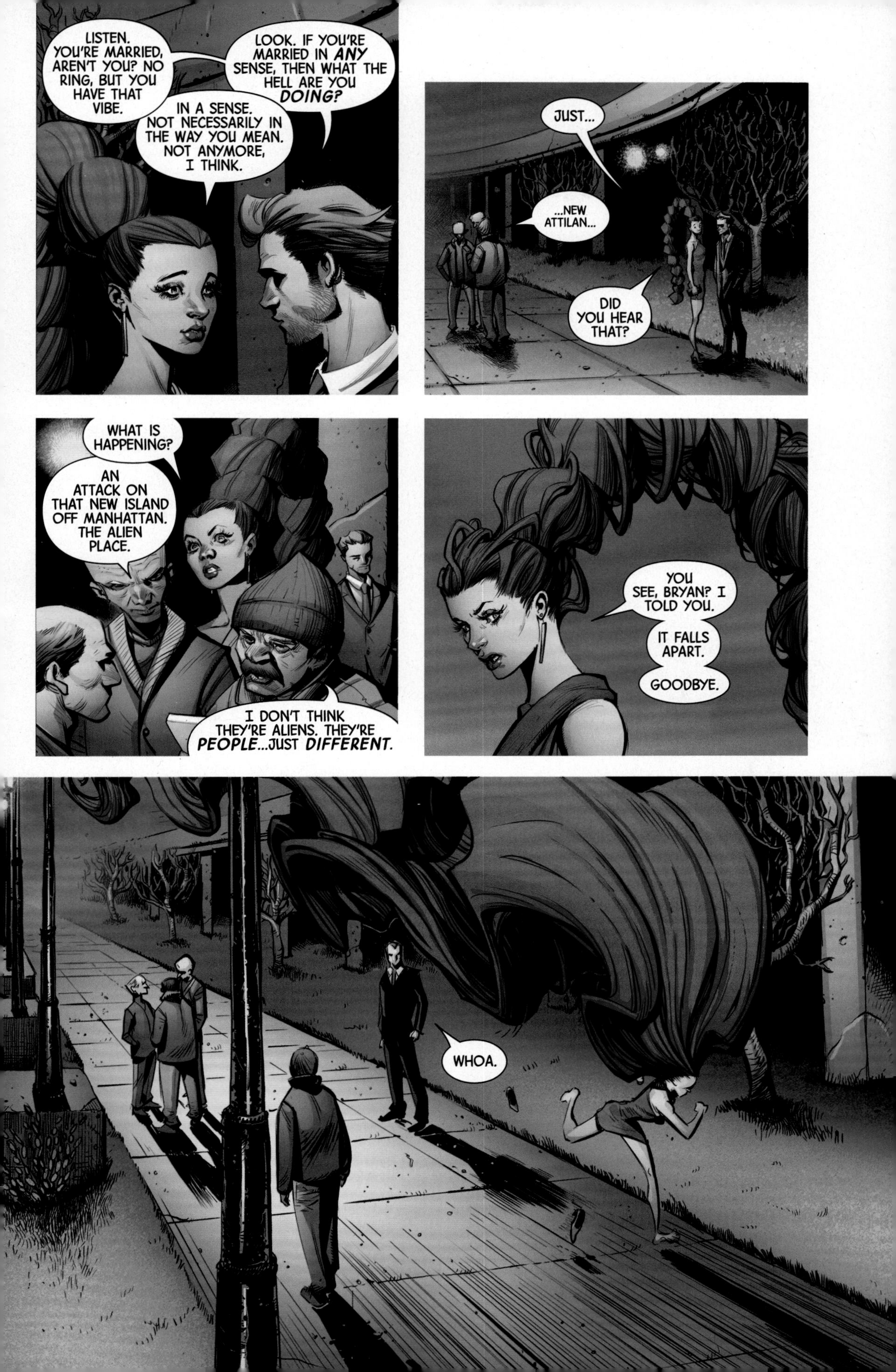

LISTEN. YOU'RE MARRIED, AREN'T YOU? NO RING, BUT YOU HAVE THAT VIBE.
IN A SENSE. NOT NECESSARILY IN THE WAY YOU MEAN. NOT ANYMORE, I THINK.
LOOK. IF YOU'RE MARRIED IN ANY SENSE, THEN WHAT THE HELL ARE YOU DOING?
JUST...
...NEW ATTILAN...
DID YOU HEAR THAT?
WHAT IS HAPPENING?
AN ATTACK ON THAT NEW ISLAND OFF MANHATTAN. THE ALIEN PLACE.
I DON'T THINK THEY'RE ALIENS. THEY'RE PEOPLE...JUST DIFFERENT.
YOU SEE, BRYAN? I TOLD YOU.
IT FALLS APART.
GOODBYE.
WHOA.

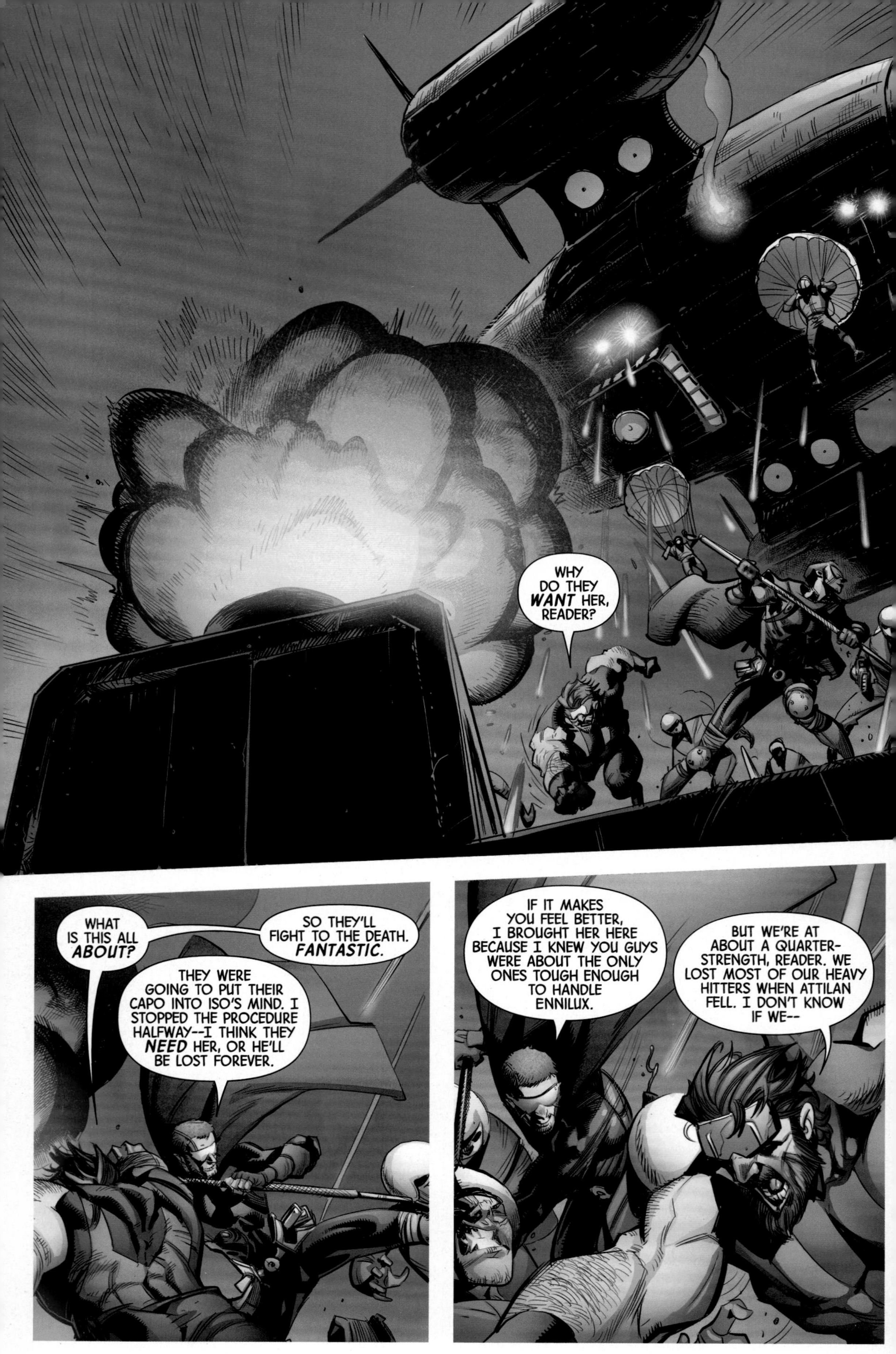
WHY DO THEY *WANT* HER, READER?
WHAT IS THIS ALL *ABOUT?*
SO THEY'LL FIGHT TO THE DEATH. *FANTASTIC.*
THEY WERE GOING TO PUT THEIR CAPO INTO ISO'S MIND. I STOPPED THE PROCEDURE HALFWAY--I THINK THEY *NEED* HER, OR HE'LL BE LOST FOREVER.
IF IT MAKES YOU FEEL BETTER, I BROUGHT HER HERE BECAUSE I KNEW YOU GUYS WERE ABOUT THE ONLY ONES TOUGH ENOUGH TO HANDLE ENNILUX.
BUT WE'RE AT ABOUT A QUARTER-STRENGTH, READER. WE LOST MOST OF OUR HEAVY HITTERS WHEN ATTILAN FELL. I DON'T KNOW IF WE--

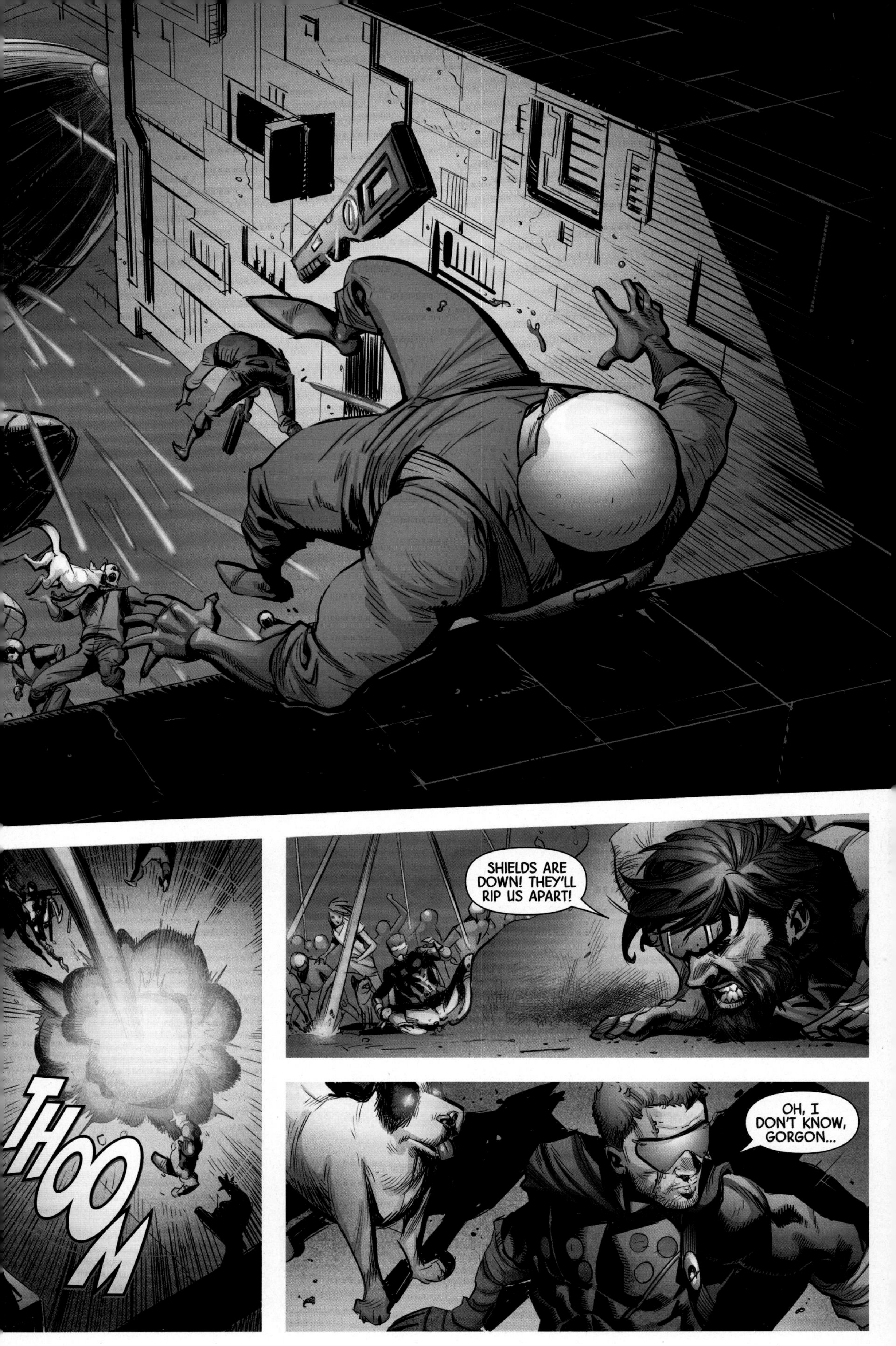
THOOM
SHIELDS ARE DOWN! THEY'LL RIP US APART!
OH, I DON'T KNOW, GORGON...

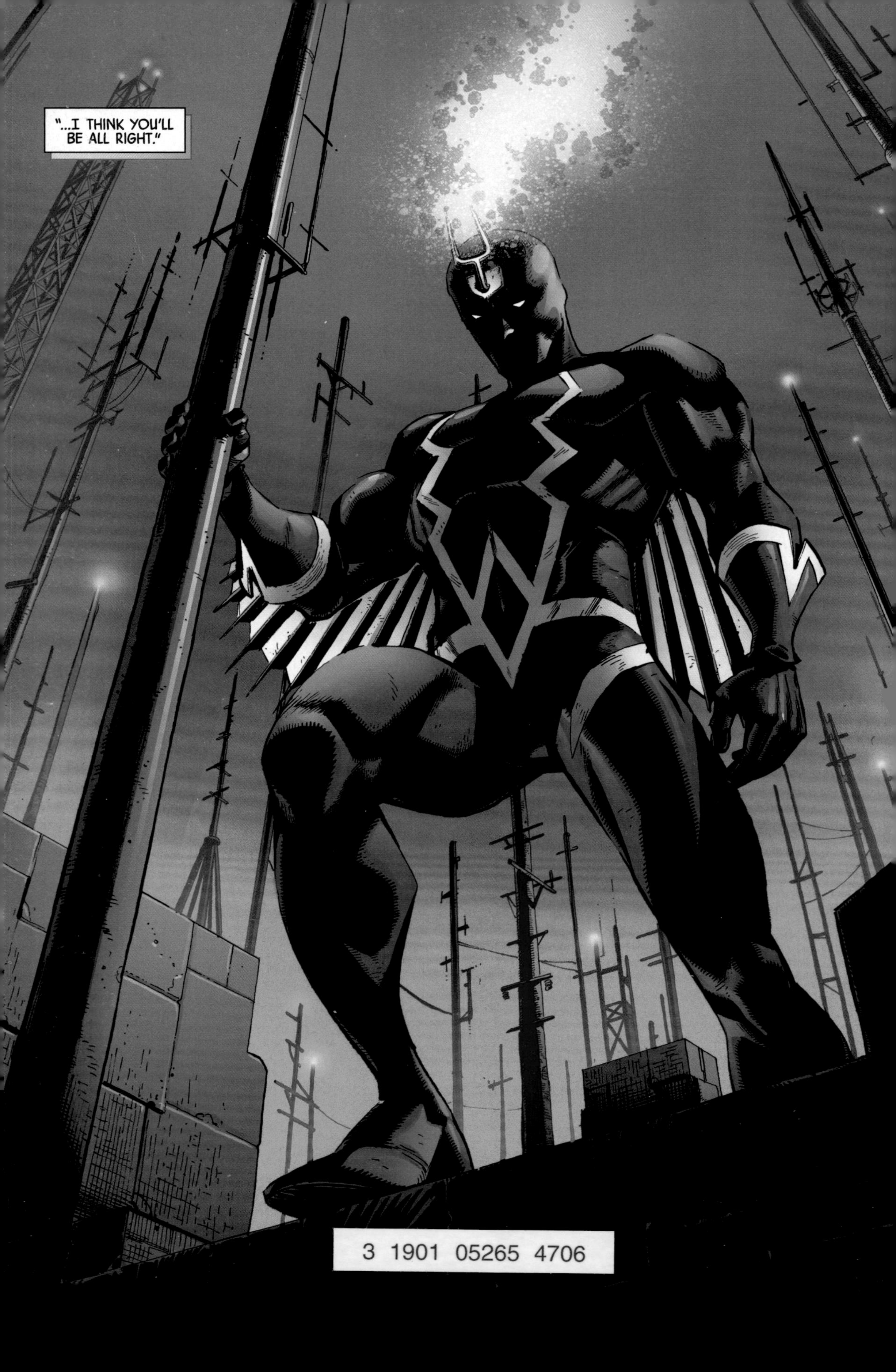
"...I THINK YOU'LL BE ALL RIGHT."